Keetsahnak / Our Missing and Murdered Indigenous Sisters

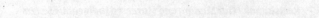

KIM ANDERSON, MARIA CAMPBELL & CHRISTI BELCOURT, *Editors*

Keetsahnak
Our Missing and Murdered Indigenous Sisters

The University of Alberta Press

Published by

The University of Alberta Press
Ring House 2
Edmonton, Alberta, Canada T6G 2E1
www.uap.ualberta.ca

Copyright © 2018 The University of
Alberta Press

LIBRARY AND ARCHIVES CANADA
CATALOGUING IN PUBLICATION

Keetsahnak / Our missing and
murdered Indigenous sisters /
Kim Anderson, Maria Campbell &
Christi Belcourt, editors.

Includes bibliographical references
and index.
Issued in print and electronic formats.
ISBN 978–1–77212–367–8 (softcover).—
ISBN 978–1–77212–391–3 (EPUB).—
ISBN 978–1–77212–392–0 (Kindle).—
ISBN 978–1–77212–390–6 (PDF)

1. Native women—Crimes against—
Canada. 2. Native women—Crimes
against—Canada—Prevention. 3. Native
women—Violence against—Canada.
4. Native women—Violence against—
Canada—Prevention. 5. Missing
persons—Canada. 6. Murder victims—
Canada. 7. Native women—Canada—
Social conditions. I. Campbell, Maria, editor
II. Anderson, Kim, 1964–, editor
III. Belcourt, Christi, 1966–, editor
IV. Title: Our missing and murdered
Indigenous sisters.

E98.W8K448 2018   305.48'897071
C2018–901685–X
C2018–901686–8

First edition, fourth printing, 2020.
First printed and bound in Canada by
Houghton Boston Printers, Saskatoon,
Saskatchewan.
Copyediting and proofreading by
Joanne Muzak.
Indexing by Judy Dunlop.

The University of Alberta Press is
committed to protecting our natural
environment. As part of our efforts, this
book is printed on Enviro Paper: it contains
100% post-consumer recycled fibres and is
acid- and chlorine-free.

The University of Alberta Press gratefully
acknowledges the support received for its
publishing program from the Government
of Canada, the Canada Council for the Arts,
and the Government of Alberta through the
Alberta Media Fund.

Dedicated to spirits of our relatives who continue to guide their families from the spirit world.

Contents

Prologue XI

Waking Dreams: Reflections on Walking With Our Sisters

CHRISTI BELCOURT

I HAD A DREAM shortly before Walking With Our Sisters
(WWOS) opened for the first time in the fall of 2013 in Edmonton.
I was wondering how all those vamps were going to be set up. I
knew the red cloth would be covering the floor and people would
remove their shoes to walk along side the vamps. But I wasn't sure
exactly how that many pairs would be laid out. I didn't yet understand the extent to which community involvement would be
essential. I also didn't yet understand how this Indigenous-led
commemoration was ceremony and not just "art."

By the time Edmonton was set to open, 1,763 pairs of vamps
had arrived, 65 beading groups had sprang up, over a dozen people
had joined me on the national collective to help organize, and
thousands had been inspired to express their care and concern by

---

Walking With Our Sisters is a memorial installation of over two thousand moccasin tops
(sometimes called vamps) to honour the lives of Indigenous women, girls and two-spirit
people. The travelling memorial runs until 2018. For more information, see www.
walkingwithoursisters.ca. This publication emerged as an idea by the WWOS national
collective under the guidance of Elder Maria Campbell, who wanted to increase the
amount of resources available for post-secondary studies.

either making vamps, organizing to help, or making donations. It was a whirlwind and outpouring of care and compassion. We were all feeling the same way: like we needed and wanted to do something. We needed to express our support and care for the families.

In my dream, the one I had before Edmonton, I was standing in a big long lodge, the kind you see with longhouses or Midewewin lodges. There were women standing all around the edge, shoulder to shoulder. About three rows of us standing like that, looking at each other, wondering what to do. Suddenly a drum appeared in the middle, and then some men appeared and started singing. Just then, Elder Maria Campbell, who was standing beside me, walked out and began to dance with her hands faced upwards. I followed her. Other women followed as well. We all danced, hundreds of us, and then one by one everyone disappeared until I was left alone in the lodge, and I woke up.

This dream formed the basis of how the installation of wwos is set up. The vamps are placed in pairs, one beside another, as if women are standing shoulder to shoulder in their moccasins facing the people who have come to pay their respects.

I thought, at the beginning, when I first made the call out for vamps, that wwos was an art exhibit. It isn't. Walking With Our Sisters defies categorization. It's a commemoration, it's ceremony, it's an honouring, it's art, it's community taking action, it's a way to demonstrate we care.

It is compassion that guides it. Nothing else. And it has no other purpose except for communities to come together to hold ceremony to honour the lives of missing and disappeared sisters and two-spirit loved ones, and to support family members who attend. wwos is not an organization. It's never been registered and it will never be. It's merely a collective of caring souls.

We set no expectations or goals and allowed the ceremony to guide what needed to happen. We asked the spaces where wwos goes to turn their space into a community-owned space. Even if it was a gallery, museum, or another type of space that is typically run by a dedicated staff, we asked that wwos be entirely run by community and that the space become transformed into a sacred space where grandmothers, Elders, and traditional knowledge keepers could feel comfortable being there every day to sustain the ceremony.

At the beginning, Walking With Our Sisters set out four guiding principles. Everything we do flows from these principles:

- All who attend are equal. All are welcome.
- The memorial in each community is Indigenous led.
- Practice kindness, gentleness, patience, and love.
- We are all volunteers. No one is paid. No profits are made.

We also have not accepted government funding or resource-extraction money. Communities that hosted WWOS held many fundraisers. We also fundraised online with auctions to raise money so we could not only continue but also share our proceeds with other community groups such as Tears4Justice, Two-Spirited People of Manitoba, Families of Sisters in Spirit, the Native Youth Sexual Health Network, Maisy's Foundation of Hope, Butterflies in Spirit, Awasis Sacred Journey, and Got Bannock.

Sault Ste. Marie, Ontario, was the fifth community to host WWOS. It was installed in Algoma University, in what was the Shingwauk Indian Residential School inside the former auditorium of the school. Naturally, we felt uncomfortable with this site. But it was the grandmothers and Elders, who were part of the Children of Shingwauk Alumni Association, who brought such beauty to the Walking With Our Sisters "bundle." "Bundle" is a traditional ceremonial term to describe a collection of sacred items. WWOS began to be referred to by community members as a "bundle" because of the sacred items that were added by traditional ceremonial people at each stop along the way.

The residential school survivors of Shingwauk Residential School suggested that a specific call for children's vamps be sent out to survivors or family members of survivors via social media. The call invited them to create a pair of children's vamps to honour the lives of the children who attended residential schools but never made it back home because they died as children at the schools or on their way home from the schools.

In the end, 108 pairs were sent in.[1] A special ceremony was held inside the wwos memorial. A hundred chairs were set up along the entire pathway. Many residential school survivors came. Pipe carriers were at the front. Children who came with their parents were asked to help lay the children's vamps on the floor at the front. The ceremony began with smudge and with passing tobacco to everyone. After that, a water song was sung and prayers were made over the copper pails that held the water. Prayers were made for the berries. The water and berries were passed around to everyone. A feather was passed around, and residential school survivors or their family members were invited to speak. They spoke passionately about the deaths of their brothers, sisters, cousins, or friends they witnessed, and how they were told not to express emotion, even when they had to help bury them. The last part of the ceremony was done with song. As singers drummed and sang, the survivors and other attendees were invited to come one by one and pick up a pair of children's vamps and lay them down in the centre under the Eagle Staffs. It was powerful and moving. The ceremony ended with all of us dancing and going to have a feast and eat together. Food was offered to the sacred fire outside that was kept 24/7 for the entire time the memorial was in the community.

This is but one example of how a community transformed what was known as a triggering space into a sacred space. Reclaiming the space for traditional ceremony was empowering and powerful.

| On December 8, 2015, the newly elected Trudeau government announced that it would officially begin the national inquiry into murdered and missing Indigenous women and girls and women by initiating a "pre-inquiry" phase that would specifically seek the guidance and input of family members, Indigenous organizations, advocacy groups, and other stakeholders.

In the days leading up to the announcement, I had conflicting emotions—sometimes vacillating between relief and bewilderment, especially because we had just emerged from over a decade of near draconian treatment at the hands of the Harper government. But mostly what I felt was a deep sadness. So many. Too many. So many still missing. Too many gone. I felt only a deep sense of sadness for the families. In fact, the day before the announcement, the remains of Karina Wolfe were finally found and a person was charged with her death. And the day before that, a young woman named Chrisy succumbed to the injuries she suffered by violence, and a person has now been charged with her death. It never stops.

Inquiry is not the be all and end all. Until this country is willing to stare itself in the mirror and look to itself as the underlying reason why our sisters make up 25 per cent of all cases of homicide when we are only 4 per cent of the population, only then will we have taken the first step towards fixing anything.

On December 8, 2015, I heard the minister of Northern and Indigenous Affairs Canada say, "Racism and sexism in this country kills." The next day, the head of the RCMP admitted there were racist police officers in among the force. These are truths that Indigenous Peoples have always known. We are the victims of systemic racism and sexism that have their roots in the very formation of this country.

The statistics the RCMP presented back in 2012 are highly problematic. They cited 1,181 missing Indigenous women or girls, but they do not, for example, explain how they determined the ethnicity of Indigenous women, particularly among those who may not have been registered as a status Indian or are Métis.[2] There are still lingering questions about how many of those listed as "Jane Doe" may in fact be Indigenous women. In addition, there are many deaths listed as "suspicious," but without evidence to support a homicide they are not officially listed as homicides. As well there are outstanding files that are not within the RCMP jurisdiction that are not factored into the overall count. There are deaths listed as suicides or accidental that families dispute and feel were not properly investigated. There are two-spirit and transgender people who are not listed as part of the murdered and missing Indigenous women but should be. And in addition to all of this, the RCMP only went back thirty years in their count. They do not include the women and children or two-spirit people who went missing or who were murdered before 1980. The deaths of children at residential schools or within child welfare systems, for example, are still not counted. Stats before 1980 don't really exist, but there are families who are still speaking about their missing loved ones and who say that, at the time, the police simply wouldn't allow families to report people missing, or families wouldn't report them missing because of the police. Many missing have not been officially listed as missing. There are many reasons to question the statistics of the RCMP, but I don't believe they have deliberately withheld numbers. I do think, however, for all the reasons listed above, that the numbers are much higher than 1,200. In fact, since 2012, the numbers have been climbing. All of this is such cold talk about "numbers," when we should really be saying "lives." The number of *lives* that were cut short have been climbing. The number of *lives* that have been robbed or stolen.

The roots of racism in Canada go back to contact. It's no secret that European countries and monarchies were competing to colonize the world to make themselves rich off natural resources. The land grabs didn't just take place here; they took place everywhere outside Europe, wherever they possibly could reach. The systematic removal of Indigenous Peoples in Turtle Island off our lands coincided with the devaluing of Indigenous Peoples' lives and the propaganda that was perpetrated to assuage settler guilt. It's naïve to think that all that was done to us was simply out of "good intentions." The federal government's starvation policies, for example, certainly can't be argued as borne from good intentions.

The removal of Indigenous Peoples from our lands, the forced removal of children (which continues today), the forced severance from our languages, cultures, autonomy, traditional governance— all have lead to the higher incidence of our sisters being murdered or going missing. Ultimately, society and the service agencies set up as protections for Canadians have failed us. Police and justice, with their own issues of systemic racism and sexism, are failing us.

When Canadians judge themselves to be generous and tolerant global citizens, why is there such vitriol towards Indigenous Peoples?

It's ingrained. The hatred, superiority, and racism from the time of European contact has made its way into the subconscious of the citizens of Canada, and they don't even know it. Each new generation has been brainwashed by education systems that teach very little about us. They teach the myth of two founding nations, then conveniently skip over all the nasty parts about starvation policies, forced removals, and torture of children. Genocide is ugly. Somehow, in schools, Canada comes out unscathed as the greatest country in the world.

My experience with Walking With Our Sisters, however, has taught me to hope. I have seen thousands, and I mean thousands, of volunteers, both Native and non-Native working side by side. I have seen donations come pouring in to help with the memorial. I have seen tears of sincere grief flowing down the cheeks of those from all walks of life.

It is the way the project came together—the overwhelming feeling of wanting to express love, compassion, kindness, and caring to the families of missing and murdered women and girls. This is what the whole of wwos is about. The way the hundreds of volunteers work together in each community. And even the way each community drives hundreds or thousands of miles to hand deliver the "bundle" to the next host community. The gentleness and compassion and love people are demonstrating is overwhelming. It's the counter to the ugliness. It's what we need more of.

The last dream I had about wwos was a few months prior to writing this piece. I was again in a large ceremonial space, this time an arena. wwos was set up in the centre and a large circle of people were standing outside near the bleachers all the way around. Feast food was there. Songs were being sung. Elders were there. I turned to Tanya Kappo, my friend and member of the national collective and a main organizer for the first installation in Edmonton, who was standing beside me, and said, "I know what to do now. It has to be all about the children; our focus has to be on the children and we have to give everything we can to them." Since then my shift has changed. I think about the next generations constantly. I think about this world we are leaving to them. I try to think about the ways WWOS can be used to help children and youth in connecting with traditional ways or ceremonial ways.

I think, for me, overall, WWOS has been yet another example among examples from our communities, stretching back decades, of the resilience, grace, and beauty that exists among Indigenous women and communities. Yes, we continue to face the most horrific tragedies and suffer from collective grief. But, at the same time, we are strong. We are beautiful. We have survived the worst Canada had to throw at us, trying to wipe out our people and our cultures. Young people are picking up the cultures and languages with a vengeance. We are on the rise once again. This makes me proud. It makes me determined.

I am so grateful to each and every person who has marched, held a vigil, lit a pipe or a candle, held a sweat, given offerings, fasted, feasted, cooked, protested, written blogs, chapters, or books, painted, sang, blockaded, sewed vamps, hung a red dress, or put tobacco in a fire for a better future for our children.

Drawing from Elder Maria Campbell, I would like to finish with "Power to the babies." My love to all of you and to the little ones yet to come. May we find a way to end the violence.

NOTES

1. That number has since grown to approximately three hundred pairs as a second call for children's vamps was made in 2014.
2. RCMP, *Missing and Murdered Aboriginal Women: A National Operational Overview* (Ottawa: RCMP, 2014), 7, http://www.rcmp-grc.gc.ca/en/missing-and-murdered-aboriginal-women-national-operational-overview#sec3.

Acknowledgements

WE ACKNOWLEDGE the work of family, friends, and advocates who toiled for decades when no one was listening, and who never gave up on the struggle to bring awareness to the crisis of missing and murdered Indigenous women, girls, and two-spirit peoples. We acknowledge all who were murdered and continue to go uncounted and unnamed. We acknowledge all the strength and resilience within Indigenous communities.

Introduction

KIM ANDERSON

Every time I see a photo of an Indigenous woman or girl who has gone missing, I feel my spirit tighten inside of me.
—HELEN KNOTT, this volume

IN THE WINTER OF 2012, Michif artist Christi Belcourt was driving to Ottawa from her home near Sudbury, Ontario, and she kept thinking about something that had lodged in her spirit. It was the poster of a young missing Indigenous woman she had seen on Facebook. A girl who had been missing for years. A poster circulated by the family.

Like all Indigenous women in Canada, Christi was well familiar with the issue. For many of us—as described by Helen Knott above—every photo, every story of a missing and murdered Indigenous woman is deeply internalized. We can experience gnawing feelings of fear, trauma, or threat to our own safety and that of our sisters, daughters, nieces, mothers, aunties, and grandmothers. But what followed Christi as she drove along that evening were thoughts about the family. Being a mother herself, she became overwhelmed with a sense of compassion for the girl's mother. What unspeakable worry, trauma, and grief must the mother of the missing endure? And what about all the other families of missing and murdered Indigenous women and girls?

What happened next, as Christi describes it, is that an idea "just arrived; just popped into my head." She explains, "It could have come to anyone. But by the time I got to Ottawa, the idea was fully formed." This was the beginning of the commemorative installation that would become Walking With Our Sisters (WWOS).

When she got home, Christi put out a call on social media for people to send in vamps—the beaded top part of moccasins, to represent the over six hundred Indigenous women who, at that time, were reported missing or murdered according to a list compiled by the Native Women's Association of Canada. The unfinished moccasins would represent the interrupted lives of the women, and Christi would find a way to arrange them so that families, friends, allies, and community members could "walk with our sisters." It would offer one way to visit, honour, and commemorate the missing and murdered relations.

Christi set a time frame of one year for participants to send in their vamps. I recall talking to her early that summer, not long before their due date, and she was concerned that she had only received 200 pairs. But by July, the boxes started arriving daily at the small post office near her home, and by August she had over 1,763 pairs of vamps. In the end, there were over 2,000 women's pairs and 300 children's. Christi's call had clearly touched on an issue that is widely and deeply felt.

The beading of these vamps was the start of a collective commemorative act. Families got together to bead, and new community beading groups formed across the Americas and beyond, creating community, kinship, and dialogue in the process. This collaborative work has since been replicated in the touring of WWOS, as each community visit of two to three weeks has become a ceremony that requires extensive and widespread preparation and commitment. As such, it has been a tremendous demonstration of caring. By the end of the tour in 2018, WWOS will have visited thirty-one communities.[1]

From the outset, it was apparent that participants and visitors to WWOS wanted more information about the missing and murdered Indigenous women, girls, and two-sprit peoples (MMIWG2S). Those who "walk with sisters" can't help but ask, why is this happening? How can we make it stop? These long-standing questions were also those of the WWOS national collective Elder Maria Campbell, who was simultaneously working on a Trudeau Foundation–funded research project about the roots of violence against Indigenous women. Maria determined that it would be beneficial to produce some WWOS companion literature about missing and murdered Indigenous women, and her vision resulted in this book.

Writing about the issue is not new, and we are indebted to the work of activists, researchers, writers, and scholars before us. Because of them we are slowly starting to see non-Indigenous peoples, institutions, and governments focus on MMIWG2S. At the time of writing, for example, the Government of Canada had recently launched a National Inquiry into Missing and Murdered Indigenous Women and Girls.[2] This initiative follows ten years of inaction and dismissal by the previous federal government. The repeated requests for a national inquiry and other Indigenous calls to action have been supported by substantial evidence, reporting, and recommendations, with the literature gradually increasing since Amnesty International's 2004 *Stolen Sisters* report, which Beverly Jacobs describes in her chapter in this volume.[3] The work of Indigenous women, families, and their allies has thus been both persistent and consistent; by 2015, the Legal Strategy Coalition on Violence Against Indigenous women (LSC) documented that fifty separate reports had been written on missing and murdered Indigenous women. Unfortunately, as the LSC researchers note, "only a few of the more than 700 recommendations in these reports have ever been fully implemented."[4] There is work that remains to be done, including relentless and continual attention to research and writing in the interest of change.

We are honoured to walk with other scholarly anthologies on missing and murdered Indigenous women and girls in Canada, including with *Torn from Our Midst: Voices of Grief, Healing, and Action from the Missing Indigenous Women Conference* and *Forever Loved: Exposing the Hidden Crisis of Missing and Murdered Indigenous Women and Girls in Canada*.[5] Like our work here, these books document the roots of violence, the pain it has caused and the resistance, resilience, and activism of Indigenous peoples. Our book brings in new stories and voices, and touches on controversial topics such as lateral violence, challenges in working with "tradition," and problematic notions involved in "helping"— always grounded in the narratives of Indigenous women and families.

We have divided the book into four sections, starting with "All Our Relations" as we wish to foreground that the MMIWG2S crisis and related trauma is part of daily, lived experience for Indigenous women and families. The first chapter is written by women from the Downtown Eastside Power of Women Group in Vancouver, a zone described by the authors as "the poorest off-reserve postal code in Canada" and an "epicentre in the colonial gendered violence of missing and murdered Indigenous women and girls." Women from Vancouver's Downtown Eastside (DTES) have long been at the forefront of attention, leadership, and activism on MMIWG2S in Canada, and the stories of the sisters here are both a sobering reminder of the need to keep working and a celebration of the power of sisters when they work together.

Following the DTES chapter, Beverly Jacobs describes the history of her work as a MMIWG2S activist and advocate. This work led her to the presidency of the Native Women's Association of Canada (NWAC), a position that she held from 2004 to 2009. Beverly introduces us to some of the many families she worked with over the years and provides an inside view on some of the early reporting, including the Amnesty International *Stolen Sisters* report that led to the NWAC campaign of the same name. Sandra Lamouche's chapter then focuses on immediate family relations, with an essay about her experience of multi-generational missing and murdered women and the sadly inadequate police response. She shares teachings of the hoop dance, which encompasses "all of life—the good and the bad," as the dancer pushes through struggle to a position of hope and regeneration.

The final chapter in the "All Our Relations" section tells the story of Elsie Jones Sebastian, a Nuu-chah-nulth woman who disappeared from Vancouver's Downtown Eastside in 1992. This story is told by Elsie's daughter with friend Sarah Hunt, who ask the question, "How can Elsie's story be heard and her life honoured?" They point out that the voices of family members are often unheard. As we embark on the National Inquiry on MMIWG, their question about how families can remain centred amidst the flurry of activity dominated by consultants, Indigenous organizations, academics, and government officials is timely and relevant.

The second section of the book draws attention to "The Violence of History." As noted by the Legal Strategy Coalition, the fifty reports under their review showed "a general consensus about the root causes of violence against Indigenous women"[6]— and as scholars, we need to keep adding to evidence in support of these arguments.[7] We are lucky to have an essay in this section by Robyn Bourgeois, a Cree scholar who did her PHD dissertation on MMIWG2S.[8] Robyn's chapter provides a historical and sociological mapping, offering an excellent introduction to MMIWG2S and proving that the MMIWG2S is, indeed, a national sociological issue of concern, not simply an issue of "crime" as former Prime Minister Stephen Harper so infamously stated.

Other chapters in this section weave together personal histories with colonial histories of violence. Michelle Good tells a story that draws us into mid-twentieth-century prairie life, calling attention to the commonplace racist narratives that caused her settler grand-mother to be horrified when her white father married her Cree mother in 1949. She links twentieth-century misogynist racism to the violence inflicted on Indigenous women by some of Canada's "founding fathers." This chapter draws particular attention to how nineteenth-century stereotyping of Indigenous women "as commodities or currency to be bartered, used and discarded" underpins the everyday racist stories that Canadians continue to tell—like well-versed nursery rhymes—and which often constitute the entirety of what settlers "know" about Indigenous women.

Kelsey Leonard's chapter then provides evidence of the violence of history with a specific case: that of her people, the Shinnecock Indian Nation of Long Island. Drawing on her training in law and anthropology, she shows how colonial legal systems, starting with the Dutch and English in the seventeenth century, rendered Indigenous women "inherently violable" and displaced the Indigenous legal and social systems that protected women and girls. In spite of this history, as her chapter demonstrates, Shinnecock women have continually found ways to assert their personhood, and to resist.

Maya Ode'amik Chacaby provides the final chapter in the second section, combining the theoretical, poetic, and autobiographical in her story of how she came to be a missing Indigenous girl, living inside "that space between Being Missing and Being Murdered." Maya demonstrates how her story is connected to the construction of an "Indian Problem" out of European Enlightenment thought, Canadian colonialism, and the inadequate contemporary systemic supports that fail to provide a safe place of returning. Her chapter calls for us to collectively re-create a home of Indigenous culturally resilient belonging. Maya offers a challenge by "wonder[ing] if the plight of missing Indigenous women is worth that kind of effort."

The third section engages often unspoken questions of lateral violence within our communities, connecting them to the histories of colonialism and violence that were discussed in the previous sections. Helen Knott writes about the sexual violence and silencing that happens in her home community of Fort

St. John, British Columbia. Much of this abuse is connected to the rape of the land—which is rampant in Helen's territory and where the oil industry brings in the violence of "man-camps."

Another area of both lateral and non-lateral violence involves two-spirit and trans people. This subject has received too little attention within MMIWG2S work, and as Alex Wilson points out in her chapter, two-spirit and trans-identified community members are more likely to be targets of violence, while receiving fewer supports. Alex offers a much-needed critique of how patriarchy, the regulation of women's behaviours, and homophobia get woven into what is considered tradition. She offers a wonderful grounding in stories of her Swampy Cree upbringing and in stories of contemporary spaces of two-spirit resurgence to show how "two-spirit identity is one way in which balance is being restored to our communities."

In Chapter 11, Robert Innes and I raise questions about Indigenous men as perpetrators of violence—"the moose in the room"—as work to end MMIWG2S often focuses on settler violence against Indigenous women. While we feel it is critical to draw attention to the violence perpetrated by Indigenous men, we stress that colonial, contextual, and social determinant factors must be at the heart of these discussions. We also provide hopeful examples of Indigenous men and groups that are taking leadership to end violence against Indigenous women. And although not dealt with in this book, we are starting to see work coming together regarding the issue of violence against Indigenous boys and men, including murdered and missing Indigenous men.[9] While not the focus of this book, we recognize and assert that violence against all Indigenous people, of all genders, must end.

Waaseyaa'sin Christine Sy raises provocative questions about how patriarchy, male dominance, and violence are perpetuated in our communities through the stories we tell. She asks how misogynist renderings of "traditional" stories contribute to normalizing violence against Indigenous women, using the example of the Anishinaabeg story of Wenonah. In her chapter at the end of the third section, Leanne Betasamosake Simpson then gives examples of stories that allow us to think beyond heteropatriachal versions of "traditional" and contemporary stories. She looks at the gender fluidity in Louise Erdrich's work, and writes about the validation she experienced upon hearing a woman's version of the Anshinaabek creation story from Elder Edna Manitowabi. Leanne finishes her chapter by telling a story of resurgence that celebrates the agency and self-determination of a brave (and genderless) child, and of aki, the land.

The final section of our book, "Action, Always" demonstrates that activism to protect and honour Indigenous women has a long history as well as a vibrant ongoing presence. In the first chapter in this section, Darlene Okemaysim-Sicotte, Susan Gingell, and Rita Bouvier map out a model for grassroots activism, sharing their story of participation in the Iskwewuk E-wichiwitochik community group in Saskatoon. Their chapter shows how families must be at the centre of MMIWG2S work; the authors model this by starting with the story of how they provided financial, emotional, and public lobbying support for the family of Daleen Bosse, a undergraduate student and mother who went missing in Saskatoon in 2004 and was later found to be murdered.

In the chapter that follows, Pahan Pte San Win writes about working with women who have been victims of abuse and about her work as an Elder in a prison for men. As she points out, "These men were the sons of the women that I had worked with. They were hiding under the bed, trembling and afraid while she was being attacked." Pahan's twenty years of experience as a counsellor underpin her suggestion for a "three-prong approach" that includes healing for perpetrators, healing for women, and addressing mainstream stereotyping that fuels the violence. The final chapter brings us full circle to the origins of the book, as it documents the activism of Walking With Our Sisters. Authors Laura Harjo, Jenell Navarro, and Kimberly Robertson show how WWOS has engaged community through the sacred ontology of beading. This chapter provides a valuable summary of activism and strategies to end MMIWG2S, not the least of which involves dismantling dehumanizing stories and then telling new ones. As the authors point out, "the power of storytelling via beadwork maintains a cultural legacy that settlers have not been able to eliminate."

We conclude the book with an epilogue that was carved out of a two-day meeting that we held in January 2016 with members of the WWOS national collective and friends. We held this meeting to discuss insights from this collection, draw attention to gaps in our work, and set a path for what may follow. What occurred was a remarkable weekend of storytelling, language lessons, life lessons, and critical readings that will hopefully serve as a model for the kinds of discussions and actions our book might engender as it begins its own walk.

Finally, we decided to use the mother language of the editors by including the Cree word "Keetsahnak" as part of the title. It means simply "Our Sisters," and is intended to show our kinship with the women whose lives form the heart of the installation and this volume. We give thanks to everyone who takes up this important work; to the helpers, to the writers, to the families, and especially to the children/descendants of MMIWG2S. Ekosi.

NOTES

1. For more information on WWOS, see www.walkingwithoursisters.ca, as well as the final chapter in this book.

2. For more information about the National Inquiry into Missing and Murdered Indigenous Women and Girls, see www.mmiwg-ffada.ca.

3. Amnesty International, *Stolen Sisters: A Human Rights Response to Discrimination and Violence against Indigenous Women in Canada* (Ottawa: Amnesty International, 2004), https://www.amnesty.ca/sites/amnesty/files/amr200032004enstolensisters.pdf. One of the earliest scholarly calls to attention came out of work in the Downtown Eastside of Vancouver. See Dara Culhane, "Their Spirits Live within Us: Aboriginal Women in Downtown Eastside Vancouver Emerging into Visibility," *American Indian Quarterly* 27, no. 3/4 (2003): 593–606.

4. "Legal Strategy Coalition on Violence against Indigenous Women (LSC)," Women's Legal Education and Action Fund, accessed December 3, 2017, http://www.leaf.ca/legal/legal-strategy-coalition-on-violence-against-indigenous-women-lsc/.

5. A. Brenda Anderson, Wendee Kubik, Mary Rucklos Hampton, eds., *Torn from Our Midst: Voices of Grief, Healing, and Action from the Missing Indigenous Women Conference, 2008* (Regina, SK: University of Regina Press, 2010); Dawn Memee Lavell-Harvard and Jennifer Brant, eds., *Forever Loved: Exploring the Hidden Crisis of Missing and Murdered Women and Girls in Canada* (Toronto: Demeter Press, 2016).

6. "Legal Strategy Coalition on Violence against Indigenous Women (LSC)," Women's Legal Education and Action Fund, accessed December 3, 2017, http://www.leaf.ca/legal/legal-strategy-coalition-on-violence-against-indigenous-women-lsc/.

7. In addition to the aforementioned anthologies, the works that contextualize the history of violence against women and girls on Turtle Island include Sarah Deer, *The Beginning and End of Rape: Contextualizing Sexual Violence in Native America* (Minneapolis: University of Minnesota Press, 2015); Cindy Baskin, "Systemic Oppression, Violence and Healing in Aboriginal Families and Communities," in *Cruel But Not Unusual: Violence in Canadian Families*, 2nd ed., ed. Ramona Alaggia and Cathy Vine (Waterloo, ON: Wilfrid Laurier University Press, 2012), 147–48; Venida S. Chenault, *Weaving Power, Weaving Strength: Violence and Abuse against Indigenous Women* (Durham, NC: Carolina Academic Press, 2011); Hilary Weaver, "The Colonial Context of Violence: Reflections on Violence in the Lives of Native American Women," *Journal of Interpersonal Violence* 24, no. 9 (2009): 1552–63; and Jacqueline Agtuca, "Beloved Women: Lifegivers, Caretakers, Teachers of Future Generations," in *Sharing our Stories of Survival: Native Women Surviving Violence*, ed. Sarah Deer, Bonnie Clairmont, Carrie A. Martel, and Maureen L. White Eagle (New York: Altamira Press, 2008).

8. Robyn Bourgeois, "Warrior Women: Indigenous Women's Anti-Violence Engagement with the Canadian State" (PHD diss., University of Toronto, 2014).

9. See Introduction to *Indigenous Men and Masculinities: Legacies, Identities, Regeneration*, ed. Robert Alexander Innes and Kim Anderson (Winnipeg: University of Manitoba Press, 2015).

I | All Our Relations

1 | *Voices from the Downtown Eastside*

DEBRA LEO, BEATRICE STARR & STELLA AUGUST

DOWNTOWN EASTSIDE POWER OF WOMEN GROUP

THE THREE PIECES by Debra Leo, Beatrice Starr, and Stella August included here are part of the Downtown Eastside Power of Women Group "In Our Own Voices" writing series facilitated by Harsha Walia. Eleven stories in total were published in 2011 on the Vancouver Media Co-op website with the aim of uplifting the direct voices and stories of hope, struggle, love, and resistance of women living in Vancouver's Downtown Eastside.

The stories here have not been updated and are included in their original (now, slightly dated) form. Beloved Heiltsuk Elder Beatrice Starr, one of the authors and a matriarch of the group and community, passed away in 2015. Our participation in this book is dedicated to her cherished memory.

The Downtown Eastside of Vancouver is known as the poorest off-reserve postal code in Canada. The neighbourhood is characterized by high rates of homelessness, mental and physical health issues, substance use and/or addiction, and criminalized street-level economies. Although Indigenous peoples make up 2 per cent of the city's overall population, they represent over 10 per cent of the Downtown Eastside community. Indigenous women in particular continue to experience high rates of violence, and the neighbourhood is an epicentre in the colonial gendered violence of missing and murdered Indigenous women and girls. The provincial Missing Women Commission of Inquiry recently investigated police misconduct and gross negligence when women were reported as missing or murdered from the Downtown Eastside.

The Downtown Eastside Power of Women Group is a trans-inclusive group of women who live in the Downtown Eastside of Vancouver, Coast Salish Territories. As they state on their Facebook page,

> *We are a group of women (we are an inclusive group) from all walks of life who are either on social assistance, working poor, or homeless; but we are all living in extreme poverty. Our aim is to empower ourselves through our experiences and to raise awareness from our own perspectives about the social issues affecting the neighbourhood.*
>
> *Many of us are single mothers or have had our children apprehended due to poverty; most of us have chronic physical or mental health issues, for example HIV and Hepatitis C; many have drug or alcohol addictions; and a majority have experienced and survived sexual violence and mental, physical, spiritual, and emotional abuse.*
>
> *For indigenous women, we are affected by a legacy of the effects of residential schools and a history of colonization and racism.[1]*

Debra Leo
Being an Addict and Working the Streets on Skid Row

When I was about fifteen years old I ran away from my parent's home in Burnaby. My parents were alcoholics and there was a lot of abusive behaviour and yelling in our home.

This is common in a lot of Native homes, but I think this is because our parents are mimicking the behaviours of abuse that they learned in residential schools. Residential schools were a terrible nightmare. White people were in charge of the schools and their main purpose was to "beat the Indian out of us." It was a means of controlling Native people and trying to subordinate us into White society. Young Native people were ripped from their homes, beaten when we spoke our own languages, and denied the right to our history, our culture, and the safety and wisdom of our families. My dad used to get beat up badly in the residential school that he was in, and so he behaved the same with us.

One night my sister and I decided we had had enough of our parents' drinking and fighting. We jumped out of the window and took nothing except the clothes on our back. I remember thinking, "What are we going to do and where are we going to go?" We hitchhiked all the way from Burnaby to Main and Hastings, the heart of the Downtown Eastside (DTES).

Once we got to Main and Hastings, we ran into two older guys who allowed us to stay with them and they introduced us to pot and alcohol. But of course, we could not stay with them for free. We had to have sex with these two men. They would get us drunk and then force themselves on us. Although they took advantage of us sexually, we stayed with the two men, because we felt it was safer than the alternative of being alone on the streets or back in our parents' abusive home. As with many other women fleeing parental or partner violence, my sister and I became re-victimized as women without homes and thus vulnerable in our relationships with men.

The police were often looking for us because we were reported as missing by our family. Until we became legally recognized as adults, the police would track us down and drag us back home, where we would get locked into our rooms. Because the abuse did not stop at home, we kept running away. The police never asked us why we kept running away; they just keep dragging us back to the same situation at home that we were running from.

At the age of sixteen, I started hooking (working on the street as a sex worker) in the DTES. I learned how to talk to guys, how to ask for money, and how much to charge. But I did not know much about safety—such as using condoms to protect against STIs and pregnancy. I had four abortions while working on the street. Working the street was also very dangerous because you never knew if you would come back alive. According to a 2001 PACE report, one-third of surveyed women in the survival sex trade in the DTES said they had survived an attack on their life.[2] A guy could beat you, rape you, or murder you. I feel lucky that I wasn't one of serial killer Robert Pickton's victims, though I know that I easily could have been. I remember hearing that he was driving around the area where I was working and I knew three of the women who were murdered on his farm.

One night a guy picked me up in his van. He grabbed me by my hair while I was in the backseat and tried to rape me. I was screaming so loudly that someone walking by knocked at the van door. The guy opened the back door, pushed me out, and drove away. I never reported this incident because I was too scared and I believed that the violence committed against me was my own fault. Also, I do not trust the police. They judge those of us who live in the DTES, particularly the working girls. My friend once tried to report an incident and was told by the police, "You are a hooker. What do you expect?" Just like many other people in our society, the police stigmatize women in the sex trade, which is exactly why men prey on street-level sex workers as targets for violence and know that their crimes will either not get reported or not be taken seriously.

Working the street was the only way to make enough money to support myself and to get my own place, away from those two men. I was also addicted to drugs by then, which I did to forget the violence of my parents' home and the pain of the streets. I started by snorting cocaine and then I started smoking crack in a pipe. Doing drugs is fun at first; it helps ease the everyday pain of just wanting to end your life. But over time, I started to realize how dangerous it was—three of my personal friends overdosed and died. Over 4,700 injection drug users live in this neighbourhood, and until recently, overdose deaths outstripped all other North American cities.

It is not just the probability of overdosing that worried me, but also the risks associated with the street-level drug trade. People are often trying to steal your drugs. If you have a drug debt with your dealer, they show no mercy. Women have all of the hair on their heads shaved off, are kidnapped and tortured for days, or are pushed out of their windows. I knew a woman who was raped all night by several different men because she owed money to the drug dealers.

After fifteen years, I realized I wanted a better life for myself and I believed that I deserved a better life for myself. Even though I had a drug habit and needed money to survive, I decided to get out of the sex trade. My boyfriend at the time helped me realize that I could get other work and take better care of myself. So I started volunteering and working on furthering my skills. I am proud of myself now.

I really wish my life had turned out differently, but I had few options back then. There are things that can be done so that no one else has to go through what I had to go through. I believe there should be housing available for young girls so they do not end up homeless or in an unsafe housing situation. If I had a younger sister, I would do everything possible to prevent her from entering the sex trade. I believe it is important for young girls to know that the street is disappointing and dangerous.

The government should make it easier to get on welfare and raise the welfare rates so women do not have to work the streets to survive. Welfare for a single person without disability is $610, made up of $375 for rent and $235 for support. Even in the DTES average rents in slum buildings are above $450, forcing people to rent in unsanitary housing and leaving us hardly enough money for food. Our society should also make it easier for people who live in the DTES to work because no one is willing to hire people who have the DTES as their address or who have no address at all. Finally, I think people should have more understanding and compassion towards us. We should not be judged for who we are or what we do for trying to support ourselves when no one else even seems to cares whether we live or die.

Beatrice Starr
My Story of Domestic Violence and Child Apprehension

I was abused by my ex-partner, who is also my children's father, for ten and a half years. I had four children with him: Angela, Rosalie, Mike, and Jackson. I was beat all throughout my first pregnancy, and as a result my girl Angela was born a month early. She did not develop properly and was born with her heart on the right side of her body. She was a Mother's Day baby, born on May 13, 1973 at 5 pounds 11 ounces. I named her Angela Michelle because she looked just like an angel. She only lived to the age of 16 and died on January 17, 1990 in Prince George.

It is for her and in her memory that I tell this story.

You might be wondering why I stayed in a violent relationship for that long. I grew up without a dad and was often called a "bastard." I was always taunted with sayings such as, "Do you even know who your dad is?" It hurt a lot to be bullied and I did not want my own children to go through the same experience. So I silently suffered the abuse. At the time I did not realize that is was equally bad, if not worse, for my children to witness the violence of their father beating up their own mother.

I tell this story for the women who are still in abusive relationships so that they will have the courage to get out. Anyone who controls you and physically and emotionally hurts you does not love you. We have to understand that violence against women is always unacceptable, and as Native women, we are five times more likely than other women to die as the result of violence.

I became an alcoholic while I was in the relationship. The alcohol would numb the pain of being beaten; it would numb me for when he got home in the evenings so I could tolerate all the kicks and punches; it would numb me against his false accusations of me cheating on him when he was the one cheating on me with other women.

As a result of my drinking, the Ministry of Child and Family Development (MCFD) became involved in my children's lives. I had several visits from MCFD over the years and they told me to stop drinking and to get counselling, but I could not stop drinking. They also told me to leave my ex-partner, but I had nowhere to go. For years, MCFD kept apprehending my children. Sometimes they would take my children away for a few weeks; sometimes it was for a few months.

Then in December 1981, in a surprise visit, MCFD workers came to my home. I was not home, but my children's father was supposed to be home. However, he had left them alone in the house and the upstairs neighbour called MCFD. MCFD apprehended my children, this time seeking a permanent order. That meant that my young children, ages one to five, were going to essentially be kidnapped from me forever.

I broke down and started drinking even more heavily. I felt that if I did not have my children, then I had nothing to live for and would rather drink myself to death. One night in March 1982 I drank so much that I felt my heart was going to stop. That night I decided that I did not actually want to die an alcoholic and that I had to fight for my children.

I quit drinking cold turkey. I went for alcohol counselling at the Native Courtworkers and Counselling Association of BC and also enrolled at Native Education College to get my GED. I finally left my partner. After a few months I was able to get two-hour supervised visits with my children every six to eight weeks, but only after I appealed the decision by MCFD to deny me visits entirely.

After I won my right to supervised visits, I decided to appeal MCFD's decision to apprehend my children permanently. I did not even know that I could appeal this decision until I was informed by an advocate at Native Courtworkers that I could. I realized that

MCFD had not informed me of my basic legal rights as a parent and did not actually care to fulfill their responsibility and mandate to keep families together. I felt that as a survivor of violence and as a Native woman, I was being re-victimized by being labelled as a bad mother who was unable to protect her children.

After four years of fighting in the court system, I finally won my case and my children were given back to me in 1986. Throughout the four years, I often felt like giving up but I knew I had to fight for my family. The MCFD social worker reported to the court that I was "not showing love and affection" to my children. But the court-ordered psychologist determined that there was lots of affection between us and said that it was clear that my children wanted to come back home. I thank Dr. Diane Mitchell for helping me win my case by recommending that my children be returned. It is frustrating though that we have to rely on these professionals to validate us.

The whole system of child apprehension is grossly unfair and unjust. From my experience and those of other women I know, it seems that the ministry is interested in keeping children in the foster system rather than returning them to their parents. Most of the children in MCFD's custody are Native children. In BC, Native children are 6.3 times more likely to be removed from their homes than non-Native children. I believe this is both a continuation of the residential school experience—where children are torn away from their families and communities are destroyed—as well as a consequence of residential schools, which has forced Native families into social dysfunction with rampant alcohol/drug use and abuse in the home. I feel like the odds are stacked against us, but still we continue on.

I am now twenty-nine years sober and my three beautiful children—Rosalie and Michael and Jackson—are parents themselves. Once I had my children back, I told my boys to never hit a woman because it is like hitting your mother. I still live with the guilt about what happened to my deceased daughter Angela. I also felt responsible when my other daughter Rosalie was in an abusive relationship worse than mine. I felt that she thought it was okay to be abused because she watched me take it. But now my daughter Rosalie is happy and has a beautiful eight-year-old daughter named Kayla. My son Michael is thirty-one years old and has been clean from heroin for several years now. He is working and has a two-year-old daughter named Tayla. My youngest son Jackson is thirty years old and recently graduated from the Academy of Learning. He has a wonderful ten-month baby girl named Gianna. I am so proud of my children and thank the Creator for every new day. Love to all my family and friends.

Stella August
Residential Schools and My Journey to the Downtown Eastside

I was six years old when I was taken away from my parents and grandparents in Ahousat, BC, and forced into a residential school. The Department of Indian Affairs came to our reserve every year in the 1950s, taking Native children away and placing them in residential schools to learn the White way of life.

In residential schools, under the federal policy of "aggressive assimilation," we were stripped of our language, our culture, and our customs. We had to scrub ourselves clean until we were White. It is estimated that approximately 150,000 Native children were removed from our communities and forced to attend residential schools, with the last school closing only as recently as 1996.

I was forced to attend the Christie Indian Residential School and then the Mission City St. Mary's Residential School. I felt like I was in a concentration camp. In these schools, we were punished for speaking our language. Our punishment was being kept in isolation in a dark room for the whole day. Often we would be fed food from the garbage and be forced to drink raw cow milk. We were strapped and beaten until we were too sore to stand.

If we did not get up on time in the mornings, the nuns would drag us across the floor, beat us, and make us go without breakfast. I remember every morning they would wake us up by saying,

"You are not on the reserve; you are in White Man's land. Indians are liars, filthy and good for nothing. You don't want to live like an Indian."

When we were silent, they made us talk. But when we talked, they did not like what we had to say and persistently hit us while repeating, "God doesn't like you talking like that." We were too scared to do anything. We would often go without food and there would be no activities. At nighttime we would often see the children taken out of their dorm rooms and they would come back crying and bleeding.

I was incredibly lonely in the residential schools. The priests and nuns did not like us making friends with each other. Even brothers and sisters were kept apart and forced to act like strangers with one another. From the time I was placed in residential schools, I did not have a single kind word said to me. No one appreciated me for the individual I was, or the culture I came from. All I remember is being punished for anything and everything. I still have horrible flashbacks. I grew up with a tremendous amount of shame and loss of dignity. I believe that residential schools were prisons for young children.

I managed to get out of residential school earlier than the other children because one day my brother managed to sneak a phone call to my grandparents and told them to come get me. The nuns had beaten me so badly across my head with a stick and a ruler that my ears would not stop bleeding. My grandparents got me out of the school for a special doctor's visit. The doctor determined that I had permanently lost my hearing in both ears. My grandparents were furious and kept me at home, refusing to send me back to the residential school. When the school called the Indian band office looking for me, my grandparents told the school and the Indian agents that the nuns had given me a severely damaged ear. The officials hung up the phone and did not try forcing me back.

When I was older, I moved to the Downtown Eastside. Almost 60 per cent of Native people and 72 per cent of Native women now live in urban settings with the erosion of the land base of our communities and Indian Act regulations limiting women's access to housing on the reserves. I, too, drifted here from the Island and found work at a fish plant. Since then, this neighbourhood has become my permanent home.

Like me, most people here carry deep scars. It is hard to describe all the different experiences that women have—for example, the history of abuse that has brought many of us here to the DTES, the brutality of child apprehensions that many of us have borne as a direct result of poverty, the fact that many of us do not know our parents because of the legacy of residential schools and colonization has destroyed our families, the chronic and often fatal illnesses such as AIDS and hepatitis C that break our bodies, the grief of living through the deaths of our missing and murdered sisters, and much more. People who drive by us every day to work have no idea what nightmares we live with. My heart wants to shatter when I hear some of the stories about why people have turned to drugs and alcohol.

The Downtown Eastside is the poorest part of town. Low-income housing in the DTES is of such substandard quality that many prefer to sleep on the streets. Problems in the single-room occupancies include absence of heat, toilets, and running water; presence of mould, bedbug infestations and rats; and illegal practices by landlords, including refusal to return damage deposits, entering rooms without permission, and arbitrary evictions.

In the DTES Power of Women Group, we support our people to get proper homes. The government should provide a living wage and a decent home for all people so that we have somewhere to stay and so that no one has to work the street. A lot of our young people are working for drug dealers. Women who owe drug debts have much harm come to them, sometimes even death, like the murder of twenty-two-year-old Ashley Machisknic last year. A lot of girls who have to work in the sex trade are further abused by their clients and their pimps and often don't get paid.

And then there is the constant harassment on the street by police officers. I have seen officers walk by and kick people while they are passed out or sleeping on the street. Our people are not able to defend themselves against guns and tasers. It hurts me to see people slammed to the pavement by police officers just because they are poor and nobody cares what happens to poor people.

But the hidden truth of the Downtown Eastside is that despite the poverty, criminalization, and trauma, we all care for each other and socialize with one another. Especially in the DTES Power of Women Group, where we are like one family and support the community on issues such as police brutality, child apprehensions, violence against women, and housing. Whether people are sober or high on drugs, we listen to each other's dreams and desires to make this neighbourhood a better place for ourselves.

NOTES

1. DTES Power of Women Group (Facebook group), "About This Group," Facebook, accessed December 4, 2017, https://www.facebook.com/groups/DTESPowerofWomen/about/. For more information about the DTES Power of Women Group, see their Facebook page.

2. PACE Society is a non-profit organization that provides sex-worker-led programs and services to sex workers in Vancouver's DTES. For more information, see www.pace-society.org/.

2 | *Honouring Women*

BEVERLY JACOBS

THIS CHAPTER IS TO HONOUR ALL WOMEN, to honour the lives of the women who are missing, and to honour the lives of women who have been senselessly murdered. This article was written on the heels of the horrific murder trial of Cindy Gladue, an Indigenous woman and victim whose spirit was also victimized by the legal system.[1] This article is in honour of her and the many Indigenous female victims of murder, sexual violence, and relationship violence.

This article is intended to demonstrate my love and dedication to the spirits of those women who sacrificed their lives. They left us with so many reminders and powerful messages to our families, to our communities, and to our Nations. I give thanks to them for guiding me to places that I never thought I would be. I give thanks to them for honouring me with the gift of loving relationships with their families. I give thanks to them for showing me the sacredness of life and the sacredness of our traditional teachings. It is my intention to highlight my amazing journey with the spirits of those women and with their families and to share the many messages that they have gifted us with.

My journey begins with the explanation of my Mohawk, Bear Clan name: Gowengyuseh, which means "She's Visiting." I was given this name as a very young child and was told that this is a very old name. Now that I am older, I realize what this name means to me. With the work that I do and the places I have been, I acknowledge that I am just a visitor in this physical world. I am able to visit with people in the physical world and in the spirit world. This is a gift that I now understand. I have been visited by many of the spirits of the women who are missing and who have been murdered. It is hard to explain, really, because the visits are really not explainable. I just know that there are some instances when I am visited by them. I just know. There is one instance that is very powerful that I would like to share before I begin telling my stories and relationships with families of the missing and murdered Indigenous women (MMIW).

Over the years, I have been honoured to present at various events around the globe about the horrific crises of MMIW. I have also been honoured to meet so many Elders and have heard so many powerful teachings of different First Nations (e.g., Cree, Anishinaabe, Mi'kmaq, Coast Salish, etc.) One of those teachings says that the spirit of each one of us is like a star. During an event in London, Ontario, in 2005, the spirits of the MMIW were being honoured and feasted. I remember looking up into the ceiling of the room where I was speaking and it was beautifully painted with stars. During that presentation, I was shown the twinkling of stardust that was shooting down and literally landing on specific people who were to become more aware and take action about the issue. It was totally amazing because I could see it happening as more and more people and communities were gathering and taking responsibility. It was and continues to be the spirits of those MMIW who are reminding all of us of our responsibilities.

My connection with the spirits of the MMIW began when I participated in a meeting at Caldwell First Nation with Darlene Ritchie in 2001. Many women had gathered to share their experiences of oppression and resistance. It was found that killing and maiming Aboriginal women was not uncommon, and it was far too common to have women disappear and killed without any investigation. As a result of this meeting, a report titled "Stop the Undeclared War against Aboriginal People" was prepared for the World Conference Against Racism in August 2001.[2]

Around this time, I also started focusing on the impacts of colonization on Indigenous women in Canada, and I was contracted by the Native Women's Association of Canada (NWAC) in 2002 to write a report to the United Nations Special Rapporteur on the situation of human rights of fundamental freedoms of Indigenous peoples, Rodolfo Stavenhagen.[3] That report provided a detailed history of colonization (i.e., government control, the Indian Act, residential schools, and child welfare, court, and prison systems), documented the specific impact on Indigenous women, and included a section on MMIW. Stavenhagen never followed up on this report; however, incumbent UN Special Rapporteur James Anaya did during his visit to Canada from October 7 to 15, 2013.[4]

In the report to the UN Special Rapporteur, I wrote about nineteen-year-old Helen Betty Osborne, who was killed because she was an Aboriginal woman and because four white men thought she was "easy."[5] I also advised Amnesty International that they had to at least begin the discussion of human rights violations against Indigenous women in their *Stolen Sisters* report with the human story about what had happened to Helen Betty Osborne.[6]

Osborne was a young Cree woman with hopes and dreams to become a teacher and to help her people. She had to leave her community to attend high school, which she did when she turned seventeen. She moved to the town close to her community called The Pas, which, in 1971, had a population of six thousand. The Pas was "sharply divided between Indigenous and non-Indigenous residents."[7] As Amnesty International explains in *Stolen Sisters*, "According to the testimony of one of the men, the four had decided to pick up an Indigenous woman for sex. When Osborne refused, they forced her into their car. In the car, she was beaten and sexually assaulted. She was then taken to a cabin owned by one of the men where she was beaten and stabbed to death. According to the autopsy report, she was severely beaten around the head and stabbed at least 50 times, possibly with a screwdriver."[8] One of the saddest aspects of the so-called police investigation was the fact that the police began their investigation within the Aboriginal community. When no suspects were found, the police dropped their investigation. There were some reports that four men were bragging about Osborne's death. It was found that many of the people in The Pas knew the names of the murderers but nothing was done for sixteen years. In the end, only one of the men was convicted and served any jail time. The handling of this case demonstrates a complete disregard for the life of an Aboriginal woman. It also shows the failure of the Manitoba police to properly investigate Osborne's death.

The Manitoba Justice Inquiry's mandate was to look into the circumstances surrounding the investigations of the murders of Helen Betty Osborne and J.J. Harper. Osborne's murder took place in 1971, but the inquiry began after three months of J.J. Harper's murder in 1988, and the final report was published in 1991. The inquiry noted the racism and a pattern of sexual harassment that existed in The Pas, where Osborne was abducted and murdered. As Amnesty International notes, "Police officers who testified before the Inquiry described 'white youths cruising the town, attempting to pick up Aboriginal girls for drinking parties and for sex.' The Inquiry found that the RCMP failed to check on the girls' safety. The Department of Indian Affairs also ignored the practice, failing to work with the schools to warn Indigenous students of the dangers."[9] These patterns still exist throughout Canada; there are continued safety risks for Indigenous women and girls. Canada, through its police force and political departments, has failed to ensure that Indigenous women and girls are safe and secure in today's society.

The Manitoba Justice Inquiry further determined that the most important factor of obstructing justice in this case was the failure of members of the non-Indigenous community to bring forward evidence that would have assisted the investigation. The inquiry concluded that the community's silence was at least partly motivated by racism. The question remained, however, "why the police waited more than ten years to publicly seek the assistance of the community."[10]

The stories of other murdered Indigenous women were included in my report to the UN Special Rapporteur in 2002. I wrote about my hero and mentor, Anna Mae Aquash, a Mi'kmaq warrior woman, who died in an execution-style murder after violence broke out between the FBI and the American Indian Movement at Wounded Knee in South Dakota. Fortunately, with her daughters' push for investigations and charges, the murderer, an Indigenous man, was found guilty. I also wrote about another Mi'kmaq woman, Cheryl Ann Johnson, whose drowned and partially nude body was found in shallow water off Sydney's popular boardwalk in Nova Scotia. Her death was investigated by police for only one day. The horrific details of the murders of Calinda Waterhen, Eva Taysup, Shelley Napope, and Mary Jane Serloin were also included in the report to the UN Special Rapporteur. These Indigenous women were all victims of a white rapist and serial killer John Crawford, who journalist Warren Goulding described as "the beneficiary of disinterested media and an equally impassive public."[11] Goulding placed Crawford amongst the likes of "David Berkowitz, New York City's 'Son of Sam,' the charming and deadly Ted Bundy, New Brunswick's Michael Wayne McGray and Canada's worst offender, the child killer Clifford Olson."[12]

Crawford was convicted (as a result of a plea) of manslaughter and served a ten-year sentence. Goulding met with Mary Jane Serloin's sister, Justine, who informed Goulding that no one contacted her regarding the death of her sister, nor about the charge, the trial, the conviction, or Crawford's sentencing. Goulding notes that throughout the trial and sentencing, none of Mary Jane Serloin's family appeared in court. He writes,

It would have been a simple matter for justice officials to locate Serloin's family and brief them on the case. Similarly, the local media could have shown some interest, even a little compassion for a family that had suffered the loss of a loved one. But when John Martin Crawford appeared in court and entered his plea, there were only a few observers, and Mary Jane Serloin's family was not among them. Their role in seeing that justice was meted out to the man who had taken Mary Jane's life was neither sought nor offered.[13]

I also referred to the life and brutal death of Pamela George in the UN Special Rapporteur report.[14] George was a Saulteaux mother with two children from the Sakimay First Nation community near Regina, Saskatchewan. She lived in poverty and was forced to work occasionally in the sex trade in Regina.[15] On April 17, 1995, Pamela George was killed by Tyler Kummerfield and Alexander Ternowetsky, two young drunk white male students who bragged to friends that they had picked up an "Indian hooker." Both were charged with first-degree murder and were eventually convicted of manslaughter and sentenced to six and a half years in prison. Both men admitted to hitting Pamela George but did not admit to killing her. According to a friend who testified at the trial, Ternowetsky said, "She deserved it. She was an Indian."[16]

The issue of Pamela George being a "hooker" and not a victim was prevalent throughout the trial. During the trial, presiding Justice Ted Malone instructed the jury to remember that George was "indeed a prostitute" when considering whether she consented to the sexual assault.[17] The issue of consent was important in determining whether the young men should be convicted of manslaughter rather than first-degree murder. Both of these men are now paroled and out of prison.

In the report to the UN Special Rapporteur in 2002, I also acknowledged the horrific numbers of Indigenous women who were missing from Vancouver's Downtown Eastside (DTES).

The women began disappearing in 1983, although the majority
of them went missing in the six years prior to Robert Pickton's
arrest in February 2002. When I wrote the UN report, Pickton had
just been arrested. The trial did not begin until January 22, 2007,
and it took almost a year to complete. Pickton pleaded not guilty
to twenty-seven charges of first-degree murder. I attended the
first few days of the trial and then went sporadically throughout
that year. I attended mostly with Sandra Gagnon, sister of victim
Janet Henry, about whom I wrote to the UN Special Rapporteur.
I continue to be friends with Sandra, who has been such a strong
advocate for her sister. The mysterious disappearance of Janet
Henry has touched the lives of hundreds, perhaps thousands, of
people. She is still missing and her sister and family continue to be
traumatized.

   While attending the Pickton murder trial, I also became friends
with Georgina Papin's sisters. Georgina Papin was another of
Pickton's victims. I vividly remember Georgina's sisters walking
back to the hotel after court one day. It was pouring rain and I was
driving, so I picked them up and asked if they needed help. They
did. We spent the rest of the day together. We laughed and they
shared their memories of Georgina with me. It struck me that I
already knew some of their stories, and it was then I realized that
the spirit of Georgina had visited me many times. There were
statements that they made about her and various descriptions of
her silliness that I had already known. In the years that followed,
I invited them to participate in many of the NWAC's Sisters in
Spirit gatherings. I met them at many different places across the
country, including Edmonton, Ottawa, Vancouver, and New
Westminster, BC. I love them dearly. And later, when Georgina's
body parts were released to the family, they asked me to honour
the spirit of Georgina, to carry her remains and bury her. It was an
experience I will cherish forever.

   Writing the report to the UN Special Rapporteur on the rights
of Indigenous peoples, and working with the stories of the MMIW
began my journey with the spirits of the women. While writing

that report at my office at Six Nations, I recall a cold chill racing up my spine. I did not know the missing and murdered women, but I was beginning to. I could see their faces and I could hear them speak and I could hear them cry. I remember a strong voice telling me, *This is bigger than you know.* I did not realize then exactly what that meant, but now I do.

Amnesty International's Stolen Sisters Report

After completing the report to the UN Special Rapporteur, I was contracted by Amnesty International Canada to be the lead researcher and consultant for a report titled *Stolen Sisters: A Human Rights Response to Discrimination and Violence against Indigenous Women in Canada* (2004). During this work, my personal relationship with the MMIW's families deepened. I travelled across the country and met family after family who told me their traumatic and emotional stories about the loss of their loved ones. I remember too well the emotional trauma I felt as well. Too often I heard families tell me that no one had ever sat with them to listen and to support them. I was honoured that they allowed me into their homes and trusted me to share their stories in the Amnesty report. One of the huge messages was that we all need to support and honour any individual or family who has been traumatized as a result of losing someone.

The Amnesty International report focused on the lives and brutal deaths of nine missing and/or murdered Aboriginal women who lived primarily in the Western provinces, even though I had met with many more families. I advised Amnesty that it would take time to develop trust with the families of the MMIW, and that there was a need to educate families about the human rights work of Amnesty International and what the organization does. It was also important that the family members knew exactly what the project was about and what their responsibilities would be in participating. As part of the reciprocity, Amnesty agreed to bring the families together at a gathering at Six Nations Grand River Territory after the release of the final report in October 2004.

During my travels for Amnesty International and while meeting with families from coast to coast, I heard of the trauma that these families were dealing with on a day-to-day basis. I sat with some of them for days at a time, some for just a few hours. They trusted me; they trusted that I would tell their truths. Most of them felt that their voices were silenced, that there was nowhere to turn. They told me about how they were doing all of the work to bring attention to the issues. They were putting up the poster boards and pictures. They were doing all of the searching and investigating, not the police. It was a stark reminder of the societal indifference to Indigenous women.

I met with Anna Mae Pictou Aquash's daughter Denise Maloney Pictou more than once, and I maintain a friendship with her to this day. Denise and her sister Debbie have had to deal with so much regarding their mother's murder. To lose a mother is one of the most difficult things to go through by any means, but to have to deal with the violence of murder from one of our own Indigenous men must compound the trauma. This case also reinforced one of the biggest messages that I encountered: no one has the right to take another person's life—especially a mother's life. Anna Mae's message was about peace and our relationship to the land, and I honour her spirit for this. She was fighting for all of our rights. She stood at the front lines without hesitation. She was a Woman Warrior, and I honour her for that. She is my mentor.

One of the MMIW that did not make it into the *Stolen Sisters* report was Deborah Anne Sloss, whose death was never investigated. In 2003, I organized and facilitated a powerful and moving family healing circle in Hamilton, Ontario, for her family. They believed that Debbie was murdered in Toronto in the summer of 1997, but there was no police investigation into her death. The healing circle allowed family members to talk freely. Debbie's sister Mary Lou Smoke and her husband, Dan Smoke, were integral to the gathering, as they provided healing songs and prayers throughout. Each of the family members was given the opportunity to talk about Debbie's life and to describe when they had heard about Debbie's passing. When Debbie's daughter, Laura, spoke, it became immediately apparent that this discussion was going to be very healing for the family. Everyone started sharing information about Debbie's death. They were upset and disappointed with the Toronto police because they did not investigate. The family felt that the police did not investigate because she was labelled a street person. As a result, the family was left searching for answers.

I could see that the healing circle enabled many of the family members to have closure for Debbie's death. They felt that she was now at peace and in the Creator's hands. They also felt that her death helped bring the family together. I honour the spirit of Deborah Anne Sloss: her message was to bring family back together. Dan Smoke, Debbie's brother-in-law, closed the gathering with these words: "It is important to honour the missing and murdered women. It is unacceptable to marginalize these women. The Creator did not create garbage. He created beauty. Debbie was a beautiful flower."

Another beautiful flower that did not make it into the *Stolen Sisters* report was Carrieann Larocque. She, like so many Indigenous women, was murdered by her common-law boyfriend when she was twenty-nine years old. Carrieann was a Mi'kmaq woman from the Gesgapegiag First Nations community in Quebec. She was the sister of seven siblings. She grew up in her community as well as in New Hampshire and Massachusetts. She moved back to her community in 1996. Her sister Denise described her as someone who would do anything for anyone. She was a very kind person. As Denise said during an interview with me in 2003, "She helped everybody. She would spend her last dollar on a birthday present for you and you knew the gift came from her heart. She always made your birthday special."

Carrieann was in an abusive relationship with her boyfriend, Noel Condo. When I met with her sister, she told me that many people had warned Carrieann to leave but she wouldn't. She always thought it would get better. There were restraining orders against Condo; he was not supposed to come near Carrieann.

However, Condo did not follow these restraining orders, and, on January 2, 2002, he murdered Carrieann. Condo was charged with murder, but he was convicted of only manslaughter. Rhonda, Carrieann's sister, stated that Carrieann did not deserve to die this way, nor should any other woman.

There are horrific statistics of Indigenous women being murdered by their partners,[18] and the most high-risk times are during separation or divorce. I honour the spirit of Carrieann: her message to all of us is to become more aware of the risks so that the situation does not become lethal. Her death was also a message for police to become aware of the cycle of violence, and to come up with solutions when the system breaks down—especially when restraining orders are not working. It was over ten years ago that Carrieann's sister Denise urged the police to take up more training on violence against women. This is a message that still requires action. Denise also recommended training or awareness workshops for families who know that their mother, daughter, or granddaughter is being abused. She called for finding ways to assist them. This is what we can take from the loss of Carrieann: a reminder that we can no longer be a bystander, that we all have to take responsibility in providing safety to our loved ones who may be going through a horrific relationship like the one that Carrieann suffered.

Native Women's Association of Canada's Sisters in Spirit Initiative

Another amazing journey with the spirits of the MMIW and their families occurred while I was president of the Native Women's Association of Canada. In fact, it was the families of the MMIW that I had met during my time with Amnesty International who pushed me to run for president of NWAC. I made a conscious choice at that time to support those families, and to bring awareness to the issues surrounding MMIW, as well as many other issues related to Indigenous women in Canada.

I had already been part of a team that designed the initial national proposal for the Sisters in Spirit (SIS) initiative, which had requested $10 million over two years from the federal government. Paul Martin's Liberal government gave us $5 million over five years, so the Sisters in Spirit initiative began in the spring of 2005 and ended in 2010. It was a "long-term research, education, and policy initiative designed to increase public knowledge and understand the impacts of racialized, sexualized violence against Aboriginal women that often leads to their disappearance or death."[19]

One difficulty that I had with the SIS initiative was that it did not directly support families of MMIW. We were able to have little bits of money to have family gatherings, but it became more and more difficult to ensure that all families participated. I began to feel the difficulties of having this issue of MMIW funded by government, with its control over the dollars and how it would be spent. Many times, I felt the families' angst in not being able to participate in gatherings, or to have the resources that they needed for searches or to attend murder trials.

The SIS initiative did bring the public's attention to the issue of MMIW, and grassroots organizations and individuals did a lot of work to support many families across the country. As a result, awareness of the issue spread like wildfire at the grassroots level, but I still feel that the Canadian public is not as aware as they should be about MMIW. I also feel that the affected families need to be directly supported—whether it be for searches for their loved ones or resources for families while they attend murder trials. At the time of writing, the federal government had just committed to implementing the National Inquiry into Missing and Murdered Indigenous Women and Girls, which will hopefully make the Canadian public more aware of these issues. Also, the federal government should immediately provide the resources that families require as the inquiry is launched.

An ongoing difficulty is that families are not made fully aware of what happens at murder trials. They need the support from legal counsel or legally trained people to advise them about the process; after all, the criminal legal process largely does not support victims of crime. Families need support while going through a murder trial and especially around what to expect when evidence—that is, the details of the murder of their loved one—is presented for the first time. Families need to be prepared for this! I learned this at Pickton's murder trial. It was during that trial that many of those families first heard the horrific details of how their beloved mother, sister, aunty, cousin, grandmother had been murdered. It made me physically sick to hear these details, so I can't even imagine how the immediate family members and friends felt.

One of my first meetings as president of NWAC was with Bridget Tolley, whose mother, Gladys Tolley, was struck and killed by a Sûreté du Québec police cruiser in 2001. A police investigation closed the case by reporting that the death was accidental. Bridget maintained that her mother's death was not accidental, and was adamant that the police failed her family and her mother. When I first met Bridget, she was already working hard to obtain justice for her mother and her family, and was calling for an inquiry into her mother's death. I supported Bridget instantly, which prompted other organizations to jointly sign a letter requesting that the Quebec government reopen the case and conduct an independent inquiry into the supposedly accidental death of Gladys Tolley. The letter, dated July 17, 2009, was signed by the Native Women's Association, Assembly of First Nations, Quebec Native Women's Association, the Algonquin Nation, Kitigan Zibi Anishinabeg, Amnesty International Canada, and Amnesty Montreal. The Quebec government ultimately denied the call for an inquiry in 2010. It was heartbreaking to see the pain and grief that Bridget was going through and continues to go through. It was Bridget who had suggested that we start a vigil on Parliament Hill in Ottawa. So, once Sisters in Spirit began, we co-ordinated the first Sisters in Spirit Vigil on the Hill on October 4, 2005, and it has now become a yearly event around the world. When NWAC's Sisters in Spirit initiative ended in 2010, Bridget refused to allow the momentum to stop and co-founded the Families of Sisters in Spirit organization. Bridget has become one of the strongest advocates for the families of MMIWG to this day. She and her family deserve justice.

Also as president of NWAC and later as a lawyer, I assisted the Muskego family—Pauline and Herb from Onion Lake Cree Nation in Saskatchewan. They had originally contacted me just as I had handed in my first draft of the *Stolen Sisters* report to Amnesty International in April 2004. I was not able to get the story of their daughter Daleen Bosse into the report, as Daleen had been missing for only two weeks at that time. They were referred to me by our mutual friend Patricia Monture, who is also now in the spirit world. Unfortunately, four years later in August of 2008, Daleen's remains were found and she had been murdered. The trial did not proceed until May 2014 and the Muskegos had requested that I represent them at their daughter's murder trial. I would like to share my journey with the Muskegos, which continues.

Like all of the families of MMIW, the Muskegos had the horrific job of bringing attention to the issue and doing the hard work of searching for their daughter when she was missing. I remember the conversations with them when they received a tip, and how they travelled across the country to look for her. They organized a run for Daleen four years in a row (2004 to 2008) in the hopes of bringing her home. Many of the youth and young family members participated in those runs, and I had the pleasure of meeting most of them, as I travelled to all of them except for one. Herb gifted me with an eagle feather at one of the runs, and I carried this feather with me while I was president of NWAC and during my work for Aboriginal women and MMIW. I carried this feather at the Statement of Apology to former students of residential schools in June 2008. The last run was in July 2008 and the Muskegos had decided that this would be the last one—not knowing that their daughter's remains would be found just a month later. When their daughter's remains were found four years after she was reported missing, it was a traumatic and terrifying time for the family. It came after many hopes and dreams that Daleen would return home. I watched the family through some very emotional times and supported them the best that I could.

Daleen's murder trial finally took place in 2014—ten years after she first went missing. One of the most unusual processes occurred at the murder trial. The defence for murderer Douglas Hales argued that Daleen was drunk and died from alcohol poisoning, and requested her medical records. Drawing on *R. v. O'Connor*, the Supreme Court of Canada set out a test for trial judges to determine whether privileged medical records can be disclosed as evidence. As a result, the trial judge in this case wanted to hear from Daleen's family to determine whether her medical records should be made available. As I attended a meeting with Pauline and the Crown attorney, I was designated by Pauline to represent the family, and I argued that Daleen's medical records should not be presented as evidence. This was an amazing opportunity to speak for the family and on Daleen's behalf, to respect her spirit, as I argued that any medical records were totally private and protected under law as privileged evidence.

I was not prepared to argue at the Superior Court of Saskatchewan, where I was required to wear a gown, so the Muskego family and community in Saskatoon gathered up the required lawyer garb that I had to wear in court the next day. I was quite honoured but very nervous to do this for the family and for Daleen, but I remember feeling that her spirit visited me and provided me with the words that needed to be said in court. Unfortunately, it was not her own physical voice that could be heard.

My Personal Experiences of Violence

During my professional life as an entrepreneur, lawyer, consultant, and professor, my focus has been on understanding and bringing awareness of the impacts of trauma and violence on Indigenous peoples, specifically Indigenous women. I never believed that after supporting and advocating for families of the missing and murdered, I would have to experience the same loss and trauma. Yet my own cousin, Tashina General, went missing in January 2008 when she was three months pregnant. She was found murdered in April 2008. That was one of the most traumatic experiences our family has ever been through, and it resulted in post-traumatic stress. I had to move away from my family and my community when I retired from NWAC in 2009 in order to heal. I have now returned home and will use my life experiences and healing experiences to revitalize our teachings that focus on peaceful relations, and to continue to advocate for families of the missing and murdered women.

While on my healing path, I began to learn about Haudenosaunee teachings that were cut off from me, from my mother, and from my grandmother—my matrilineal ancestors who were directly impacted from the residential school system. I began to understand our teachings around women being honoured and respected because of their decision-making instincts and their responsibilities in carrying and bringing life into this physical world. I began to understand that our men are Warriors and are responsible to protect women and children and to protect our lands and territories. I began to understand that how colonization had such a detrimental effect upon these roles and responsibilities.

I have learned about not being safe in my own home and community. I have learned what an abusive relationship is. In an abusive relationship, the abuser feels the need to have power and control. When an abuser feels that his power and control are taken away, he has to strike out at his most vulnerable victim to regain that power and control. The victim loses her voice and feels that she does not have any control of the situation during the abuse. I remember being silent and knowing that I could not say a word to anyone about the abuse that was happening. I remember that silence well.

When an abusive relationship ends, the victim makes a decision to take her power back. I remember saying that I will no longer be

beaten or abused—not mentally, emotionally, spiritually, physically, or sexually. I remember saying that no one will ever hurt
me again. I acknowledged that I would no longer be a victim. I
had found my voice and regained respect for myself. As a survivor
of violence, I have learned not to blame anyone else but to take
responsibility for myself. I can celebrate my life and learn from the
lessons that have been taught to me.

The abusive relationships that happen to our women are also
borne out in the larger context of Canada's colonial relationship to
Indigenous peoples. Canada's colonial government has been an
abuser since it began. First, it violated peace and friendship treaties,
which were based on nation-to-nation relationships, by unilater-
ally establishing its government through legislation in which it
had control over Indians and lands reserved for Indians with section
91(24) of the British North America Act, 1867. This legislation
then gave the government authority to establish the most racist
piece of legislation: the Indian Act. These unilateral acts were the
beginning of the abusive relationship. As a result of generations of
abuse and control, Indigenous peoples have become victims in a
longstanding abusive relationship and have been silenced through
the lack of control over lands and resources, the genocidal policies
of the residential school system, and the disrespect and violence
against Indigenous women.

Conclusion

The spirits of the MMIW remind all of us that the violence against
women and the violence occurring against Mother Earth are
directly connected. Haudenosaunee planting ceremonies acknowledge that the women are the seed—the connection between the
Creator and Mother Earth. The loss of connection of Indigenous
women to their lands and territories through legalized genocide
(i.e., the Indian Act policies and law) or murder means that the
lifeblood and carrier of future generations are also cut off. Since the
inception of the Indian Act, there have been missing Indigenous

women who were forcefully displaced from their traditional territories for "marrying out." This was the beginning of missing Indigenous women. The genocidal policies of the Indian Act also had an impact on Indigenous governance systems where the women's decision-making qualities were silenced and no longer part of the balance of these systems. And we already know what the residential schools did to our families, including the roles of mothers and fathers and the losses of family bonding, and the loss of the most basic tenets of a relationship: love and emotional well-being.

To become survivors of this abusive relationship, all victims, including Indigenous men and women, must take their power back. Many have already. This is what decolonization means at a very practical level—taking our power back. The language and actions about violence against Indigenous women has to shift to actually begin the decolonization process.

What do I mean by shifting our language? It means that we have to stop behaving and talking like a victim. One of the most difficult things to do along our healing path is to stop blaming the abuser and to take responsibility for our own actions. We have to teach our next generations about healthy relationships and healthy sexual relationships and how to treat each other with respect. We need to practice our teachings by making a conscious choice about the decisions that we make today and how each of those decisions have an impact seven generations from now. I know my ancestors did that for me seven generations ago. The decisions include how we teach our sons to respect themselves and to be good men, to honour the women in their lives, to honour their children, to be good fathers and good grandfathers; the decisions to teach our daughters to respect themselves and their bodies, to respect all of the relationships in their lives, to know that they are the life givers and nurturers to the next generations.

Decolonization means bringing the safety back and living in a society where we feel safe and where we respect each other as people. It means that our men are taking back their rightful responsibilities to be the Warriors of our nations, to protect the women and the children, and the lands they are all connected to, to protect the lands for our future generations. It means that our women are taking back their rightful responsibilities to be respected decision makers, to carry and nurture life, and to bring those future generations into this physical world. It is the responsibility of all generations (mothers, fathers, grandmothers, and grandfathers) to ensure that we maintain those connections to our lands and territories, with our strong languages and ceremonies intact. It means that we celebrate our resiliency in the face of an abusive relationship and choose positive relationships that honour ourselves, our communities, our women, and our lands. These are the lessons that I believe have come from the spirits of the MMIW and from their families and friends.

I have been very honoured to present these stories of the families and friends of MMIWG who, at one time, might have felt that their voices were not being heard. I hope I have done them justice as they are now quite strong enough to share their own stories, and they are very much being heard today. Their voices are powerful and amazing, and I am so grateful to be on this journey with them. We now have an opportunity to ensure that the public is aware of the impacts of the losses of MMIWG and to delve into the positive changes that are coming ahead.

NOTES

1. "Cindy Gladue Case Sends a Devastating Message to Aboriginal Women," *The Current*, CBC Radio, March 31, 2015, http://www.cbc.ca/radio/ thecurrent/the-current-for-march-31-2015-1.3016006/cindy-gladue- case-sends-a-devastating-message-to-aboriginal-women-1.3016011.

2. "Stop the Undeclared War against Aboriginal People" presented by Terri Brown at the World Conference Against Racism, Durban, South Africa, August 2001.

3. Beverly Jacobs, "Native Women's Association of Canada's Submission to the United Nations Special Rapporteur Investigating the Violations of Indigenous Human Rights," Ottawa, December 2002.

4. James Anaya, *Report of the Special Rapporteur on the Rights of Indigenous Peoples*, UN General Assembly, A/HRC/27/52/Add.2, 2014, http://unsr.jamesanaya.org/docs/countries/2014-report-canada-a-hrc-27-52-add-2-en.pdf.

5. A.C. Hamilton and C.M. Sinclair, *Report of the Aboriginal Justice Inquiry of Manitoba: The Deaths of Helen Betty Osborne and John Joseph Harper*, 3 vols. (Winnipeg: Aboriginal Justice of Manitoba, 1991).

6. Amnesty International, *Stolen Sisters: A Human Rights Response to Discrimination and Violence against Indigenous Women in Canada* (Ottawa: Amnesty International, 2004), https://www.amnesty.ca/sites/amnesty/files/amr200032004enstolensisters.pdf.

7. Amnesty International, *Stolen Sisters*, 22.

8. Amnesty International, *Stolen Sisters*, 22.

9. Amnesty International, *Stolen Sisters*, 22.

10. Amnesty International, *Stolen Sisters*, 23.

11. Warren Goulding, *Just Another Indian: A Serial Killer and Canada's Indifference* (Calgary: Fifth House, 2001), xiii.

12. Goulding, *Just Another Indian*, 46.

13. Goulding, *Just Another Indian*, 75.

14. Sherene Razack, "Gendered Racial Violence and Spatialized Justice: The Murder of Pamela George," in *Race, Space, and the Law: Unmapping a White Settler Society*, ed. Sherene Razack (Toronto: Between the Lines, 2002), 125–47.

15. Razack, "Gendered Racial Violence."

16. Amnesty International, *Stolen Sisters*, 26.

17. Razack, "Gendered Racial Violence," 152.

18. Shannon Brennan, "Violent Victimization of Aboriginal Women in the Canadian Provinces, 2009," *Juristat*, Statistics Canada cat. no. 85-002-X, May 17, 2011, http://www.statcan.gc.ca/pub/85-002-x/2011001/article/11439-eng.htm#a4. As Brennan reports, 15 per cent of Aboriginal women who had a current or former spouse reported being a victim of spousal violence in the five years preceding the General Social Survey, compared with 6 per cent of non-Aboriginal women.

19. Beverly Jacobs and Andrea Williams, "Legacy of Residential Schools: Missing and Murdered Aboriginal Women," in *Truth to Reconciliation: Transforming the Legacy of Residential Schools*, prepared for the Aboriginal Healing Foundation by Marlene Brant Castellano, Linda Archibald, and Mike DeGagné (Ottawa: Aboriginal Healing Foundation, 2008), 132, http://www.ahf.ca/downloads/from-truth-to-reconciliation-transforming-the-legacy-of-residential-schools.pdf.

3 | Sacred Sisters and Sacred Circles

A Story of One Nehiyawak Family and the Power of Spirit

SANDRA LAMOUCHE

IT HAS BEEN OVER FIFTEEN YEARS since I first heard about the Stolen Sisters and Sisters in Spirit campaigns during my first few years in university. I was immediately overcome by the facts and statistics and decided to get involved. Since 2003, I have collected signatures for the Stolen Sisters petition, been part of a panel discussion on Christine Welsh's film *Finding Dawn*, danced in and co-created a dance film with Cara Mumford called *When It Rains*, which has played nationally, danced for several awareness events, marched in Stolen Sisters rallies, and attended a rally in Vancouver's Downtown Eastside.[1] Most recently, I was invited to co-create a contemporary dance piece with Sydney Murdoch. R E (A) D, uses spoken word, quotes, and poetry from Indigenous scholars, artists, and the Truth and Reconciliation Commission to explore the connection between Mother Earth, residential schools, and Missing and Murdered Indigenous Women and Girls.

In 2005, wanting to learn more about my family history, I asked my mother what happened to my Nohkom (my grandmother), her mother. She told me the story of my Nohkom, Sarah Cardinal, and how she had attended residential school, which she was only able to leave at the age of sixteen if she married Nimosom (my grandfather), who was Métis. She told me how Nohkom Sarah had been hit by a drunk driver on the Bigstone Cree Nation (Wabasca) in northern Alberta when my mother was still a young girl. Her body was thrown into the lake, only to be discovered a while later, frozen. This happened over fifty years ago and remains an unsolved murder case today.

My mother, Margaret (Cardinal) Lamouche, and her siblings had a tough childhood without their mother to care for them. Nimosom was a trapper and would leave for long periods during the winter to attend to his trapline, leaving my mother and her older sisters to care for the younger children. My mother fondly remembers hearing the sound of the bells from his team of sled dogs and the joy of knowing her father had returned.

In 2006, my youngest sister, Julie, went missing from our home for one month. She was with an abusive and controlling boyfriend who would take her without letting her or anyone else know where they were going. Usually, she would be gone a few days, which is why we were so concerned for her this time. During this period, her boyfriend drove over her cell phone and threatened her, as we later learned. Although we contacted police, they did nothing more than put out a poster. Determined to do something, my parents sought spiritual help from an Elder in Saskatchewan; with these prayers they returned home. They next spoke with my auntie, a deeply spiritual person, who used a pendulum to help locate my sister. Recently, I spent a weekend with my auntie as she shared how she came to recognize the movement of the pendulum in a spiral as relating to the Native world view.

Through her spiritual gifts, my auntie shared an image of where my sister was. She described it as a large parking lot with a lot of big trucks and lights. She said it looked like she was at a carnival. It was the middle of summer so we searched for all the different fairs and carnivals in Alberta. My brother found her working at a carnival near Edmonton, and he brought her home. Today, Julie is living a good life: she is in college, working, raising her son, and living a drug- and alcohol-free lifestyle, as well as returning to hoop dancing and other cultural practices.

The story of Nohkom and my sister, respectively, tell the worst-case and best-case scenarios for Aboriginal women who go missing in Canada. For my Nohkom, as an unsolved murder case, it is obvious that the police have not done enough to bring justice to her murderer(s). In my sister's case, again, the police did not find her. It was my parents and family who looked for help and were able to find her through the spirituality.

The experience and history of my family is a testament to the spiritual power of our people and the relevance of Native culture in our contemporary world. The ancient knowledge of Native people is needed today more than ever, as many Elders have been stressing to younger generations for so long. Our culture is a vital part of our healing and well-being as Native peoples. It has been my goal to learn, share, and promote Native culture as much as I can.

Sacred Circles

In 2005, I began learning the hoop dance, and decided to bring both of my younger sisters to learn with me. Our teacher was Jerry First Charger (Kainai/Blood Reserve), who shared the story of the hoop dance with me. This story can be found in Basil Johnston's *The Manitous: The Spiritual Life of the Ojibway*.[2] The story is about Pukawiss (the disowned one), whose real name has been forgotten. The middle child of three brothers, Pukawiss was fascinated with nature since childhood. His father hoped he would become a good warrior and hunter like his older brother, Maudjekawiss. Pukawiss tried to please his father but always returned to his ways of exploring the world around him. Eventually, his father disowned him and gave all his attention to Maudjekawiss. Pukawiss left his family and travelled to different villages as a performer. He created dances and performances based on what he saw around him, mimicking animals and humans alike. He became well known,

receiving gifts and offers of marriage as he travelled village to village.

One day he decided to create a dance that encompassed all of life—the good and the bad—and thus he created the hoop dance. The beautiful designs reflect the beauty all around us—in birds, butterflies, flowers, and other beings. The hoop dancer's transitions from one shape to the next represent life's struggles. The transitions also show how everything in life is interconnected; the hoop itself represents interconnectedness, equality, and balance. Johnston writes that today people often see only the beauty in the dance and fail to see the struggle; therefore, they do not understand the full meaning of the dance. Johnston explains that Pukawiss used the hoop dance to act as a counsellor:

> In the Hoop Dance, Pukawiss dramatized the trauma that people often go through, their disorientation, and finally their recourse to a counselor for guidance. But instead of giving answers, directions, and encouragement to enable a person to get out of his or her predicament, the dancer who portrays the counselor presents the distressed person with wooden hoops made of willow. The act represents the perception that troubles cannot be transferred to or resolved by another and that the advice dispensed is actually a return of the troubles to the distressed person for sorting out…And like the distressed person who seeks refuge or solutions outside himself, even in spiritualism and religion, the dancer who portrays Pukawiss forms figures of spiritual patrons and manitous. The manitous are unmoved; they offer no help. Desperate, Pukawiss twists and turns and, commencing with the last turn, pressed himself through the hoops until he works his way through all of them, reminiscent of the person who must live and work his own

< *The author's sister, Julie Lamouche, in performance.* [photo: Kyle Fowler]

way through his adversities from last to first until he has them
all hand in hand, under control.[3]

The story of my family, as well as the story of Pukawiss, follows
a cycle of creation–destruction–re-creation as described in Leanne
Betasamosake Simpson's *Dancing on Our Turtle's Back: Stories of
Nishnaabeg Re-Creation, Resurgence, and a New Emergence.*[4] In her
analysis of the Seven Fires Prophecy of the Anishnaabek, Simpson
explains,

There is a mirroring of the cycle of creation–destruction–
re-creation within Nishnaabeg thought. This cycle sets the
stage for interpretation of re-creation as a new emergence or
resurgence. This theme is also echoed to current generations
through our Re-creation Stories. Within Indigenous thought,
there is no singular vision of resurgence, but many...[This means]
we all carry responsibilities in terms of resurgence; and that
we are also responsible for re-creating the good life in what-
ever forms we imagine, vision and live in contemporary times.[5]

In the story of my family, creation would have been in the
period of my ancestors, before Nehiyaw ways were disrupted by
European beliefs, and the subsequent period of destruction that
resulted in the unsolved murder of my Nohkom Sarah. Now my
family is living in a period of re-creation, my sister being found
through spiritual gifts once celebrated in Aboriginal culture. My
family's story is evidence of just how vital Aboriginal culture can
be in the case of missing and murdered women. These traditional
practices and spiritual gifts can be more successful and accurate
when searching for our stolen sisters than the police. Through a
return to culture and spirit we can take charge of our own safety,
ensure our own health and happiness, and reclaim our strength

< *The author, Sandra Lamouche, performing her own choreography—*
"Sagowsko," Lethbridge, Alberta. [photo: Kyle Fowler]

and beauty as Aboriginal women. This is not to imply, however, that we don't need multiple strategies—including holding the Canadian state accountable for improving police service.

For Pukawiss, creation was the period in childhood where he was being himself—interested in nature. Destruction was the opposition and oppression he faced from his father, and re-creation was his life as a traveller and performer, which led to his creation of the hoop dance. Being true to his identity and continuing to be himself led him to a great life as a performer, artist, leader, and teacher.

For Aboriginal women, creation was the original role and teachings of women in traditional Aboriginal societies. Destruction occurred with colonization and assimilation. Before Europeans came to the "new world," Aboriginal women had respected roles and positions of value and importance within a community. Women were once considered sacred in the circle of life. They were important are keeping families and communities together; they ensured culture and language were taught to children. "Old world" opinions about the subordination of women, and especially Aboriginal women, meant that women were no longer considered equals within the sacred circle of life. The re-creation period is occurring now as Aboriginal women strive to regain and relearn this vital role that ensures the well-being of all. We are returning to our position as an essential part of the circle as Sacred Sisters, re-creating a life based on the Sacred Circle.

Hiy hiy (Thank you)
Kisaageetin (You are loved by me)

NOTES

1. *Finding Dawn*, directed by Christine Welsh (NFB, 2006), https://www.nfb.ca/film/finding_dawn/; *When It Rains*, directed by Cara Mumford, available on YouTube, posted December 30, 2012, https://www.youtube.com/watch?v=w_Ec9ujP55k.

2. Basil Johnston, *The Manitous: The Spiritual Life of the Ojibway* (New York: HarperCollins, 1995).

3. Johnston, *The Manitous*, 31–32.

4. Leanne Betasamosake Simpson, *Dancing on Our Turtle's Back: Stories of Nishnaabeg Re-Creation, Resurgence and a New Emergence* (Winnipeg: ARP Books, 2011).

5. Simpson, *Dancing on Our Turtle's Back*, 68.

43

4 | *Honouring Elsie*

Was She Just a Dream?

ANN-MARIE LIVINGSTON & SARAH HUNT

IN NOVEMBER 1992, *at the age of forty, my mother, Elsie Jones Sebastian, went missing from the streets of Vancouver's Downtown Eastside. I had seen her only a few months before, when I visited her in the summer after I finished grade twelve. But my sister, Donalee, and I haven't seen her since. In fact, no one, including loved ones, friends, and family, has been able to find out what happened to her. Over the years, my sister and I have participated in a number of women's memorial marches in Victoria and Vancouver, BC, and have also testified at the Missing Women Commission of Inquiry, as we have joined in the social and legal efforts to find answers for the missing women. But I have also become concerned about the gaps between the experiences of family members like myself and the larger political issues, funding, and legal issues that have developed as the missing women have become a social cause along with broad issues of violence against Indigenous women. Aside from the legal realm of court cases and inquiries, how can Elsie's story be heard and her life honoured? How can we connect the intimate acts of mourning and remembrance with the societal efforts to address the issue of missing women?*

In this essay, I will share some of my stories and observations emerging from the years of coping with my mother's disappearance, as the issue of missing and murdered women has gained national attention. Along with my collaborator and family friend, Sarah Hunt, who has worked on these issues for more than fifteen years, I will talk about how my own experience as the daughter of a missing woman differs from the perspectives of the ever-growing list of "experts" on this issue, who are largely the ones accessing funding ear-marked for this cause. I question the credibility of these consultants to be the voice of the missing, given that the voices of family members and their unique experiences and insights often remain unheard. These experts may focus on missing women's lives after they are already gone, but family members are able to share individual histories of colonial oppression as well as resilience and strength that each woman carried. These insights change how we see the issue of "missing women," as we are called to make Indigenous women's lives matter at a personal level. I will also share some of the complex ways that personal mourning has been brought into the legal realm, as we are confronted with unthinkable decisions around the legal processes in how to deal with my mom's "missing" status. I end by sharing some of my ongoing personal struggles to deal with my mom's loss and confront the judgement of those who fail to understand the nature of my grief, as missing and murdered Indigenous women becomes an "issue" or a "cause." My first-person perspective will be written in italics, as it is here, while the text that Sarah and I wrote collaboratively will be in regular font.

Voices of the Missing and Murdered Women
Personal to Political

In 2007, the issue of missing and murdered Aboriginal women rose to international attention as a serial killer Robert Pickton was convicted of the murder of six women, after the remains or DNA of thirty-three women were found on his rural farm in British Columbia. Yet many more women were suspected to have met

their death on this property—Elsie Jones Sebastian was one
of them.

In the years leading up to the surfacing of this horrific story,
people began talking about "the missing and murdered women"
from Vancouver's Downtown Eastside (DTES)—a group of
women who were targeted for violence in this neighbourhood
where poverty, drug use, sex work, and homelessness are commonplace. Women here were also targeted due to the lack of systemic
response to the violence, as community advocates had been calling
for a police investigation into their murders and disappearances for
many years, to no avail. But even before the community activism
began, and before the public became aware of the missing women,
family members were searching for, talking about, and mourning
the loss of their loved ones. Individual women who had disappeared
were more than just faces on a poster of "the missing"; for those
who loved them, they had long been a source of good memories,
complex histories, and unending hope that they would some
day return.

Although Elsie's life has become known publicly through her
status as "missing" from this notorious Vancouver neighbourhood, her personal history reveals both the longstanding legacy
of colonial violence facing Indigenous women in this country, as
well as the personal legacy of love and resilience she left behind.
The complexity of her story, along with many other missing
and murdered women, is often left out of national representations of "the missing women." The emotional landscape of family
members' intimate loss, grief, memories, and hope differs in
significant ways from the aggression and anger than often fuels
rallies and awareness campaigns that have come to represent the
issue. We suggest that the personal and ongoing ways family
members cope with losing their loved ones is an important part of
the story of the missing women.

In the years since investigations began into the missing women
from in the DTES, violence against Indigenous women and girls
has been shown to be rampant in both rural and urban areas

throughout the country.[1] This growing recognition led to the designation of funding from provincial and federal governments in Canada, targeted at addressing violence against Indigenous women, specifically the issue of missing and murdered women. Although the funding has contributed to important education and research, the family members of women like Elsie have had little involvement in these initiatives, little say in prioritizing government funding, and little benefit from the designated funds.

Federally funded organizations such as the Native Women's Association of Canada (NWAC), along with individual consultants and other "experts" have become known as the voice for "the missing and murdered women," while the voices of individual family members as well as community advocates in the DTES and along the Highway of Tears and other communities, have largely been overlooked. Ann-Marie, the co-author of this paper, has been told by some professional consultants about invitations they received to speak nationally or internationally, yet these same consultants fail to ask Ann-Marie for consent to speak about her mother's case or invite her to speak alongside them. How ethical is it for academics, who have no personal connection to a missing woman, to be paid a consulting fee to speak as an expert on this topic, while family members are still limited in their choices for counselling? Others, such as artists who painted portraits of missing women from the DTES without permission from their family members, have been called out for capitalizing on the issue of missing and murdered women.[2]

Sarah—the second co-author of this paper—has been working on this issue as a community-based and academic researcher and educator for many years and is frequently invited to speak about the issue of missing and murdered women at events where family members' voices are absent. This question of who is invited to represent this issue is what led to our decision to collaboratively write this paper, rather than Sarah authoring her own paper to contribute to this volume on the issue of missing women.

Academics, employees of government-funded organizations, and consultants who work on Aboriginal issues must continue to reflect on the way they use their power and position to advocate for change. In speaking up, how might other voices be silenced? In accessing funding, how might family members lose out? How can academics and advocates instead be useful in holding up the voices of family members and others who are normatively unheard? In addition to creating more spaces for family members to make their voices heard when they choose to speak, we advocate for others to always ask permission to represent the stories of missing women, as a demonstration of respect and to follow protocol. This act of gaining permission from the family members of missing women also supports the development of relationships between family members and other stakeholders, which is vital for the families' continued healing.

Like Ann-Marie, Bridget Tolley of Families of Sisters in Spirit also speaks out about the death of her mother, bringing her personal outrage, grief, and mourning to her activism on this issue.[3] Each time she speaks, Bridget begins with the painful story of how her mother died and then she explains the lack of justice in her case. Keeping the individual women's lives at the centre of the issue is key, for Bridget, Ann-Marie, and other daughters of missing and murdered women. Importantly, the perspectives of family members reveal aspects of Indigenous women's lives that are not captured in the educational campaigns that receive government funding—this includes insights into the compounded impacts of colonial policies and individual violence that preceded their disappearance. This larger context reveals that Indigenous women are not only targeted for interpersonal violence or abuse but have experienced a continuum of violence at the hands of government systems, including residential schools.

Elsie at Residential School
A Continuum of Violence

As dominant representations of "the missing women" generally focus on their deaths or disappearances and the legal processes that unfolded after they went missing, other stories about Elsie shed light on why her life and her story should have mattered long before she went missing. Her story demonstrates the intimate sites of colonialism she experienced as a child and the complex factors that shaped her life as an Indigenous woman.

My mom, Elsie Jones, was born in the mid-1950s in Port Alberni, BC, to Walter and Mary Jones, who were Nuu-Chah-Nulth from the West Coast of Vancouver Island. Mary, my grandmother, explained to me that when her children were young they didn't have much money to raise nearly ten children and life was hard due to poverty and family dysfunction such as alcoholism and physical abuse. When the children were school aged, about five or six years old, they were apprehended by the Department of Indian Affairs (DIA) and taken to attend Alberni Indian Residential School. In looking at documents obtained from the government about my mom's attendance at the school, I found she was there from age six to about age sixteen.

My mom, Elsie, told me that at around sixteen she left the residential school, as it was a lonely, miserable existence there. Students were verbally and physically abused at residential schools. I have heard terrible stories of how gifted children were often targeted by sexual predators in the system—adults who were supposed to be their guardians and protectors. It has been confirmed by family members that, at home, Elsie was sexually and physically abused by family members (who will remain anonymous at this time). Consequently, Elsie often used violence to discipline me and my sister, Donalee, when we were small children.

As Elsie's story suggests, the violence experienced by missing women is not specific to whatever act may have led to their disappearance or death. While the circumstances surrounding Elsie's disappearance remain a mystery that haunts Ann-Marie daily, questions about her treatment as a child are much clearer. For ten years, Elsie was a student at a residential school that was notorious for rampant sexual and physical abuse. Conversations between Ann-Marie and her mom revealed that it is likely that Elsie faced violence during these years that was too painful to name. This colonial legacy of violence continues to shape the lives of Indigenous women—both those who are living and those whose lives have already been lost. Connecting these forms of violence is an important aspect of creating a fuller portrayal of the individual lives of missing women, and can help with strategies to prevent violence. The voices of family members are therefore vital to any conversations about how to address violence against Indigenous women—how to prevent the list of missing women from growing.

The Life She Could Have Lived
Remembering Elsie's Strengths

In addition to remembering the complex histories of colonial violence that Elsie experienced, Ann-Marie also remembers her mother's strengths and potential. One of the difficulties of losing a mother to an unknown fate is continually revisiting the possibility that she might be living somewhere and doing well. Although Ann-Marie is quite certain her mother would have called if she were still alive and has come to believe that she has died, others continue to wonder, which leads to difficult conversations for Ann-Marie. Family members of missing women do not only remember the women for the way they left this world, but for the legacy they left behind, including the unfulfilled potential their lives held. Every missing woman had hopes, dreams, and aspirations—dreams that Indigenous women who are living today also hold and that should be nourished. Preventing violence against Indigenous women is not only about stopping individual acts of harm but upholding and nurturing the full vitality and humanity of our lives at this intimate level. As the daughter of a missing woman, Ann-Marie takes up everyday acts of remembrance and mourning that honour Elsie's vitality and the very personal, intimate qualities that made her who she was.

Elsie told me that she was a very fast runner and often won races in track and field. She said she could've gone on to become a successful athlete, given the opportunity, as it was her passion. She was also very pretty and socially popular among her peers. I've met a few of her fellow students from the residential school who said she was a smart and gifted student. She had nice clothes, even though none of the kids had the kind of disposable income that many average middle-class teenagers might have today. Family members told me that this was because Elsie could sew her own clothing. She even sewed the bridesmaids' dresses for my aunt's wedding. I also have a button blanket and ladies dress that she made with Native designs sewn on them. Most notable of all were her lovely hairdos. I have pictures of her as a teenager in the mid-1960s with the trendsetting beehive. Elsie was also a good cook and I remember her baked bread and bannock that were almost perfect. She seemed to be a perfectionist— if something didn't turn out right, she was disappointed. I recall being in the third grade and working on my badges for Stepping Stones (similar to Brownies). She was watching me do my project and was getting frustrated with me as it didn't appear I was doing a good job. She urged me to "do it again and do it good!"

It seems as though my mom could've gone on to do almost anything she wanted to do. She was talented in so many ways. She was politically astute as a young person. My uncles told me she was involved in the Native youth movement and apparently she even went to San Francisco for an AIM (American Indian Movement) event. She participated in the Victoria Native Friendship Centre beauty pageant and won the Indian Princess title. I saw pictures of her in my late grandmother's photo album.

Ann-Marie and other daughters of missing women continue to live with the questions they will never be able to ask their mothers, the conversations they wish they had, and the memories they wanted to create. The loss of a mother is not easily grieved and does not end; it remains ever-present. The process of mourning this loss is compounded, however, by the questions that remain around how Elsie went missing, whether or not she is dead, and what justice is being sought on her behalf.

The Personal Becomes Public
The Inquiry and Other Legal Realms

The increased visibility of this issue, and the impact of colonialism, racism, and other systemic oppression, moves Elsie's death from being an intimate loss to being part of public discourse. The public nature of information around the missing women is fraught with misunderstandings as individuals come to know about women like Elsie as part of a broader social, legal, and political issue— poster campaigns, hashtags, and mugshot-like photos that flash on the TV screen. Yet engaging with legal processes and connecting with social movements to seek justice for missing and murdered women has been a necessary part of dealing with the ramifications of Elsie's disappearance.

Legal actors and legal processes have had a central presence in Ann-Marie's life since she began to seek answers for the loss of her mother. Bringing Elsie's death into the legal realm has felt jarring at times, as the legal status of her mother's case hinges on decisions that Ann-Marie and her family are forced to make. As Ann-Marie explains, *we must uncomfortably determine whether or not Elsie should be recognized as "deceased" and whether or not to obtain a death certificate. We have also had to decide whether or not to apply for Elsie's "Common Experience Payment" for pain and suffering during her attendance at an Indian residential school, as well as filing a civil suit to the Province of British Columbia for a negligence claim or wrongful death suit.*

These engagements with legal processes can be re-traumatizing, as can everyday experiences of talking to people about her mother's disappearance. Although the increase in public awareness about the missing women has been positive in many ways, it has also meant that a growing number of people are using second-hand knowledge to talk about something that is very intimate and personal for Ann-Marie and other family members of missing women. Ann-Marie is often faced with the unnerving experience of having complete strangers talk to her about the issue as though they're familiar with it, when they've only ever heard about missing women on the news. On the other hand, Ann-Marie has found that many people, including friends and family, are uncomfortable talking about the specifics of her mother's death, Ann-Marie's experience participating in the inquiry, and the ongoing ways she is coping with the loss. Thus, it seems that while some people are comfortable talking about the missing women as a generalized social issue, they're less willing to sit with the sadness, grief, anger, uncertainty, and many other complex feelings experienced by family members.

Dealing with these interpersonal dynamics over many years has made it difficult for Ann-Marie and her family to choose whether or not to talk publicly about their loss in formal legal processes, although it can have some benefits. In the wake of Robert Pickton's conviction, a public inquiry was held in to the police response to the missing and murdered women in Vancouver's Downtown Eastside. While many people were left out of the inquiry, family members of missing and murdered women were invited to make statements.[4] Ann-Marie and her sister, Donalee, were encouraged by their aunt to participate. She found that the inquiry created one of few spaces for family members of missing women to develop relationships with one another and come together in their shared experience. As part of her testimony, Ann-Marie urged the commissioner to set aside funding for the family members of missing and murdered women, as a way for them to get counselling, pay for education, or support their future well-being in some other way. This recommendation was taken up following the inquiry, and a settlement was made in which family members of the women who were on the list of sixty-seven missing and murdered women were given the option to sign on.

*My siblings and I were faced with the difficult question of whether
or not to settle when the children of the missing women were offered
$50,000 each to drop the current and all future civil suits against
the government and the Vancouver Police Department. Our lawyer
instructed us that most civil suits in BC have a precedent of about
$40,000 for wrongful death settlements. We had to ask ourselves,
"How much is a life worth?" When I asked my sister what she
thought, she said, "Well, mom would've wanted us to have something from her and you know she would've given us everything she
had, so even though it's not a lot of money it's still something and
mom would've wanted us to have it." For that reason we decided to
join the settlement for families of missing women. We also decided
that with these funds we would put something away for our children
and use the money for them or put it towards a home of our own.*

When I was interviewed by CBC *and other media about the
settlement,[5] I stated that clearly this money doesn't erase what
happened, but it's a success in that it at least acknowledges where the
police and the authorities failed to protect Elsie and other women like
her. These women were vulnerable and targeted either because they
were Aboriginal, addicted, or worked in the sex trade, or a combin-
ation of all these factors. Certainly, this money won't replace
our mother, but it will help us move ahead in life. And finally, this
settlement at least came to fruition from one of the many recommendations that the families of the missing women made to Wally
Oppal, the commissioner appointed and tasked with overseeing the
public inquiry into police conduct in investigating the* DTES *cases.[6]*

Ann-Marie's lawyer received a phone call from a reporter
requesting an interview about the settlement that saw a total of
$4.9 million distributed to ninety-eight children of the sixty-
seven missing women. However, her lawyer phoned Ann-Marie
to see if she would like to be interviewed instead, saying that it
would be more appropriate for her to tell her own story rather
than having him speak for her. This was a respectful gesture that
gave Ann-Marie a choice of whether or not to speak, which she

chose to do.[7] The news report shared that Elsie's case illustrated the extreme barriers family members faced in trying to report their loved ones missing. Although Elsie's family reported her missing in 1993, 1994, and 1999, it wasn't until 2001 that her case was officially documented and investigated. These kinds of injustices are what compelled the compensation for the victims' families, and caused Ann-Marie to experience mixed emotions as the ruling was announced. No amount of money will make up for the loss of her mother or the mistakes that police made along the way. Yet the compensation showed that her voice was heard in the inquiry and it will help her to move forward.

Engagements with these legal and public processes have been facilitated by legal and government representatives, some of whom have clearly respected Ann-Marie as the best person to make decisions about how and when her mother's story is heard. Individual lawyers and other support people have been vital to the complex legal decisions Ann-Marie and her sister have had to make, as their mourning has been brought into the legal realm. Yet interacting with lawyers, police officers, counsellors, and others in helping roles can be uncomfortable or even re-traumatizing for family members, as these individuals—like the general public— may bring their own biases, misinformation, or lack of compassion into their professional roles.

Following the financial offer to settle from the courts, I was sent a package of forms to fill out. One of these forms required a lawyer to notarize it. I made an appointment with a nearby lawyer who often deals in routine real estate transactions that need legal notarization. I thought that because this lawyer is generally swift and precise in his other transactions, he would be a good candidate to sign off on my documents. I made an appointment to see him and went to his office. As I explained the process for the forms, and explained the history of the missing women's case I began to sense his discomfort. Looking back, when I walked into his office he was immediately uncomfortable with my presence. I asked if I could shut the door as I wanted a bit of privacy in his office since we were close to the front door and this is still a difficult and very personal issue for me to discuss. He refused and stated that there was no need to close the door, as his entire staff would keep all matters confidential. Then when I asked if he would bill the Province for the notarization (which is a standard process), he also refused and insisted that I pay him upfront instead and then get reimbursed. After I said no to him, he still insisted we proceed with the notarization and was about to start writing on my documents. I had to ask him two times to return my forms back to me. In the end, I abruptly ended the appointment and left the office in tears. I was frustrated and angry about the whole scenario. I then chose to see a female lawyer who was also Aboriginal as I did not want to have to go through that type of humiliation ever again— of having to explain myself to some asshole who neither cares nor understands my predicament of having to settle for the loss of my mother.

This lawyer was insensitive, and perhaps even racist. He didn't understand the dynamics of my situation and was blatantly uncom- fortable with the subject matter, which is a common occurrence when I talk about my mom. I sense that most people, especially white, middle-aged men, don't like to hear about the issue of the missing women. Strangely enough, this demographic represents the majority of employees of the Vancouver Police Department, polit- icians, and bureaucrats. Perhaps this group is the ones who suffer from the most collective colonial guilt of white society as these men are generally the ones who've made decisions for our people and regarded us as legal wards of the state under the Indian Act or subjected Aboriginal peoples to the same legal stature as children. This demographic is also the same group as the man who targeted our women as a sexual predator and facilitated the sexualiza- tion of Aboriginal women in the Downtown Eastside as disposable and subhuman. All these thoughts raced through my head when I left that lawyer's office and I refused to see another lawyer who wouldn't understand. When I went to see a female lawyer who is in her thirties and is also from the Nuu-Chah-Nulth First Nation, she was not only sympathetic to my situation but also refused to charge me for the service, which took all of fifteen minutes for her to complete. She said she was happy to assist me, especially because it had to do with one of our people. Clearly, only another Aboriginal woman would relate to these matters and be able to help me move forward with this issue.

Remembering Elsie
Life as the Daughter of a Missing Woman

Now forty, Ann-Marie is the same age Elsie was when she went missing, and she finds herself engaging in some of the same coping behaviour as her mother, including struggling with addictive behaviours. These coping mechanisms are part of the ongoing effects of Elsie's disappearance, which is often not acknow-ledged by friends and family who judge her for her choices. This judgement can get in the way of people being able to fully hear the continued pain experienced by family members of missing women. People routinely fail to understand the ongoing personal and emotional nature of this loss, and how it is compounded by the very public political efforts to address this issue. When we see the missing women talked about on the news, it isn't just another story or purely a public awareness campaign. It might be gut wrenchingly sad for family members like Ann-Marie to see a photo of her mom on the news. Each time the issue is raised, the personal nature of her loss is intensified along with witnessing an extensive array of experts who claim to be the voice of the issue, while she deals with her loss in isolation. Sometimes these experiences are hard to articulate, as Ann-Marie is aware of the fact that she is living while her mother is gone, that she holds a more privileged position than her mom in many ways, and yet can also pass over in to the spaces her mom occupied as an Indigenous woman.

I've been thinking about how some words in First Nations languages don't have translations in English, and how some of my experiences don't have literal translations in either language. A lot of times as I go through various experiences with the settlement and the issue of my mom being missing, I feel like I'm treated different than my mom would've been treated. She was less educated, she was living in poverty, on welfare, had an active drug problem, lived on the streets, had an icky street boyfriend. I feel like I'm treated different because of how I talk, how I look, my educational background, my job. When I think of the word for someone who is a half-breed, there is no word for that in my mom's language. The term is just "white girl." You're either Native or white. No half. She used to call me "white girl." You are or you aren't white. I feel that way sometimes. I feel like I can cross into both worlds: white or Native. I can go to the Eastside. I've gone to look for my mom and was not threatened or scared by people who are drunk or using. They are not intimidating to me. I'm welcomed because I look Native too. So I can play different parts, wear different masks, have a parallel existence going in and out of different experiences. Sometimes it's actually amusing because I get to see things others wouldn't see. But sometimes it's really heartbreaking. I can fit in there in the Downtown Eastside, but know that I can fit in ways she couldn't in the white world. I've learned to know how someone else would want me to be in order to cope, to get by. I can be a business type. I can be heard in ways she couldn't.

Although Ann-Marie is taken seriously in ways her mother wasn't because of her class and educational status, when she raises the issue of missing women, the stigma surrounding her mother's disappearance clouds her ability to be heard. Talking about Elsie and about the ongoing legal and social processes to find justice for missing women requires the support of individual friends and family members, and sometimes lawyers, counsellors, or police. Although it might be uncomfortable to hear the experiences of family members of missing women, it is important to remember that Ann-Marie's mourning is far from comfortable. Being able to truly hear the stories of family members of missing women requires allowing for personal discomfort and letting go of any stigma surrounding the circumstances of the women's lives and deaths. It is at this emotional and embodied level that mourning, grief, and remembrance unfold, not at the more analytic level of research reports or government policy tables. As we hope we have shown here, listening to the voices of family members of missing women is where the intimate tributes to missing women are possible.

The few times I lived with Elsie, she was a doting mother who put me on a pedestal. Elsie often told me I was smart and better than most. As a very young child, I recall her telling me these things and I didn't understand why. She would say, "You are beautiful and talented and you won't be kicked around like a dog like I was." I see now that was merely her way of instilling in me a sense of pride; it was also her own defensive mechanism to protect me from the abuse and suffering she experienced as a child in her own family and at residential school.

Elsie was also funny and childlike in her humour. I recall us housecleaning on Saturday mornings and she would play disco and country music and dance around the house with a mop and a broom. She loved to sing and dance. I can remember all of the lovely ballads she loved to sing along to. When I hear "The Rose" by Bette Midler or "Stand by Your Man" by Tammy Wynette, I remember Elsie. She had so much heartbreak in her short time, yet still did the best she could, laughed about life, smiled, and was at least successful in leaving behind us children before she disappeared. It is because of her that I am here. These memories are my most cherished ones and it is particularly heartbreaking when I think about the successful achiever Elsie could have been if she was given the chance. She wanted to be a teacher, and for a few years she even went to Camosun College for upgrading. I remember riding on the bus with her and feeling so optimistic, thinking, "My mom is going to be a teacher!" Today when I see other young women with their mothers sharing conversation or affection with each other, I long for her and feel ripped off. My sister, Donalee, once said to me, "It seems like mom was just a dream." What other young women take for granted in a mother, I secretly wish for and daydream about when I'm frustrated or distraught. In particular, when my son was a baby, I often thought, "I wish my mom was here to guide me or babysit for me."

Remembering Elsie, her aspirations, her strengths, and her mothering encouragement—this remembrance expresses the love shared between Elsie, Ann-Marie, and other members of their family, a powerful reminder that Elsie was not "just a dream." The missing women are memorialized not only in public rallies or news reports but also in the very intimate and quiet spaces of family members' homes, hearts, and daily struggles to reconcile unthinkable loss. This chapter is also a space of tribute to Elsie and the legacy she left behind in her daughter, who continues to seek space for her story to be heard.

NOTES

1.   Amnesty International, *Stolen Sisters: A Human Rights Response to Discrimination and Violence against Indigenous Women in Canada* (Ottawa: Amnesty International, 2004), https://www.amnesty.ca/sites/amnesty/files/amr200032004enstolensisters.pdf; Beverly Jacobs and Andrea Williams, "Legacy of Residential Schools: Missing and Murdered Aboriginal Women" in *Truth to Reconciliation: Transforming the Legacy of Residential Schools*, prepared for the Aboriginal Healing Foundation by Marlene Brant Castellano, Linda Archibald, and Mike DeGagné (Ottawa: Aboriginal Healing Foundation, 2008); Maryanne Pearce, "An Awkward Silence: Missing and Murdered Vulnerable Women and the Canadian Justice System" (LLD diss., University of Ottawa, 2013), https://ruor.uottawa.ca/handle/10393/26299; Shannon Brennan, "Violent Victimization of Aboriginal Women in the Canadian Provinces, 2009," *Juristat*, Statistics Canada cat. no. 85-002-X, May 17, 2011, http://www.statcan.gc.ca/pub/85-002-x/2011001/article/11439-eng.htm#a4.

2.   Artist Pamela Masik painted a portrait series of missing and murdered women using photos from a missing persons poster. Family members were troubled by the fact that the artist did not follow the protocol of asking for permission to paint their portraits. Following a public outcry, a 2011 exhibition of Masik's missing women series at the University of British Columbiau's Museum of Anthropology was cancelled. For more on this story, see Canadian Press, "BC Missing Women Art Exhibit Called Off: Museum Cites 'Serious Concerns,'"

CBC *News*, January 13, 2011, http://www.cbc.ca/news/canada/ british-columbia/b-c-missing-women-art-exhibit-called-off-1.1048707.

3. Families of Sisters in Spirit (FSIS) is a grassroots, volunteer, non-profit organization led by families of missing and murdered Indigenous women and girls in Canada. FSIS strives to create and nurture an anti-oppressive and safe space where Indigenous and non-Indigenous communities can come together to show their love, support, and solidarity for missing and murdered women and their families. For more information, see https://fsismmiw.wordpress.com/.

4. For an analysis of the gaps in the inquiry, see D. Bennett, D. Eby, K. Govender, and K. Pacey, *Blueprint for an Inquiry: Learning from the Failures of the Missing Women Commission of Inquiry*. (Vancouver: British Columbia Civil Liberties Association, West Coast Women's Legal Education and Action Fund, and Pivot Legal Society, 2012).

5. CBC is the Canadian Broadcasting Corporation, a publicly funded national radio and television news company.

6. Wally T. Oppal, *Forsaken: The Report of the Missing Women Commission of Inquiry*, vol. 1, *The Women, Their Lives and the Framework of Inquiry, Setting the Context for Understanding and Change* (Victoria: Province of British Columbia, 2012).

7. To read the news story about the settlement, see Camille Bains, "Pickton Compensation: Children of Victims Split $4.9 Million Fund," *Huffington Post*, May 18, 2014, http://www.huffingtonpost.ca/2014/03/18/ pickton-compensation-children-victims_n_4986590.html.

II | The Violence of History

5 | *Generations of Genocide*

The Historical and Sociological Context of Missing and
Murdered Indigenous Women and Girls

ROBYN BOURGEOIS

THERE IS LITTLE DOUBT that missing and murdered
Indigenous women and girls is one of the most pressing social
issues facing Indigenous communities across Canada today. As the
Royal Canadian Mounted Police (RCMP) operational overview on
missing and murdered Aboriginal women found, more than one
thousand women (1,017) have been murdered between 1980 and
2012, and 164 women were officially listed missing as of November
4, 2013—confirming the long-held claims of Indigenous women,
their organizations, and communities about the scope of this
problem in contemporary Canadian society.[1] Political support has
led to a Canadian state-funded national public inquiry into the
issue of missing and murdered Indigenous women and girls—albeit,
after many years of lobbying and a change from Prime Minister
Stephen Harper and his Conservative government, which was
unwilling to entertain this political option. In response to intensification in calls for this inquiry resulting from discovery of fifteen-
year-old Tina Fontaine's (Sagkeeng First Nation) body in the Red
River in Winnipeg in August 2014, Prime Minister Harper refused

on the basis that "we should not view this as a sociological issue," but as "crime." "It is a crime against innocent people," he explained, "and it need to be address as such."[2] He reaffirmed this position in a December 2014 interview with CBC, stating that the issue of missing and murdered Aboriginal women and girls "isn't really high on our radar, to be honest."[3]

In one aspect, Prime Minister Harper was correct—this is a crime against innocent people: it's settler colonial genocide committed against Indigenous women and girls and their nations (although I am fairly certain this is not the "crime" that Mr. Harper is imagining). However, he was very wrong in claiming it isn't a sociological issue: this contemporary phenomenon of missing and murdered Indigenous women and girls, as this chapter demonstrates, is the direct by-product of dominant social systems of oppression, such as colonialism, racism, and patriarchy, that hierarchically order the social world and ensure the distribution of privilege and the fruits of citizenship accordingly. Constructed in dominant Canadian discourses as inherently inferior and, moreover, inherently violable, Indigenous women and girls find themselves extremely vulnerable to all forms of violence while simultaneously being excluded from the protection of the Canadian state. And while "missing and murdered Indigenous women and girls" is generally understood as a contemporary phenomenon, violence against Indigenous women and girls isn't—the seeds of this contemporary injustice have been planted over the course of settler colonial history in Canada. This chapter attempts to trace not only the historical roots of the contemporary violence of missing and murdered Indigenous women and girls, but also the sociological factors involved in this contemporary phenomenon. Additionally, this chapter out-lines the Canadian state's ongoing role in perpetuating and enabling this violence, with generations of Indigenous females and their nations subject to genocidal elimination (bureaucratically, assimi-lation, and death). This serves a secondary goal: to raise important questions about the Canadian state's role in ending violence against Indigenous women and girls. Please note, for the purposes of this discussion, the *Canadian state* refers to both the federal and provincial/territorial governments, as well its institutions and agencies including educational systems, the criminal justice system, and child protection services.

Settler Colonialism and the Ideology of Genocide

Making sense of the contemporary social phenomenon of missing and murdered Indigenous women and girls in Canada requires a theoretical understanding of settler colonialism as a dominant system of oppression that has long organized, and continues to organize, life in Canadian society. Settler colonialism involves the domination of Indigenous lands and peoples by non-Indigenous peoples (and predominantly those racialized as white). As critical anti-racist feminist scholar Sherene Razack explains,

> A white settler society is one established by Europeans on non-European soil. Its origins lie in the dispossession and near extermination of Indigenous populations by the conquering Europeans. As it evolves, a white settler society continues to be structured by a racial hierarchy. In the national mythologies of such societies, it is believed that white people came first and it is they who principally developed the land; Aboriginal peoples are presumed to be mostly dead or assimilated. European settlers thus become the original inhabitants and the group most entitled to the fruits of citizenship.[4]

As Razack highlights, racial hierarchy underpins settler colonialism (both ideologically and practically), with white settler supremacy confirmed through the portrayal of Indigenous peoples as inherently pathological: deviant, dysfunctional, and, ultimately, subhuman. In turn, this ideological ejection of Indigenous peoples from the realm of humanity secures settler colonial social and material relations: Indigenous sovereignty and the right to self-determination is denied, as is Indigenous occupancy and use of their traditional territories. Moreover, Indigenous peoples are excluded from the rights, freedoms, and spoils accorded to citizens of those white settler societies. A consequence of this domination, however, is that Indigenous peoples/nations are made threatening to the colonial order of things—that is, while Indigenous people are needed to confirm white racial supremacy and settler colonial domination, they also represent a significant threat to the colonial order of things: a living testament to the illegitimacy of white settler society. As a result, settler colonial society seeks to eliminate Indigeneity, and as Patrick Wolfe argues, a genocidal "logic of elim-ination" directed at Indigenous peoples is a central organizing principle of settler colonial societies.[5] In addition to "frontier homicide," Wolfe contends, this logic of elimination is repre-sented by practices such as "officially encouraged miscegenation, the breaking-down of native title into alienable individual free-holds, native citizenship, child abduction, religious conversion, resocialization in total institutions such as missions or boarding schools and a whole range of cognate bicultural assimilation."[6] Significantly, while violence against Indigenous peoples is central to settler colonial domination, so too is the denial and erasure of this violence. As Razack writes, "a quintessential feature of white settler mythologies is…the disavowal of conquest, genocide, slavery, and the exploitation of peoples of colour," and "in North America, it is still the case that European conquest and coloniza-tion are often denied, largely through the fantasy that North America was peacefully settled and not colonized."[7]

Indigenous women have unanimously identified settler coloni-alism as a root cause of all forms of violence committed against Indigenous women and girls,[8] including the contemporary phenomenon of missing and murdered Indigenous women and girls.[9] While "colonization has taken its toll on all Aboriginal peoples," Métis scholar Emma LaRocque contends, "it has taken perhaps the greatest toll on women," and "we can trace the diminishing status of Aboriginal women with the progres-sion of colonialism."[10] Importantly, Indigenous women are in no way suggesting that violence originated with colonialism: they acknowledge its existence in pre-colonial Indigenous societies, but also point out that the matriarchal organization and/or strict anti-violence policies of many Indigenous societies provided Indigenous females with security against violence.[11] However, the arrival of settler colonialism undermined all of this. As Indigenous women have argued, the racial ideologies and practices of settler colonialism have specifically but simultaneously gendered dimensions organized around patriarchal domination of Indigenous women and girls.[12] The oppression of Indigenous females, as Andrea Smith writes, is essential to the operations of settler colonialism: "in order to colonize a peoples whose society was not hierarchical," she explains, "colonizers must first naturalize hierarchy through instituting patriarchy" and, thus "patriarchal gender violence is the process by which colonizers inscribe hierarchy and domination on the bodies of the colonized."[13] This process, as Indigenous women and non-Indigenous scholars have demonstrated, has been powerfully enabled through the settler colonial discourse of the "squaw" that constructs Indigenous females as inherently sexually available ("easy") and, therefore, inherently sexually violable.[14] The portrayal of Indigenous females as "dehumanized sex objects," argues Emma LaRocque, constitutes a "double objectification": "Aboriginal women have been objectified not only as women but also as Indian women," where "racism sets up or strengthens a situation where Aboriginal women are viewed and treated as sex objects" and "the objectification of women perpetuates sexual violence." In this way, she contends, "the dehumanizing portrayal of Aboriginal women as 'squaws'…renders all Aboriginal female persons vulnerable to physical, verbal, and sexual violence."[15] This violence, as Smith suggests, is integral to settler colonial domination: "the violence of settler colonial sexual violence," she writes, "establishes the ideology that Native bodies are inherently violable—and by extension, that Native lands are also inherently violable," thus facilitating the theft of Indigenous lands required for the establishment of settler colonial societies.[16]

Furthermore, as both Smith and Razack have persuasively demonstrated, this violence is productive of the multiple social identities that underpin the hierarchical order of things in settler colonial society.[17] The denigration and violation of Indigenous females, according to Smith, helps establish and secure the supremacy of white males over not only Indigenous women and their nations, but also white females: within the settler colonial imagination, discourses of Indigenous female inferiority are entwined with the construction of Indigenous males as inherently "savage" and "violent," who are then positioned as a perceived racial threat to the purported "purity" (and, thus, respectability) of white women—all of which justifies domination by superior males, who are required to protect white women from the colonized, racial other (men and women included).[18] Violence, as such, is indispensable to settler colonial domination—dominant subjects, as Razack argues, seek to establish that they are "indeed in control and [live] in a world where a solid line marks the boundary between [themselves] and racial/gendered Others," and "violence establishes the boundary between who [they are] and who [they are] not," as "it is the surest indicator that [they are subjects] in control."[19]

As this discussion makes clear, settler colonialism requires violence against Indigenous women and girls to secure domination over Indigenous peoples, nations, and territories. As this violence plays a fundamental role in establishing the hierarchical order of things that privilege masculinity and whiteness in settler colonial societies like Canada, it will persist as long as the underlying social systems of oppression (colonialism, racism, and sexism) persist. In the next section, I map the persistence of settler colonialism and, thus, violence against Indigenous women and girls within the Canadian nation-state to historically situate and contextualize the contemporary phenomenon of missing and murdered Indigenous women and girls in Canada.

Canada and Settler Colonialism

Securing a Nation through Violence against Indigenous Women and Girls

Settler colonialism requires Indigenous lands, which in Canada has been secured through violent physical and legal dispossessions enabled through discourses of white settler supremacy and Indigenous inferiority, and justified through manipulations of settler colonial law.[20] The subjugation of Indigenous females was also integral to this process as lands were organized matrilineally in many pre-colonial Indigenous nations, with Indigenous women holding power over possession and usage.[21] Thus, as Smith argued above, denigrating and violating Indigenous females became important to imposing settler colonial notions of patriarchally controlled private property. Indigenous nations were removed from the most productive and resource-rich land on Turtle Island (a term many Indigenous people use to refer to the lands that now make up the Americas) through confinement to reserves and reservations, with the added effect of disrupting traditional patterns of subsistence and local economies.[22] Following the formation of the Canadian nation-state in 1867, colonization of Indigenous lands was codified through the Indian Act, which since 1876 has dictated all aspects of Indigeneity in Canada, including identity. The Indian Act, for example, determines who legally counts as "Indian." It rules certain First Nation people—those who can establish lineage as laid out by the Canadian state—as deserving of treaty obligations, and excludes other First Nation peoples— particularly women—and Métis and Inuit peoples. Critically, while reserve lands belong, in theory, to Indigenous nations, the Indian Act extends state control over those lands to other areas, including use, sale, and inheritance. This theft of Indigenous lands to establish the Canadian nation-state has resulted in endemic poverty that has plagued Indigenous nations for generations—which, in turn, has created greater Indigenous economic dependence on the Canadian state and, therefore, further enhanced Canadian state control over Indigenous nations.[23] At present, Indigenous people in Canada experience high rates of poverty: a 2009 statistical profile produced by the Canadian state reported that Indigenous people were more than twice as likely than non-Indigenous populations to live below the low income cut-off, a designation set to establish poverty in Canada (18.7% compared to 8.4%).[24] Notably, the 2006 Canadian Census showed that the number of Indigenous women and girls living in poverty was more than double the number of non-Indigenous women (36% compared to 17%), and that one in three Indigenous children live in poverty.[25] This economic marginalization produced by the theft of Indigenous lands and Canadian state domination over Indigenous nations, in turn, produces violence—poverty is regularly identified as a significant contributing factor to violence against Indigenous women and girls in Canada,[26] including in the cases of missing and murdered Indigenous women and girls.[27] Consequently, as long as the Canadian nation-state continues to occupy Indigenous lands and reap the economic benefits of this theft, it does so at the expense of the lives of Indigenous women and girls in Canada.

The settler colonial violence of the Canadian state strikes at the heart of Indigenous nations through the Indian Act and its control of Indigenous identity—determining, on the state's terms, who *officially* counts as "Indian" in this country and, therefore, to whom that state is officially accountable in terms of Indian rights and treaty obligations. It also, as outlined above, excluded certain First Nation individuals and both Métis and Inuit, preventing these groups from accessing treaty rights and obligations from the Canadian state. The imposition of these foreign membership codes on Indigenous nations has had particularly detrimental consequences for Indigenous women and their children, who have long been targeted through discriminatory provisions that exclude only Indigenous women who married non-Indigenous men and their children from status under the Indian Act (a situation that persists to this day).[28] As Bonita Lawrence notes, "the phenomenal implication hidden in this legislation is the sheer numbers of Native people lost to their communities"—because "for every individual who lost status and had to leave her community, all of her descendants…also lost status and for the most part were permanently alienated from Native culture."[29] This loss of status also translated into a loss of treaty obligations, which means that excluded Indigenous women and their children faced significant financial losses, including treaty monies, educational funding, child care funding, health benefits, and tax benefits.[30] Physically severed from their communities, excluded Indigenous women and their children were also severed from the support offered by their families and communities. In this way, the Indian Act has and continues to directly contribute to the economic marginalization and social isolation of Indigenous women and children that makes them extremely vulnerable to violence.

Violence against Indigenous women and girls was also foundational to the residential school system implemented by the Canadian state between the early 1800s and 1996. In conjunction with Canadian Christian churches, the federal government created residential schools across the country to ensure the speedy assimilation of Indian children into mainstream Canadian society—and between 1920 and 1951, the Indian Act made attendance mandatory. The ultimate goal of residential schools was elimination: as Deputy Superintendent of Indian Affairs Duncan Campbell Scott notoriously proclaimed upon making attendance mandatory in 1920, "I want to get rid of the Indian problem… Our objective is to continue until there is not a single Indian in Canada that has not been absorbed into the body politic and there is no Indian Question and no Indian Department."[31] Children were forcibly removed from their families and communities and confined to institutions founded in the belief of the inherent inferiority of Indigenous peoples.[32] They were shamed for being Indigenous and punished for speaking their Indigenous languages or engaging in their cultural practices.[33] As the residential school system progressed, emphasis on formal education decreased in order to free up students to undertake the physical labour required to operate these institutions.[34] And as is now becoming more well known, the majority of Indigenous children experienced extreme physical and sexual abuse at the hands of those involved in running residential schools.[35] Importantly, while residential schools may now exist chronologically in the past, the effects of this heinous act of genocide continue to be lived out by Indigenous peoples. For more than a hundred years, residential schools tore apart Indigenous families in ways that cannot be easily mended by official state apologies and meagre financial compensation. The patterns of violence and abuse taught to Indigenous people through residential schools continue to manifest themselves in our interpersonal relationships, resulting, for example, in high rates of family violence in Indigenous communities. The survivors of residential schools frequently struggle with mental health issues related to this violence, and many have turned to drugs and alcohol as means to coping with their pain—as do many of those subject to the interpersonal intergenerational violence learned from residential schools.[36] Notably, addictions and mental health issues have been identified as significant factors impacting the vulnerability of Indigenous women and girls to violence in contemporary Canadian society,[37] perhaps best exemplified in the cases of Vancouver's Missing Women.

With the decline of the residential school system, the Canadian state has increasingly relied on its child protection mechanisms to further the elimination of Indigenous peoples. Since the 1960s, provincially run child protection agencies have forcibly removed untold thousands (and potentially millions) of Indigenous children from their families and communities and put them into foster care and/or placed them for adoption primarily with non-Indigenous families.[38] This intensification of apprehensions is commonly referred to as the Sixties Scoop—and while this dated reference may offer the impression of it being an issue of the past, these apprehensions continue apace to this day. Research suggests that there are currently more Indigenous children in the custody of the Canadian state than during the height of the residential school system.[39] Data collected as part of the 2011 National Household

Survey shows that Indigenous children made up almost half (48%) of the roughly thirty thousand children, aged fourteen and under, in foster care in Canada. Significantly, it also revealed that Indigenous children were twelve times more likely to be in foster care than non-Indigenous children.[40] As this suggests, racial discrimination has been integral to this system: in rural areas, argue Suzanne Fournier and Ernie Crey, "often the only difference between the parents whose children were stolen away and those who took in foster children for a little extra cash was the colour of their skin."[41] They also suggest that "culturally inappropriate judgments" frequently led to the removal of Indigenous children cared for by parents or grandparents living in the impoverished conditions endemic on reserves.[42] While the primary goal of these apprehensions has, like residential schools, been the elimination of Indigenous nations through the destruction of Indigenous families, they have also contributed significantly to the contemporary phenomenon of missing and murdered Indigenous women and girls. Children in foster care are notoriously vulnerable to violence, and over the last decade several provinces, including British Columbia, Alberta, and Manitoba, have had to organize formal governmental mechanisms to address deaths of children in state custody, many of whom were of Indigenous ancestry.[43] Through its Sisters in Spirit research, the Native Women's Association of Canada (NWAC) demonstrated that many of Canada's missing and murdered Indigenous women and girls had been taken as children into the child welfare system and/or had children removed from their custody, and NWAC has identified the role of the child welfare system in the social marginalization Indigenous women and girls that increases their vulnerability to violence.[44]

The contemporary Canadian state's complicity in this violence has also been exhibited in its formal responses to violence against Indigenous women and girls. At all levels, the Canadian legal system has failed to protect Indigenous women and girls from violence or to hold those who perpetrate this violence accountable. Canadian police forces have been indicted for over-policing but under-protecting Indigenous women and girls,[45] perhaps best exemplified by the highly problematic policing efforts involved in the Missing Women cases in Vancouver. As the final report of the Missing Women Commission of Inquiry (British Columbia, Commissioner Wally Oppal) concluded, these women were "forsaken" by the police: " The pattern of predatory violence was clear and should have been met with a swift and severe response by accountable and professional institutions, but it was not."[46] Notably, the report makes clear that the criminalization of women in the Downtown Eastside (primarily as prostitutes, but also as participants in the open drug trade) produced an extremely strained relationship between police and these vulnerable women that seriously hindered the investigation.[47] Police failings—including refusals to accept missing persons reports, racism and discriminatory treatment of families, and inadequate investigations—were also highlighted in many of the life story case studies of individual missing and murdered that formed the cornerstone of NWAC's Sisters in Spirit initiative reports.[48] Canadian courts have also been notoriously lenient on perpetrators of violence against Indigenous women and girls, making use of the pernicious racist and sexist stereotype of the "squaw" to minimize the violence and/or justify/excuse the behaviour of perpetrators.[49] As Sherene Razack argues in her analysis of the case of the two young white men accused of murdering Pamela George (Saulteaux) in Regina in 1995, "because Pamela George was considered [within the court] to belong to a space of prostitution and Aboriginality, in which violence routinely occurs, while her killers were presumed to be far removed from this zone, the enormity of what was done to her and her family remained largely unacknowledged."[50] " The men's and the court's capacity to dehumanize Pamela George," she writes, "came from their understanding of her as the (gendered) racial *Other* whose degradation confirmed their own identities as white—that is, as men entitled to the land and the full benefits of citizenship."[51]

Importantly, scholarly historical analyses make clear that the over-criminalization and under-protection of Indigenous women and girls has long been a pattern of the Canadian justice system—and, significantly, these analyses also suggest that the stereotype of the squaw and the perceived and/or actual involvement of Indigenous females in prostitution has been integral to this process. For example, while the implementation of the pass system in 1885, which required Indian peoples to obtain permission from an Indian Agent to leave their reserve, was no doubt directed at suppressing Indigenous resistance following the Métis and Nehiyawak (Cree) North West Rebellion, Sarah Carter argues that "a central rationale for the pass system was to keep away from towns and villages Aboriginal women 'of abandoned character who were there for the worst purposes': prostitution."[52] "Classified as prostitutes," she writes, "Aboriginal women could be restricted by a new disciplinary regime."[53] The work of Carter and historian Lesley Erickson also shows that the Indian Act specifically targeted Indian females through prostitution law. According to Erickson,

> Just as the Indian Act rendered alcohol consumption a crime only if the accused was Aboriginal, it also designated prostitution-related offences involving Aboriginal men and women as a special category of crime. Amendments to the Indian Act in the early 1880s also prohibited white settlers from allowing Indian women or prostitutes on their property or in tents and wigwams...It became illegal in 1886 for any Indian to keep, frequent, or be found in a disorderly house, tent, or wigwam. By contrast, prosecutors had to prove that a white man caught in the same situation was a habitual frequenter. The 1892 Criminal Code reaffirmed the legislation but restricted it to women who were Status Indians, and it categorized Aboriginal prostitution as an offense against morality. By contrast, keeping a common bawdy house (the

category under which non-Aboriginal prostitutes were
commonly prosecuted) was subsumed within the vagrancy
provisions of the Code. Whereas Aboriginal prostitution was
an indictable offence, vagrancy was a summary offence that
fell under the rubric of "common nuisances."[54]

Thus, as Carter notes, "separate legislation under the Indian Act
and, after 1892, under the Criminal Code governed Aboriginal
prostitution, making it easier to convict Aboriginal women than
other women."[55] These laws, Erickson contends, "reflected
fears about miscegenation and a desire to preserve racial boundaries. The legislation also reinforced stereotypes about Aboriginal
women as dangerous and dissolute and did much to link prostitution and Aboriginal women in the minds of white settlers."[56]

Finally, Joan Sangster's examination of Indigenous women's
encounters with the Ontario criminal justice system between
1920 and 1960 suggests that prostitution was integral to the criminalization of Indigenous women during this time. As Sangster
writes, " That issues of sexual morality and public propriety were
central to Native incarceration can be seen in the increasing use of
the Female Refuges Act (FRA), which sanctioned the incarceration
of women aged sixteen to thirty-five, sentenced, or even 'liable
to be sentenced' under any Criminal code or bylaw infractions for
'and dissolute' behaviour. While this draconian law was used most
in Ontario [during] the 1930s and 1940s, for Native women it was
increasingly applied in the 1940s and 1950s."[57] Authorities, she
claims, "were especially concerned with the links between visible
sexual behaviour and alcohol consumption" and "Native women
suspected of prostitution, or who engaged in sex for no money
and with no obvious moral regret, were especially vulnerable
to incarceration." Sangster contends that these concerns "were
fuelled by the racist stereotype of the Indian woman easily
debauched by alcohol, and lacking the sexual restraint of white
women. By the late nineteenth century, political and media
controversies had created an image of the Native women in the

public mind: supposedly 'bought and sold' by their own people as 'commodities,' they were easily 'demoralized' sexually, and a threat to both public 'morality and health.'"[58]

Yet while the Canadian criminal justice system increasingly criminalized Indigenous women, it also established leniency for perpetrators of violence against Indigenous women and girls. Erickson's examination of Prairie law during the late 1880s and early 1900s shows how that conflation of Indigenous femininity and prostitution was used to excuse violence against Indigenous women and girls. In the mid-nineteenth century in Rupert's Land and British Columbia, she notes, "judges and magistrates often dismissed Aboriginal women's complaints of sexual assault at the hands of white men because colonial discourses on sexually available women coloured their responses to individual cases."[59] Erickson's work also exposes how these stereotypes worked in court cases involving men accused of sexually attacking Indigenous women and girls, where these men frequently attempted to manipulate stereotypes about Indigenous females as sexually available— including accusations of prostitution—to their legal advantage.[60] "Negative representations of Aboriginal women as promiscuous and immoral," she contends, "circulated as subtexts in these trials, and they served as an underlying rationale for Canadian legislation that created Aboriginal prostitution as a distinct category of crime."[61] Thus, Erickson concludes, " The diverse record consulted here suggests that the confluence of various trends—particularly the lenient treatment of Aboriginal men found guilty of committing serious acts of violence and the criminalization of Aboriginal women through prostitution, liquor, and trespassing laws— helped to create the conditions by which Aboriginal women's complaints of physical and sexual violence fell, and continue to fall, on deaf ears."[62] As this discussion suggests, the failure of the Canadian criminal justice system to protect Indigenous females from violence and/or hold perpetrators accountable for this violence is clearly not a new problem.

Conclusion

Violence against Indigenous women and girls is not a "new" problem, but one that has plagued Indigenous nations since the advent of settler colonial domination in Turtle Island. The social systems of oppression—including settler colonialism, racism, and patriarchy—that structure settler colonial societies like Canada not only contribute to the denigration of Indigenous women and girls, but also require the use of violence against Indigenous women and girls to protect and reinforce the social boundaries of domination. As this chapter makes clear, the Canadian state has long relied on violence against Indigenous women and girls as a means of dominating and controlling Indigenous nations—indeed, Canadian colonial history is a history of violence against Indigenous females. A recognition of this history leads to an important insight in terms of ending violence against Indigenous women and girls in Canada: that is, if this violence is integral to settler colonial domination, then only decolonization and the regeneration of Indigenous sovereignty and self-determination can hope to end this violence. This means, as other Indigenous women have argued, that violence against Indigenous women and girls is an issue of Indigenous sovereignty and self-determination.[63] In turn, this raises a significant question about the role of the Canadian state in ending violence against Indigenous women and girls: if, as the histories in this chapter suggest, the Canadian state has been and continues to be deeply invested in violence against Indigenous women and girls to establish and maintain its national power—profoundly exemplified by the refusal of Prime Minister Harper to call a formal inquiry into missing and murdered Indigenous women and girls—how likely is the state going to disrupt this process? Given what is at stake for the Canadian state—after all, if violence against Indigenous women and girls is product of colonial domination and, thus, only a dramatic reconfiguration of the contemporary Canadian state will end this violence—it is highly unlikely that the state will willingly pursue meaningful responses to violence against

Indigenous women and girls. Thus, as Andrea Smith has argued, it is inherently problematic to rely on the state to resolve issues that it is primarily responsible for creating.[64]

This raises some important questions: How should Indigenous women and their communities proceed with their efforts to end violence against Indigenous women and girls? Do we continue to engage in state-sponsored anti-violence responses? While I acknowledge that engaging the Canadian state is inherently perilous for Indigenous nations given that any reinforcement of the current settler colonial state also reinforces its colonial domination over Indigenous nations and lands, I also don't believe that turning our back on the state will effectively end settler colonial domination and violence against Indigenous women and girls. As this chapter makes clear, this violence is the product of interlocking social systems of domination and, as such, requires collective social resolutions to disrupt these social hierarchies and their violences. The Canadian state is unlikely to willingly engage in dismantling its own supremacy and, thus, the persistent energies of Indigenous women and their supporters are required to educate, expose, and disrupt settler colonial domination and violence against Indigenous women and girls. However, the contradictory existence of the Canadian state as both saviour and perpetrator also impresses the need for Indigenous community-based solutions independent of the state—as Indigenous peoples and nations, we need to invest in our own solutions to the problem of violence in our communities. Critically, whether pursuing state-sponsored or community-based solutions, we must foreground our efforts in the sociological, and focus on dismantling the dominant social systems of oppression—settler colonialism, racism, patriarchy—that provide the ideological justification for the hierarchical ordering of Canadian society that make this violence possible in the first place. For as long as these systems of oppression continue to exist, Indigenous women and girls will continue to pay the price with their lives.

1. Royal Canadian Mounted Police, *Missing and Murdered Aboriginal Women: A National Operational Overview* (Ottawa: Government of Canada, 2014), 3, 8–9, http://www.rcmp-grc.gc.ca/en/missing-and-murdered-aboriginal-women-national-operational-overview. Indeed, the RCMP shaped the date parameters of their operational overview to coincide specifically with those used by the Native Women's Association of Canada's (NWAC) in their statistical research on missing and murdered Aboriginal women and girls as part of their Sisters in Spirit initiative. This alignment, according the RCMP, was sought to "allow comparisons and corroboration with recent public work on missing and murdered Aboriginal women and girls" (7).

2. Canadian Press, "PM Rules out National Inquiry into Missing and Murdered Aboriginal Women after 15-year-old Found Dead," *National Post*, August 21, 2014, http://news.nationalpost.com/2014/08/21/pm-rules-out-national-inquiry-into-missing-and-murdered-aboriginal-women-after-15-year-old-found-dead-in-river/.

3. Tanya Kappo, "Stephen Harper's Comments on Missing, Murdered Aboriginal Women Show 'Lack of Respect,'" *CBC News—Indigenous*, December 19, 2014, http://www.cbc.ca/news/aboriginal/stephen-harper-s-comments-on-missing-murdered-aboriginal-women-show-lack-of-respect-1.2879154.

4. Sherene H. Razack, "Introduction: When Place Becomes Race," in *Race, Space, and the Law: Unmapping a White Settler Society*, ed. Sherene H. Razack (Toronto: Between the Lines, 2002), 1–2.

5. Patrick Wolfe, "Settler Colonialism and the Elimination of the Native," *Journal of Genocide Research* 8, no. 4 (2006): 387–409.

6. Wolfe, "Settler Colonialism," 388.

7. Razack, "Introduction," 2.

8. See, for example, the Aboriginal Circle of the Canadian Panel on Violence Against Women, "Aboriginal Women," in *Changing the Landscape—Ending Violence—Achieving Equality: The Final Report of the Canadian Panel on Violence Against Women* (Ottawa: Minister of Supplies and Services Canada, 1993), 117–70; Emma LaRocque, *Violence in Aboriginal Communities* (Ottawa: Clearinghouse on Family Violence, 1994).

9. See Andrea Smith, *Conquest: Sexual Violence and American Indian Genocide* (Cambridge, MA: South End Press, 2005); Anita Olsen Harper, "Is Canada Peaceful and Safe for Aboriginal Women?" *Canadian Woman*

Studies 25, no. 1–2 (2006): 33–38; Native Women's Association of Canada, *Voices of Our Sisters in Spirit: A Report to Families and Communities*, 2nd ed. (Ottawa: Native Women's Association of Canada, 2009), https://www.nwac.ca/wp-content/uploads/2015/05/NWAC_Voices-of-Our-Sisters-In-Spirit_2nd-Edition_March-2009.pdf; Rauna Kuokkanen, "Globalization as Racialized, Sexualized Violence," *International Feminist Journal of Politics* 10, no. 2 (2009): 216–33.

10. LaRocque, *Violence in Aboriginal Communities*, 74.

11. See LaRocque, *Violence in Aboriginal Communities*; Kim Anderson, *A Recognition of Being—Reconstructing Native Womanhood*, 2nd ed. (Toronto: Canadian Scholars' Press, 2016); Barbara Alice Mann, *Iroquoian Women: The Gantowisas* (New York: Peter Lang, 2000); Dawn Martin-Hill, "She No Speaks and Other Colonial Constructs of the 'Traditional Woman,'" in *Strong Women Stories: Native Vision and Community Survival*, ed. K. Anderson and B. Lawrence (Toronto: Sumach Press, 2003), 106–19; Smith, *Conquest*.

12. See LaRocque, *Violence in Aboriginal Communities*; Smith, *Conquest*; Native Women's Association of Canada, *Voices of Our Sisters*; Kuokkanen, "Globalization."

13. Smith, *Conquest*, 23.

14. See LaRocque, *Violence in Aboriginal Communities*; Janice Acoose (Misko-Kìsikàwihkwè), *Iskwewak—Kah'Ki Yaw Ni Wahkomakanak: Neither Indian Princesses nor Easy Squaws* (Toronto: Women's Press, 1995); Sherene H. Razack, "Gendered Racial Violence and Spatialized Justice: The Murder of Pamela George," in *Race, Space, and the Law: Unmapping a White Settler Society*, ed. Sherene H. Razack (Toronto: Between the Lines, 2002), 122–56; Smith, *Conquest*.

15. LaRocque, *Violence in Aboriginal Communities*, 74.

16. Smith, *Conquest*, 12.

17. Smith, *Conquest*, 21–30; Razack, "Gendered Racial Violence."

18. Smith, *Conquest*, 21–30.

19. Razack, "Gendered Racial Violence," 136.

20. See Dara Culhane, *The Pleasure of the Crown: Anthropology, Law and First Nations* (Vancouver: Talon Books, 1998); Cole Harris, *Making Native Space: Colonialism, Resistance, and Reserves in British Columbia* (Vancouver: UBC Press, 2002); Bonita Lawrence, "Rewriting Histories of the Land: Colonization and Indigenous Resistance in Eastern Canada," in *Race, Space, and the Law: Unmapping a White Settler Society*, ed. Sherene

ROBYN BOURGEOIS

H. Razack (Toronto: Between the Lines, 2002), 21–46; and Renisa Mawani, "Law's Archive," *The Annual Review of Law and Social Science* 8 (2012): 337–65.

21. See Kim Anderson, *A Recognition of Being: Reconstructing Native Womanhood*, 2nd ed. (Toronto: Canadian Scholars' Press, 2016); LaRocque, *Violence in Aboriginal Communities*; and Barbara Alice Mann, *Iroquoian Women: The Gantowisas* (New York: Peter Lang, 2000).

22. See Harris, *Making Native Space*; Howard Adams, *Prisons of Grass: Canada from a Native Point of View* (Saskatoon: Fifth House Publishers, 1989); and Hugh Shewell, *"Enough to Keep Them Alive": Indian Welfare in Canada, 1873–1965* (Toronto: University of Toronto Press, 2004).

23. See Shewell, *"Enough to Keep Them Alive."*

24. Chantal Collin and Hilary Jensen, *A Statistical Profile of Poverty in Canada* (Ottawa: Library of Parliament, 2009), 16.

25. Aboriginal Affairs and Northern Development Canada, *Aboriginal Women in Canada: A Statistical Profile from the 2006 Census* (Ottawa: Government of Canada, 2012), 70.

26. See Ontario Native Women's Association, *Breaking Free: A Proposal for Change to Aboriginal Family Violence* (Thunder Bay: Ontario Native Women's Association, 1989), http://www.onwa.ca/upload/documents/ breaking-free-report-final_1989-pdf.doc.pdf; Aboriginal Circle of the Canadian Panel on Violence Against Women, "Aboriginal Women"; and Douglas A. Brownridge, *Violence against Women: Vulnerable Populations* (New York: Routledge, 2009).

27. See, for example, Amnesty International, *Stolen Sisters: A Human Rights Response to Discrimination and Violence against Indigenous Women in Canada* (Ottawa: Amnesty International, 2004), https://www.amnesty. ca/sites/amnesty/files/amr200032004enstolensisters.pdf; Native Women's Association of Canada, *Voices of Our Sisters*; and Kuokkanen, "Globalization"; Wally T. Oppal, *Forsaken: The Report of the Missing Women Commission of Inquiry* (Victoria: Province of British Columbia, 2012).

28. For detailed information on the sex discriminatory provisions within the Indian Act, see Bonita Lawrence, *"Real" Indians and Others: Mixed-Blood Urban Native Peoples and Indigenous Nationhood* (Vancouver: UBC Press, 2004); Martin J. Cannon, "Revisiting Histories of Legal Assimilation, Racialized Injustice, and the Future of Indian Status in Canada," in *Racism, Colonialism, and Indigeneity in Canada*, ed. Martin J. Cannon and

Lina Sunseri (Toronto: Oxford University Press, 2011), 89–97; Martin J.
Cannon, "Race Matters: Sexism, Indigenous Sovereignty and *McIvor*,"
Canadian Journal of Women and the Law 26, no. 1 (2014): 23–50.

29. Lawrence, *"Real" Indians and Others*, 55.

30. Lawrence, *"Real" Indians and Others*, 54–55.

31. Duncan Campbell Scott quoted in Chiefs of Ontario, *Our Children, Our
Future, Our Vision: First Nation Jurisdiction over First Nation Education in
Ontario* (Toronto: Chiefs of Ontario, 2002), 13.

32. See Randi Cull, "Aboriginal Mothering under the State's Gaze," in *"Until
Our Hearts Are On the Ground": Aboriginal Mothering, Oppression,
Resistance and Rebirth*, ed. D. Memee Lavell-Harvard and Jeanette
Corbiere Lavell (Toronto: Demeter Press, 2006), 141–56; and Truth
and Reconciliation Commission of Canada, *They Came for the Children:
Canada, Aboriginal Peoples, and Residential Schools* (Winnipeg: The Truth
and Reconciliation Commission of Canada, 2012).

33. See Truth and Reconciliation Commission of Canada, *They Came for the
Children*; Celia Haig-Brown, *Resistance and Renewal: Surviving the Indian
Residential School* (Vancouver: Aresenal Pulp Press, 1998); and Suzanne
Fournier and Ernie Crey, *Stolen from Our Embrace: The Abduction of
First Nations Children and the Restoration of Aboriginal Communities*
(Vancouver: Douglas & McIntyre, 1997).

34. See Truth and Reconciliation Commission of Canada, *They Came for the
Children*, 25–28, 35–37.

35. Truth and Reconciliation Commission of Canada, *They Came for the
Children*, 37–45.

36. Truth and Reconciliation Commission of Canada, *They Came for the
Children*, 79–80.

37. See Amnesty International, *Stolen Sisters*; and Native Women's
Association of Canada, *Voices of Our Sisters*.

38. For detailed discussions of these child welfare apprehensions, see
Fournier and Crey, *Stolen from Our Embrace*; Nico Trocmé, Della Knoke,
and Cindy Blackstock, "Pathways to the Overrepresentation of Aboriginal
Children in Canada's Child Welfare System," *Social Service Review*
(December 2004): 577–600; and Cull, "Aboriginal Mothering."

39. See Trocmé, Knoke, and Blackstock, "Pathways to Overrepresentation,"
579.

40. Statistics Canada, "2011 National Household Survey: Aboriginal Peoples in Canada: First Nations People, Métis and Inuit," *The Daily*, May 8, 2014, 2, http://www.statcan.gc.ca/daily-quotidien/130508/dq130508a-eng.pdf.

41. Fournier and Crey, *Stolen from Our Embrace*, 86.

42. Fournier and Crey, *Stolen from Our Embrace*, 86.

43. For the overrepresentation of Indigenous children in British Columbia child welfare and high vulnerability to violence, see Mary Ellen Turpel-Lafond, *Not Fully Invested: A Follow-up Report on the Representative's Past Recommendations to Help Vulnerable Children in B.C.* (Victoria: Representative for Children and Youth, 2014), 4, 21, 26, 27–29, https://www.rcybc.ca/sites/default/files/documents/pdf/reports_publications/rcy-recreport2014-revisedfinal.pdf. For Alberta, where Indigenous children account for 78 per cent of the children who have died in care in that province since 1978, see Darcy Helton, "Deaths of Alberta Aboriginal Children in Care No 'Fluke of Statistics,'" *Edmonton Journal*, January 8, 2014, http://www.edmontonjournal.com/life/Deaths+Alberta+aboriginal+children+care+fluke+statistics/9212384/story.html. For Manitoba, see Ted Hughes, *The Legacy of Phoenix Sinclair: Achieving the Best for All Our Children* (Winnipeg: Commission of Inquiry into the Circumstances Surrounding the Death of Phoenix Sinclair, 2013), 28, http://www.phoenixsinclairinquiry.ca/rulings/ps_volume1.pdf.

44. See Native Women's Association of Canada, *Voices of Our Sisters*; and Native Women's Association of Canada, *What Their Stories Tell Us: Research Findings from the Sisters in Spirit Initiative* (Ottawa: Native Women's Association of Canada, 2010), https://nwac.ca/wp-content/uploads/2015/07/2010-What-Their-Stories-Tell-Us-Research-Findings-SIS-Initiative.pdf.

45. See John H. Hylton, "The Justice System and Canada's Aboriginal Peoples: The Persistence of Racial Discrimination," in *Crimes of Colour: Racialization and the Criminal Justice System in Canada*, ed. Wendy Chan and Kiran Mirchandani (Peterborough, ON: Broadview Press, 2002), 139–56; Amnesty International, *Stolen Sisters*; and Human Rights Watch, *Those Who Take Us Away: Abusive Policing and Failures in Protection of Indigenous Women in Northern British Columbia, Canada* (Toronto: Human Rights Watch, 2013), http://www.hrw.org/sites/default/files/reports/canada0213webwcover.pdf.

46. Oppal, *Forsaken*, vol. 1, 4.

47. Oppal, *Forsaken*, vol. 2B, 219–37.

48. Native Women's Association of Canada, *Voices of Our Sisters in Spirit: A Report to Families and Communities* (Ottawa: Native Women's Association of Canada, 2008) and the second edition of *Voices of Our Sisters* (2009).

49. See Razack, "Gendered Racial Violence"; and Nicholas Bonokoski, "Colonial Constructs and Legally Sanctioned Sexually Violent Consequences in R. v. Edmondson," *Reconstruction: Studies in Contemporary Culture* 7, no. 1 (2007).

50. Razack, "Gendered Racial Violence," 125–26.

51. Razack, "Gendered Racial Violence," 126.

52. Sarah Carter, "Categories and Terrains of Exclusion: Constructing the 'Indian Woman' in the Early Settlement Era in Western Canada," in *In the Days of Our Grandmothers: A Reader in Aboriginal Women's History in Canada*, ed. Mary-Ellen Kelm and Lorna Townsend (Toronto: University of Toronto Press, 2006), 158.

53. Carter, "Categories and Terrains," 159.

54. Lesley Erickson, *Westward Bound: Sex, Violence, the Law and the Making of a Settler Society* (Vancouver: UBC Press, 2011) 62–63.

55. Carter, "Categories and Terrains," 15.

56. Erickson, *Westward Bound*, 63.

57. Joan Sangster, "Criminalizing the Colonized: Ontario Native Women Confront the Criminal Justice System, 1920–1960," *Canadian Historical Review* 80, no. 1 (1999): 35.

58. Sangster, "Criminalizing the Colonized," 40.

59. Erickson, *Westward Bound*, 45.

60. Erickson, *Westward Bound*, 52–54, 67, 73–75.

61. Erickson, *Westward Bound*, 76.

62. Erickson, *Westward Bound*, 77.

63. See Smith, *Conquest*; Particia Monture-Angus, *Thunder in My Soul: A Mohawk Woman Speaks* (Halifax: Fernwood Publishing, 1995); and Aboriginal Circle of the Canadian Panel on Violence Against Women, "Aboriginal Women."

64. Smith, *Conquest*; Andrea Smith, "Unmasking the State: Racial/Gender Terror and Hate Crimes," *Australian Law Journal* 47 (2007): 47–57.

ROBYN BOURGEOIS

6 A Tradition of Violence

Dehumanization, Stereotyping, and Indigenous Women

MICHELLE GOOD

IT WAS 1949 when my father shared his happy news with his parents. He had proposed to my mother. They would marry in late summer. My grandmother's reaction was not quite what he'd hoped for. She took to her bed and swore that my father would be disowned if he followed through, that his choice was a disgrace and would bring the family into disrepute. My grandmother's horrified response had nothing to do with my mother's character or conduct. In fact, at the time, she was a bit of a celebrity, feted in the national press upon her return to Saskatchewan from her nurses and midwifery training in New Zealand. This and her other accomplishments would have been extraordinary for any Canadian woman in the 1940s but even more so for my mother. A member of the Red Pheasant First Nation (Indian Band at that time) she survived three years at the St. Barnabus Indian Residential School where she contracted tuberculosis and then another three years at the "Indian Hospital," a tuberculosis sanatorium in Prince Albert.

I used to wonder what made her rise up so furiously to accomplish things so beyond the reach of an Indigenous woman in Canada in the 1940s. But rise she did. Having been raised as a self-respecting person in our Cree ways, perhaps it was the outrage she felt at her treatment at residential school that triggered her wild dreams. Subjected to forced bed rest for three years, she would have had so much time to think, time for dreams and a plan to take shape. She wrote letters endlessly, looking for a way to get an education in a time when training beyond the ninth grade was prohibited for Indigenous people in Canada. Somehow she managed to find an ear or two and won a scholarship to train with the Canadian Mothercraft Society in Toronto. She was then retained by a wealthy family in Toronto as their nanny and travelled with them to places such as New York City, San Francisco, and Bermuda. It was another scholarship that took her to New Zealand for three years to train as a nurse and midwife. Upon her return, she received multiple offers from various Canadian universities to continue her studies, each offer accompanied by a full scholarship. She was thirty years old at this point, an accomplished, worldly, and educated woman who had risen against the odds and circumstance to attain the benchmarks in a life that distinguish a person and imbue them with credentials worthy of respect.

But none of this mattered to my grandmother. All that mattered was that my mother was Cree and any children from the union with my father would be even worse. Half-breeds. After my parents married, their photos revealing a tight-lipped newly crowned mother-in-law, my grandmother continued to torment my mother. During my mother's first pregnancy, my grandmother invited her to tea with her lady friends and announced her pregnancy by stating that she was "having puppies." She never missed an opportunity to degrade my mother and shame my father for marrying her.

I cast back to that time and, in spite of what I know to be true, I resist it. After all, this was 1949 and these events were playing out against the backdrop of the end of the Second World War, the role of Canadians in liberating survivors of the Holocaust fresh in the collective consciousness. These were those heady days when notions of human rights were taking on an international momentum through the League of Nations and ultimately the United Nations. *Never Again* carried a promise of a better world, a tolerant world. Paris, December, 1948 and the lofty language of the Universal Declaration of Human Rights rang out, lifting us up to stand for a world where "All human beings are born free and equal in dignity and rights."[1] How could my mother have been treated this way at a time when the world was rising up to rail against intolerance and racial hatred? Was it because my grandmother was a monster? Was she that terrible exception, the minority opinion that spews racial hatred much to the embarrassment of a tolerant majority? No. Sadly, she was a Canadian prairie woman of her time. Her attitudes, prejudices, and outright social brutality were the culmination of generations of conditioning leading to attitudes that only the most agile and critical mind could escape. Her parents, grandparents, and great-grandparents were settlers and if not active participants in the violent subjugation of Indigenous people then certainly passive observers. Even the most well-meaning of the time would have had to find a way to justify what they knew was inhumane and contrary to any notion of human dignity.

How did these people deal with the cognitive dissonance they must have experienced in the face of the brutality visited upon my ancestors? To create a place for themselves in this land, the settlers accepted the notion that success in that venture necessitated the exploitation and destruction of Indigenous peoples. I do not believe that these people were inhuman. Thus, for humans to act with such inhumanity in carrying out the violence necessary to meet their aims, a justification was required. Violence without justification is indefensible. And so, just as former Minister of Aboriginal Affairs and Northern Development Bernard Valcourt blames our people for the murder and disappearance of close to two thousand Indigenous women and girls, those in power during the days of aggressive settlement created an image of Indigenous women that justified their treatment as chattel. And that image developed into a world view that has been conveyed with a terrible efficiency by these people to their subsequent descendants, who, when pressed, cannot say why they believe the things they believe about Indigenous women. Through the everyday commentary of everyday citizens over the course of our modern history, this view of Indigenous women has become entrenched in the collective subconscious of Canada. It is this form of social communication that must be examined to understand why assumptions about Indigenous women have become so commonplace, and a critical factor in rendering them disposable in the eyes of modern Canadian society.

"Happiness is but a dream for Canada because the malice that has marked so much of human history happened here too."[2] So says James Daschuk in his arresting analysis of the role of disease and the politics of starvation in disenfranchising the Indigenous people of Canada. In *Clearing the Plains*, Daschuk provides a carefully researched analysis of how Indigenous women were reduced to items of ransom and barter as their families struggled with the horrors of famine conditions created intentionally to establish economic supremacy for the newcomers and the subjugation of Indigenous peoples.

In the context of the vicious competition between Britain and Canada for supremacy in the fur trade, a horrifying brutality was routinely perpetrated against Indigenous women by officers of the Crown and condoned by those in power. The control of Indigenous populations and their transformation into indentured servants to the fur trade was critical to the dominance of one or the other in the fur wars. As Daschuk notes,

> Canadian traders [vs. the British traders of the H B C] soon
> found ways to overcome the Chipewyan aversion to commer-
> cial trapping. By the early 1790s, they routinely took women
> from their families to ensure payment of debts and sold them
> to company employees… "If the father or Husband or any
> of them resist the only satisfaction they get is a beating and
> they are frequently not satisfied with taking the Woman
> but their Gun and Tent likewise," wrote scandalized H B C

*surveyor Philip Turnor…The chief Canadian trader along
the Mackenzie, Duncan Livingstone, was highly regarded by
his peers. "Under his management these people were modeled
anew and brought under an implicit obedience to the White's
authority," N W C [North West Company] post master Willard
Wentzel wrote to Roderick Mackenzie. That "authority" in the
Athabasca included a slave traffic in women.*[3]

To achieve the compliance of the men and to secure their
participation in enriching the settlers through the fur trade, the
women were held hostage and worse. We must understand and
acknowledge that this was not just the conduct of some rogue fur
traders. This attack on Indigenous women became a weapon in
the colonial arsenal that would be used consistently right into the
second half of the twentieth century and arguably beyond.

As Daschuk explains, the "sexual improprieties of DIA
(Department of Indian Affairs) employees" were widespread and
well known by their superiors.[4] Forty-five per cent of government
officials living in the then Northwest Territories were known to
be engaged in predatory relations with young Indigenous girls,
contrary to their stated mandate of being a moral example. Not
only did these relations cause great pain and havoc for Indigenous
people, they contributed to the escalation of violence against
predatory Indian agents for which Indigenous people paid a heavy
price. Referring to the so-called Frog Lake Massacre, Daschuk
writes, "Twenty-six years after the killings, fur-trader-turned-
missionary Jack Matheson provided a more sinister motive for the
violence…'An Indian girl more or less didn't matter; and I've seen
ration cards held back six months till girls of thirteen were handed
over to that…brute [the Indian agent].' One of the killers at Frog
Lake, Wandering Spirit, had spent eighteen months in prison for
assaulting another DIA employee, John Delaney. While he was
incarcerated, Delaney 'took his girl wife.'"[5]

In another instance, John Norrish, the farm instructor for the
Blackfoot reserve, was engaged in a practice of withholding and

trading rations for sex. He was discovered to be buying sex with flour when certain of the women from the reserve were found to have bogus ration cards that gave them three extra rations of flour. Officials within the Department of Indian Affairs believed that the women were not willing participants in this food-for-sex scenario and the Indian Act was amended in 1886 to authorize prosecution of Indigenous women prostitutes. As Daschuk notes, this amendment was made largely in response to the widespread "scandal over the traffic of Indian women involving DIA employees." It was reported to Parliament that girls as young as thirteen were being sold to white men in west for as little as ten dollars. Concern about what we now call human trafficking was rejected by Hector-Louis Langevin. He dismissed these apprehensions by stating that "(to Indians), marriage is simply a bargain and sale that the parents of a young woman are always on the alert to find a buyer for her."[6]

Likewise, it was well known that Hayter Reed, member of Parliament, took a young girl from the Touchwood Hills as his "mistress" and that she bore a child of his. Rather than being censured, he ultimately was promoted to the role of Indian commissioner and played a key role in the development of Indian residential schools and in the government's stubborn refusal to respond in any meaningful way to the concerns about sexual abuse, disease, and starvation in those schools.

In addition to simply being taken hostage and held as sex slaves, Indigenous women were forced into a form of prostitution when rations were withheld unless they provided sexual favours to the Indian agents. Daschuk explains, "Contrary to S.W. Horrall's assertion that prostitution came to the North West Territories as sex workers moved west with the railway, prostitution among aboriginal women was a survival strategy resulting from the poverty experienced in their reserve communities after the disappearance of the bison."[7] DIA employees knew that Indigenous women participated in this sex-for-food form of prostitution unwillingly, as the women were forced either in the form of human trafficking or by the desperation of starvation.[8]

Daschuk's research is invaluable in that it outlines in horrific detail the methods that were employed in the process of subjugation and dehumanization of a people in the name of settling the west. The legacy of this dark chapter of colonialism is that Indigenous women are still seen as disposable and even as commodities to be used as members of the non-Indigenous society see fit.

The idea of the role of "word of mouth" in the creation and perpetuation of the negative stereotypes that plague the lives of Indigenous women first came to me while I was teaching as a sessional history instructor. I was teaching a year-long history unit on the history of Indigenous peoples in Canada. As any Indigenous person knows, that "story" is not our story. So, out of a desire to inspire my students to challenge their preconceptions I asked them in a group discussion to share what they "knew" about Indigenous people in Canada. While I knew I wanted them to wonder a little about these things, I wasn't quite sure how I would get them to that point. I sat there, listening to all the tired, old stereotypes rolling out of these young people like memorized nursery rhymes. And it hit me. They *are*, in a hideous sort of way, memorized nursery rhymes! I thought about all those childhood rhymes: "I see London, I see France," "Ring around the Rosy," and the like. How do we come to know those chants? Ask yourself. *Where did I learn that?* I feel pretty confident that you will not, with specificity, be able to say where you learned these kinds of rhymes. So I took things a little further and when my students assertions of baldly stated and mostly wrong stereotypes petered out, I asked them, *Now how do you know these things to be true?* To their credit, they were aghast. They could not at first even speculate on how they came to know and hold as true some pretty racist stereotypes. Slowly it started to unravel. My dad told me. My grandfather used to live next to a reserve and he told me. My auntie, my mother, my grandmother. Almost invariably, the source of the "information" was familial.

So, then I turn my thoughts to the likes of Hector-Louis Langevin, Hayter Reed, Duncan Campbell Scott, and every other non-Indigenous person, and think about the things their children overheard them say as well as the things they would have actively taught their children to justify the manner in which Indigenous people were and are treated in this country. Generation upon generation of non-Indigenous Canadians have been weaned on racism and bigotry, and rather than nurturing tolerance, a bedrock foundation of disgust and disregard centuries old informs the social conception of the Indigenous woman in Canada. She is disposable. She is an object to be used and discarded. She is less than human and thus can be treated as such.

For years, a chorus of voices has been raised calling for an inquiry into the close to two thousand missing and murdered Aboriginal women in Canada. For years, we heard the common refrain, and basis for rejecting pleas for an inquiry, that one of the factors leading to their demise is the fact that these women live a high-risk lifestyle, many of them engaged in the sex trade. It was only after Maryanne Pearce's doctoral research demonstrated that a very small percentage of these women were in fact involved in the sex trade that an entirely new public perspective began to emerge.[9] Rather than hookers who contributed to their own fate, these were young girls, students, teachers, mothers, daughters, sisters. Contrary to the assumptions reinforced by government and media, these women represented a cross-section of the female Indigenous population. So how is it that media, politicians, police, and the public at large would automatically assume that these women had endangered themselves through participation in the sex trade? Even when releasing the report handed down by the RCMP in which they acknowledge the numbers of missing and murdered, the RCMP representative herself once again voiced the myth that these women had put themselves in harm's way. Granted, one might extrapolate from the sensational media coverage of Robert Pickton's trial and less prominent media coverage of John Martin Crawford, another serial killer of Indigenous women, that the only information about these women to which the public was privy was fraught with references to some of these victims who in fact were sex trade workers. But, there is something deeper afoot.

The legacy of the men, founding fathers, bureaucrats, and company men who reduced our women to disposable goods can be found in virtually every strata of society. While the women descendants of those Indigenous women live their lives in a state of fear that they might be next on the list of missing and murdered, the country glorifies the likes of Hayter Reed and Hector-Louis Langevin, whose name graced the building that houses the Prime Minister's Office and the Privy Council until very recently. It becomes easier to understand how our women became disposable when we imagine children learning at the knee of the likes of the men who brutalized our women as a strategy in the subjugation of a people.

It seems, too, that the practice of ignoring the deaths and disappearances of Indigenous women finds its roots in the history of colonialism. As Daschuk notes, the killing of Europeans was widely publicized in the media of the time, and continues to be a focal point in the broader historical examination of the various "uprisings" in Canadian history.[10] The murder of Indigenous people during these conflicts and upheavals received scant attention at the time, and the failure of the media with respect to the wholesale murder of Indigenous women today is reflective of a media committed to maintaining an illusory image of both Canada and Indigenous people.

In *Seeing Red: A History of Natives in Canadian Newspapers*, Mark Cronlund Anderson and Carmen Robertson provide a careful analysis of the media in Canada and suggest that "Insofar as the content of newspaper imagery derives from the larger culture in which its readers participate, one might reasonably expect a consonance between press content and pre-existing reader bias. The result is that the news constitutes a kind of national curriculum, which emerges organically as if nothing were more natural. In short, as curriculum news images do not present new material so much as they simply reinforce the status quo."[11] The writers conclude that colonial archetypes and behaviours have become essentialized such that wildly inaccurate ideas about Indigenous people have become normalized to form a kind of Canadian "common sense," or, as I would put it, a common sensibility that informs reactions to issues as devastating as the disappearance and murder of some two thousand women. Rather than sparking an urgent sense of something terrible happening over and over again that must be addressed, operating out of this carefully contrived national mindset, such reports elicit "nothing more than tsk tsks and knowing nods of the head." Those tsk tsks are a shorthand for a complex colonial curriculum that, if anything, culminates in the oft-reported notion that these women brought this violence onto themselves.[12]

In a very real sense, during the formation of Canada as we know it today, the idea of Indigenous women as commodities or currency to be bartered, used, and discarded emerged. It is no wonder that less than a hundred years later my grandmother would be horrified at the notion of a Cree daughter-in-law. The continuing colonial agenda, partnered with the media promulgating a curriculum of hatred and bigotry, promotes the maintenance of this idea that these women, our women, are less than human, distasteful, and entirely disposable.

Someone educated my grandmother to think of Indigenous women as less than human. At the same time her entire generation and the one before and after it received what I think of as a form of oral history passed down from one generation to the next, perpetrating these ideas such that 150 years after Confederation, these images are still superimposed on our women, and it is killing them. These images are like a permission slip for rape and murder.

Non-Indigenous populations of Canada would be well advised to take a page from the book of those Indigenous groups who argued at law that oral history must be given equal weight as written history. First in the decision in *Delgamuukw v. British Columbia* and later in *Squamish Indian Band v. Canada* and

R. v. Ironeagle, the courts began to recognize the legitimacy of the modalities of our way of keeping history.[13]

In our own struggles for recognition of our rights, we fought for the legal recognition of oral history. In the arguments we made to the courts, what the mainstream saw as our "myths" and superstitions were presented as cogent histories of our people. These arguments formed a foundation for legal recognition of the notion that information is transferred orally from one generation to the next. Our value systems and social structures were conveyed through our oral traditions. I believe that the same thing is true for non-Indigenous Canada. The way of spoken traditions passing from one generation to another is not exclusive to us and in fact played a key role in passing this tradition of bigotry, hatred, and violence through from colonial to postcolonial Canada. The values of the colonial era have been perpetuated through an oral tradition, bolstered by the media and the thinly veiled racism underlying government policy.

This triumvirate of media as curriculum, government policy, and ongoing oral history colludes to make it exceptionally difficult to replace this carefully constructed notion of who Indigenous women are with an accurate portrayal—a portrayal that would begin the process of ending the violence against our women. This profound difficulty of attempting to penetrate generations of inaccuracy in the articulation of who we are as Indigenous women is exemplified by how much work has been done and how firmly the illusion still prevails. For example, artistically, intellectually, culturally, and socially we have demonstrated in very public ways for decades that our ways of life, our social structures, our culture, and our spiritual beliefs are sophisticated and entirely contrary to the brutish notion that the Canadian mainstream proliferates and stubbornly refuses to modify. For example, consider the great artistic works of Bill Reid, Norval Morrisseau, Kenojuak Ashevak; the literary works of Lee Maracle, Thomas King, and Emma LaRocque; the legal and political advocacy of Cindy Blackstock and Mary Ellen Turpel-Lafond. The evidence is in and still we remain locked in a mirror, the reflection false, a creation of political and social forces. Why has this information that speaks with such clarity about an advanced culture and society failed miserably in revising this persistently incorrect image of who Indigenous people, and particularly Indigenous women, really are? In my view, the influence of the founding fathers was deeply successful in promulgating the idea of Indigenous women as unimportant to their own communities, much less having any value in the non-Indigenous community. This false image is as deeply entrenched in the fabric of Canadian society as is our notion of ourselves as a free and democratic nation founded on idealistic and peace-loving principles. It has been conditioned into us since those horrific times when we were being starved out of our homelands.

It is only when I look through this lens that I am able to understand how it is that my grandmother would be so shaken to her core at the prospect of my mother joining her family. It was conditioned into her and those before and after as thoroughly as the words to "O Canada."

It is from this place that horrors are perpetrated against Indigenous women in Canada with what can only be described as a silent acceptance by government and society alike. Increased policing and government programs teaching women how to be safe is not going to correct this situation. Only understanding will. Understanding and a commitment to know the truth of the brutality that was done to our women in the name of "settling the west" and how that has been institutionalized into complacent acceptance of the continued brutalization and dehumanization of our women.

Canada must know the truth of our history. Just as the door is starting to creak open in terms of education on what residential schools really were about, education about the open season on Indigenous women throughout our history must also be undertaken if we ever expect our women to be seen as we are and treated with the respect and dignity we deserve.

NOTES

1. United Nations, *Universal Declaration of Human Rights*, article 1 (1948).

2. James Daschuk, *Clearing the Plains: Disease, Politics of Starvation, and the Loss of Aboriginal Life* (Regina, SK: University of Regina Press, 2013), book jacket notes.

3. Daschuk, *Clearing the Plains*, 50.

4. Daschuk, *Clearing the Plains*, 153.

5. Daschuk, *Clearing the Plains*, 152–53.

6. Daschuk, *Clearing the Plains*, 154.

7. Daschuk, *Clearing the Plains*, 154.

8. Daschuk, *Clearing the Plains*, 154.

9. Maryanne Pearce, "An Awkward Silence: Missing and Murdered Vulnerable Women and the Canadian Justice System" (LLD thesis, University of Ottawa, 2013), http://ruor.uottawa.ca/handle/10393/26299.

10. Daschuk, *Clearing the Plains*, 155.

11. Mark Cronlund Anderson and Carmen Robertson, *Seeing Red: A History of Natives in Canadian Newspapers* (Winnipeg: University of Manitoba Press, 2011), 8.

12. Anderson and Robertson, *Seeing Red*, 8.

13. Delgamuuk v. British Columbia (1997 SCC 1010); Squamish Indian Band v. Canada (2001 FCT 480); R. v. Ironeagle (2000 2 CNLR 163).

7 The (Un)Making of Property

Gender Violence and the Legal Status of Long Island Algonquian Women

KELSEY T. LEONARD

Much of this chapter is based on my experience as an Algonquian Shinnecock woman and knowledge passed on to me from Shinnecock women and my people—the Shinnecock Indian Nation, People of the Shore or Level Land. This is my perspective. I bring these ideas in a humble way and do not presume to speak for all Native women.

Introduction

Before the European invasion and colonization of Long Island and southern New England, Algonquian women enjoyed a position in society that has long been ignored by historiography and legal anthropologists.[1] This chapter will show that the continued elevation of violence against Algonquian women is directly correlated to the legal and social disenfranchisement they suffered following the colonization of Long Island in New York. Legal scholars aim to understand the origins of violence against Indigenous women, but they often fail to examine the historical record of the colonial plural legal systems that cast the subjugation of Indigenous women as persons with less legal protections than their European counterparts and thereby inherently violable.[2]

This chapter will lay out a framework to help us examine and understand the pluralistic form that law took in the colonial period on Long Island and how it continues to shape the experiences of violence of Algonquian women. The first part of the chapter offers a starting place for envisioning the unique confluence of Dutch, English, and Indigenous legal systems that formed the inherited pluralistic legal order. The second part of the chapter explores the European and Algonquian legal definitions of personhood and how they shaped the political suffrage and later destruction thereof for Algonquian Shinnecock women. The third section discusses the historical violence waged against Algonquian Shinnecock women and the legacy of colonial laws in reshaping gender roles in Shinnecock social organization. The fourth part examines the "indirect rule" led by colonists against the Shinnecock people through an imposed government structure. The fifth section analyzes the modern conflicts between tribal and colonial laws, and the restoration of Shinnecock women's rights in spite of vestiges of colonial legal orders. The chapter concludes with the recognition of the need for further research and commitment to the study of Native women's rights in the face of gendered colonial violence and historical trauma that impacts their continued perceived violability.

Legal Pluralism in Colonial New York

In mid-seventeenth-century New York, two colonizing powers, Dutch and English, encountered one another as well as a large Indigenous population, each with their own distinct legal orders. In 1628, Isaack de Rasieres, a Dutch trader, described a "Sinnecox" Indian tribe that lived on Long Island as an agrarian society with elected political leaders and an intricate system of trade with neighbouring coastal Algonquian Nations.[3] The founding of New Netherland and later the New York Colony is marked by an early pluralistic legal culture reflective of the diverse origins and legal inheritances of the Dutch and English settlers.[4]

Legal pluralism is the co-existence of more than one legal order or system of law.[5] As scholar Dorothy H. Bracey underscores, "Legal pluralism is sometimes the legacy of colonialism."[6] Today, the Shinnecock Indian Nation and the State of New York under the United States federal government each have distinct legal systems that operate on a continuum of legal pluralism. The Shinnecock Indian Nation are a coastal Algonquian peoples whose approximately 850 acre reservation territory borders the townships of Southampton and Hampton Bays on Long Island, New York. This ancestral territory has been significantly reduced due to colonialism, but has nonetheless remained under tribal control since the pre-contact era.

During the colonial period, the English aggressively tried to suppress Shinnecock legal order and government structure.[7] As Shinnecock leaders made decisions regarding land transactions, government, and economics that did not reflect English cultural values, the colonizing forces sought to impose a system modelled after their own to override traditional Shinnecock laws and political structure.[8] European colonizers transplanted their legal systems to Long Island, creating a melting pot of Dutch and English laws. Many of these laws were drafted to diminish the political capacity of Algonquian Shinnecock women and, ultimately, Indigenous nations as they endeavoured to coexist with the colonial townships. As jurisprudence scholar Brian Z. Tamanaha notes, Indigenous systems of law were marked by the colonizers as being "customary" or "traditional" so as to distinguish them from the transplanted norms and legal orders of the European colonizers.[9]

The state of conflict among colonial and tribal systems of law permitted affluent European colonists to opportunistically select from the existing Dutch and English colonial laws to advance their personal aims. As scholar Dorothy H. Bracey states, "If law

is a method of enforcing certain norms and behaviors, it should
come as no surprise that law is a method by which one group can
enforce its norms and behaviors on others."[10] The trustee system
eliminated pre-contact forms of Shinnecock government that
included balanced roles for women and men and replaced them
with a foreign ideology that dictated the subservience of women
and ultimate dominance of men. As colonists had trouble securing
land from Shinnecock people, including women, they enforced
the European norm that women were subservient to men. When
Shinnecock women were no longer allowed to conduct land
transactions, colonists were able to advance their personal interests
in acquiring large tracts of land on Long Island. Oftentimes alcohol
was used as a tool of coercion given to Long Island Indians in
exchange for "good behaviour" or as payment for sale of land.[11]
The plural Dutch and English legal systems rendered Shinnecock
people aliens in their own land.

Defining Legal Personhood in Eras of Colonization

Prior to European arrival, Shinnecocks had a vibrant democracy
with political participation that included women as full participants in the consensus-based decision-making process.[12] In the
early colonial period, the Dutch engaged with Algonquian female
leaders. Algonquian women were even permitted to bring legal
disputes and complaints before the Court of Burgomasters and
Schepens.[13] With the English takeover in 1664, the legal proce-
dure changed dramatically as English laws, which converged and
conflicted with Dutch practice, supplemented Dutch laws. In
1665, a Court of Assizes was formed and was granted both judi-
cial and legislative powers under the new legal code.[14] Termed the
"Duke's Laws," it included rules governing all aspects of Indian
affairs.[15] Most tangibly this meant that Algonquian women saw
their personhood in the new legal order diminished irreversibly.[16]

Within English common law, women were stripped of their
legal personhood depending on their marital status through the

doctrine of coverture.[17] The English system of law eliminated all legal rights for married women, including their ability to own property. The status of married women was called *feme covert*, which meant that her legal identity was effectively non-existent, having been subsumed by her husband. Under the English common-law doctrine, if an Algonquian woman married a non-Indian man, he would then acquire her personal property and right to control any real property she brought with her.[18] Furthermore, the English legal system did not permit women to file legal suits, make contracts, or sign any legal document without her husband's permission.[19] This was in stark contrast to the Algonquian laws that allowed married women to not only own and inherit land but to possess full rights in its management, sale, or lease.

Shinnecock society represented gender roles in a dualistic symbiosis, whereby Shinnecock women had separate responsibilities from Shinnecock men, but not subordinate roles. In essence, Shinnecock gender roles were an exercise in "separate but equal" Indigenous paradigms. Birthrights among the Shinnecock were traced through the mother's lineage. Shinnecock women were very hard workers, responsible for cornfield planting and tending, making mats, building of wickiups, wampum manufacturing, and more.[20] The legal personhood of coastal Algonquian women, such as the Shinnecock, was directly linked to the land.[21] Shinnecock women believe the land and water are the life force of their existence; their spiritual and physical health is intrinsically linked to the health of their ancestral homelands.[22] As anthropologist Kathleen Bragdon states, this linkage among women and land was likely due to their role as the "principal laborers of it."[23]

To control the legal personhood of Algonquian women, the English developed a colonial policy of "deed diplomacy." In 1643, Roger Williams in his guide *A Key to the Languages of America*, noted the term *sunksqua*, which was used to describe Algonquian female leaders who served as proprietors of land and negotiators of sale or lease transactions with the colonists.[24] Historian John Strong has documented forty legal transactions involving

Algonquian women in the colonial period. Most are land sales or leases, some concern testimony on boundaries, and others are sales of whaling rights.[25] Algonquian women's authority over land may have been derived through their marriage to a sachem, a powerful male political and spiritual leader; however, there were also sunksquas, powerful female political and spiritual leaders, married to men with no position of authority within the tribe. Thus, it is less likely female leadership and autonomy were predicated on female marital status among coastal Algonquian nations.[26]

Throughout the seventeenth century, Algonquian women on Long Island had significant control over land and boundary disputes, as evidenced in English court records.[27] Native women became an obstacle in deed transactions, so the English sought to legislate their legal rights over property away from their control. With Native women out of the transactional picture, the English would be free to acquire Indian land. In 1702, the English demonetized wampum as the colonial currency, giving them further control over New York and destroying economic and trade power once held by Algonquian women.[28] After this time, it became almost effortless for the colonial powers to structure political and economic laws that attacked the core of Algonquian gender roles and the social paradigm of Indigenous societies.

During the second half of the eighteenth century, the town of Southampton struggled to secure legitimate titles to Indian lands, as Algonquian peoples would often lease or resell the same tracts of lands with the understanding that the contract was for usufruct rights. As a result, in 1764, the town of Southampton negotiated an agreement with the Shinnecock that prohibited individual Shinnecock women from leasing land without tribal approval. The agreement stated, "no Indian or squaw shall hire out any land to plant or sow upon in any cases whatsoever without the consent of the whole."[29] The New York Legislature and town of Southampton regulation of Shinnecock women's legal personhood was a powerful colonizing force, providing leverage for the dissemination of Indian assimilation policies. These laws facilitated the perceived violability of Algonquian women, granting their male counterparts superior rights and making Indigenous women "vectors for assimilation."[30] With the power to grant or deny Shinnecock women rights to lease land, marry, raise children, and control their family household, the colonial powers obtained an unprecedented hegemony over tribal society.[31]

The new legal orders effectively banished Shinnecock women to the private realm. However, Shinnecock women did not disappear; they remained integral to the survival of the nation, but their legal status as autonomous individuals changed irrevocably. Thus, the key characteristic of political violence committed against Shinnecock women was that, over time, they lost their equal standing and autonomous legal status both among the colonists and their own people.

History of Violence against Algonquian Shinnecock Women

A central theme of this chapter and this book is violence—violence against Indigenous women. American law defines violence as "the unlawful exercise of physical force or intimidation by the exhibition of such force."[32] However, this definition does not encompass the breadth of experiences of violence lived by Indigenous women. As human rights scholar Berta Esperanza Hernández-Truyol states, it is necessary for Indigenous communities to "revision the acts that constitute violence."[33] The history of Algonquian women from the Shinnecock Indian Nation demonstrates that violence has many forms of perpetration, including psychological, social, and political subjugation of women; male-dominated legal systems; and economic ostracism of women.[34] The problem of violence against Shinnecock women involves a multitude of factors: gender, colonialism, race, economics, poverty, and legal status.

It has been noted that Shinnecock occupation of Long Island, New York, dates back well over 10,000 years, during which time the thirteen tribes of the Montauk Confederacy settled and built their nations on an island carved out of the earth in such a way that, from the sky, it looks as though nations were built on a whale's back. The dispossession of the Shinnecock and violent history of their colonization has been well documented by legal scholars and anthropologists.[35] As feminist Andrea Smith states, colonial relationships are inherently gendered and sexualized.[36]

Colonial gendered violence permeates across generations, making it increasingly difficult for Native women victims to differentiate their violated persons from their violated tribal nations.[37] The victimhood is layers upon layers of sexual violence that originates in colonial contact and the language and actions of the colonizer. Historians have noted that European settlers often used language to describe the continent with references to female characteristics, including "virgin land," "woman," "her bounty," etc.[38] The language of the colonizer mirrored the language of sexual violence, such as "seizure," "taking," "pillaging," and "invasion."[39] If Algonquian women are linked to the land and the land can lawfully be raped, it is not too difficult to understand how Algonquian women became victims of sexual violence. The metaphorical relationship that equates land with women and women with land is noted by scholar Andrea Smith in *Conquest: Sexual Violence and American Indian Genocide*:

> *Native Peoples have become marked as inherently violable through a process of sexual colonization. By extension, their lands and territories have become marked as violable as well. The connection between the colonization of Native people's bodies—particularly Native women's bodies—and Native lands is not simply metaphorical. Many feminist theorists have argued that there is a connection between patriarchy's disregard for nature, women, and Indigenous peoples. The colonial/patriarchal mind that seeks to control the sexuality of women and Indigenous peoples also seeks to control nature.[40]*

English settlers on Long Island sought to control Shinnecock women through sexual violence, forced marriage, and stolen suffrage. As colonizers gained control over Shinnecock women's legal personhood and autonomy, it was only "natural" that they sought to conquer Shinnecock land and resources.

Frantz Fanon, a pioneer of postcolonial theory, argued that colonized women are subject to what Jean-Paul Sartre coined the "aura of rape" in so much that the destruction of Indigenous villages, stealing of land and property, raping of women, and ultimate usurpation of tribal governing structures has cemented Indigenous female violability in the mind of the colonizer.[41] This "aura of rape" surrounding Algonquian women is no more apparent than in the colonial intimacies of domestic servitude. Shinnecock women were often employed as domestic servants in the homes of wealthy colonial families.[42] Indian slavery was abolished in New York in 1679, but historical records indicate that Indian women and girls continued to be sold into slavery until the complete abolishment in 1857.[43] Even then, slavery conditions still existed only under the title of "indentured servitude." It is important to note that when Shinnecock girls were sent to Indian boarding schools, including Carlisle Indian School by the Bureau of Indian Affairs in the nineteenth century,[44] they were trained as domestics and used in the affluent homes of prominent American families, often without compensation, living in conditions akin to slavery. However, this practice was centuries old by then as Indian families on Long Island were forced to indenture their children to white families as early as the end of the seventeenth century. When Shinnecock women and girls served colonial households, opportunities for sexual violence increased. Furthermore, the discovery of sexual encounters outside of marriage between a Native woman and a European man often led to a public whipping for the Indian female servant and her paramour.[45]

It was the aim of European colonizing powers to subjugate Shinnecock women and erase their political power through the creation of a legal system that more closely modelled their own patrilineage. Traditional Algonquian dimensions of power were toppled over and replaced with male-dominated decision-making systems that destroyed women's roles, autonomy, and community harmony. The only remaining vestige of women's autonomy among the Shinnecock people was that membership within the tribe continued to be traced through maternal lineal descent. For centuries leading up to the modern era, Shinnecock women did not have the same autonomy as they did before European colonization. European colonization on Long Island was designed to destroy Shinnecock culture and replace it with European culture; therefore, colonists imposed the subservient role of women within European society on Shinnecock women, ushering in a new legal order that eliminated women's inherent equal rights under Indigenous customs and norms.

Imposed Legal Order

In 1792, the town of Southampton petitioned the State of New York to impose a legal system of government on the Shinnecocks that was modelled after the English trusteeship, which was already in place in many colonial towns. The trustee system aimed to control Shinnecock people through the coerced imposition of European law and order. In response to the town's petition, the New York State Legislature passed an act called An Act for the Benefit of the Shinnecock Tribe of Indians, Residing in Suffolk County (the 1792 Act), which called for adult male members of at least twenty-one years of age "belonging to the Shinnecock tribe of Indians, who for the preceding six months shall have resided on the reservation, to meet on the first Tuesday in April" each year to elect three male tribal members as trustees.[46] The 1792 Act granted the Shinnecock male trustees the power to allot lands, manage timber extraction, and "together with three justices of the peace from the neighboring Town of Southampton," lease lands for terms no longer than three years.[47]

The 1792 trustee system introduced a new form of land management that excluded Shinnecock women from positions of governance over land.[48] The system undermined traditional female authority by denying women the ability to have decision-making power in Shinnecock land transactions. Shinnecock women were the cultivators of the land as they oversaw crop planting and harvesting.[49] The new legal system usurped control Algonquian women held over land and over the distribution of the products they harvested from the land. It violated the female person-hood and identity of Algonquian women. To violate our land is to violate our bodies and our minds. This shift in legal paradigms through the disenfranchisement of Shinnecock women thus marked the gradual decline in power that women held—not only in their tribal community, but also amongst the settler colonies.

It was not uncommon in the colonial period for European settlers to marry Shinnecock women so that they might lay claim to lands, resources, and property rights. The term *marry* is used loosely. Although there were some instances of proper society marriages among Shinnecock women and male settlers, rape and abduction were more commonly used as tools to force marriages.[50] As Indigenous legal scholar Sarah Deer points out, Americans must "acknowledge that the United States was founded, in part, through the use of sexual violence as a tool, that were it not for the widespread rape of Native American women, many of our towns, counties, and states might not exist."[51] Marriage was a tool for solidifying "diplomatic bonds" among Native women and male settlers. [52] The legal contract created through marriage gave European husbands of Algonquian women greater control and proprietary interest in lands during the early colonial period. This was especially true among the Shinnecock, who created a law specifically to combat these property usurpations in the late eighteenth century.

In response to these incursions, the Shinnecock trustees voted in 1799 that "No person not being an original proprietor shall draw any land by virtue of marrying" a Shinnecock woman.[53] It was the intent of the 1799 law to combat encroachments on land and usurpation of natural resources by non-Indian men who had married Shinnecock women. In a petition for redress to the New York State Legislature in the 1800s, these non-Indian men were described as "strangers who marry in among us and by virtue of such connections, claim a right." The petition requested the State "compel such strangers so marrying to go...with their wives to retire off our lands."[54] Settler marriages to Shinnecock women destroyed the wife's rights within the tribal community. As non-Indian husbands laid false claims to Indian lands and resources, the tribal community began to resent those Shinnecock women who married-out, and attempted to ban the women from the tribe's territory.

The imposed legal order did not allow for the political participation of women, which led to the historical erasure of women in legal documents. Records kept by colonial legal systems on Long Island stopped naming women in 1799, even though in years prior Shinnecock women were named in records in equal numbers to men. Records indicated that Shinnecock women owned and leased land, as well as endorsed land sale transactions. After 1799, the colonial legal powers erased women from legal documentation. As a result, women's names were not listed in official records for almost half a century.[55] Under the imposed trustee system, Shinnecock women were excluded from voting, holding political office, or voicing their political opinions in tribal government forums for centuries.

Restoration of Rights

Over the hundreds of years following the imposition of the trustee system, Shinnecock women have continued to protect their ancestral lands despite their diminished political capacity under colonial laws. Shinnecock women have defended the land against grave robbers and illegal takings, using their bodies to block developers' bulldozers as they tried to encroach on tribal lands.[56] They have led demonstrations to protest English takings of Indian lands, as they did in 1853 when they seized a large herd of sheep that belonged to a Southampton colonist.[57] They continued on with this work into the twentieth century, as in 1952 when Shinnecock women protested the Cove Realty Company's effort to take reservation land. This is but one example of how the twentieth century saw a great resurgence of Shinnecock female leadership.

Following the imposition of the trustee system, the first recorded vote on whether to give Shinnecock women suffrage was held in 1942.[58] Male members of the tribe at that time voted to deny Shinnecock women the right to vote; furthermore, the political protests of women in public forums regarding their rights led a large margin of male voters to vote against allowing women to speak at all during tribal meetings. Leading up to the vote to give women suffrage rights in 1993, there were many tribal citizens among the Shinnecock who believed that the government structure imposed by the colonists and its male-only political enfranchisement was an important vestige of Shinnecock tradition and identity.[59] To restore women's rights in Indigenous communities, this kind of political mindset must be decolonized.

Despite the refusal of male voters to recognize women's political voice, many Shinnecock women continued to agitate for political change from the 1950s to the 1980s—often pushing to speak at meetings even with the ban. In 1967, Shinnecock women sought redress to their disenfranchisement with the local Human Relations Council.[60] However, there was little outside legal mechanisms could do in light of New York State Indian laws, which required the right of women to vote in elections or meetings to be passed by a vote of the male qualified voters of the tribe.[61] If the women of the Shinnecock Indian Nation wanted to have the right to vote, they would need the eligible male voting citizenry to recognize their rights. By the late 1980s and early 1990s, Shinnecock women slowly began to restore their political rights and legal status within the nation.

In 1987, they formed a women's advocacy organization called the Shinnecock Women's Group. The intention was to bring their concerns and political agenda to the forefront of the community and put pressure on Shinnecock male leaders to re-evaluate the imposed colonial system. It was a tumultuous period, during which Shinnecock women staged political protests regarding the lack of women's suffrage and exclusion from participation in the nation's government. Trustees opposed to women's enfranchisement would abruptly end tribal meetings when women insisted on talking and making political speeches. The women's group provided reservation women with a vehicle to exercise their criticism of the trustee system and tribal leaders. Advocacy in its many forms became a tool by which Shinnecock women began to dismantle the colonial legal and political systems imposed on the tribe. They used media outlets to bring attention to their causes and formed committees to address pressing issues of social welfare, including constitutional drafting, neighbourhood watch, and alcohol drug and substance abuse programming.[62]

Shinnecock women suffragists stated that they believed the push in the 1990s for women to have the right to vote stemmed from the increase in women as heads of households on the reservation.[63] Many Shinnecock men believed that women did participate equally in tribal elections. As one former trustee commented, "If you grew up in this community you know that the elections were just something that were done the first Tuesday in April. The decision was made Monday night at home, because the mothers told the fathers and sons who to vote for, because if you didn't vote for who they told you to vote for you weren't coming back in the house the next day. If you didn't understand that then you didn't understand power and how it was wielded here in this community."[64] Shinnecock male voters may have believed that Shinnecock women held political influence in the community through conversations they could have with their husbands, but by the 1990s Shinnecock women wanted more. They wanted to have their voices recognized and counted in the decision-making process without having to depend on their male relatives—especially if those male relatives infrequently attended meetings or for any reason chose not to heed their political concerns. Thus, to convince the male electorate to support women's right to vote, Shinnecock women took the campaign home. The women told their husbands, sons, brothers, uncles, and fathers, "either we get the right to vote or you don't eat."[65] However, even this practice was not sufficient on its own to force the change.

Shinnecock women led non-violent protests throughout the early 1990s, attending elections in large numbers, just to be turned away or to stand silent in a corner watching as their male counterparts cast their ballots. When some women tried to force the issue and speak at meetings, they were forcibly removed as they refused to have their political voice silenced. The advocacy of Shinnecock women and determination to not surrender their political voice finally led to the restoration of the right to speak in tribal meetings in September 1993. Over the course of the next few months, the women did not forsake their newly secured rights and were actively engaged in tribal meetings. As a result, on December 21, 1993, they won the right to vote in tribal elections.[66] Shinnecock women, for the first time, since 1792, were able to vote, and turned out in large numbers to cast their ballots in the trustee elections in April 1994.[67]

In spite of all this resistance and restored political rights, Shinnecock women continue to face violence. The tribe continues to work towards healing centuries of historical trauma that is the result of sanctioned colonial gender violence. In recent years, Shinnecock women have initiated a prayer fire, banding together for the movement "WAVE—Women Against Violence Everywhere." The WAVE fire was spearheaded by a Shinnecock woman who had been confronted by men armed with guns and bats, threatening her and her children at their home.[68] While she was not harmed physically, the threat of violence she and her family faced resonated with many women on the reservation who continue to be the victims of physical, emotional, and other forms of violence as a result of gangs, substance abuse, minimal security forces, and poor infrastructure. The WAVE fire will continue to burn until the women of Shinnecock are free from all forms of violence. The Shinnecock Indian Nation requires sustainable healing initiatives that are community driven and work to protect the rights of women to political participation and to live in their Indigenous community free from violence. As the Shinnecock continue on their path of decolonization, their legal reforms will continue to lead to greater protections for violence against Algonquian women.

Conclusion

Historically, women exercised rights and responsibilities of great importance in the Shinnecock Indian Nation. The goal of the analysis in this chapter was threefold. The primary intention was to examine the roles of Algonquian women in context of colonial laws and dimensions of power. Additionally, this chapter examined how European hegemony denied Shinnecock women's legal status in society. Finally, the underlying objective of this chapter was to demonstrate that colonial legal systems labelled Algonquian women as inferior to their male and European female counterparts and inherently violable.

Algonquian Shinnecock women and Native women across Canada and the United States have a common experience of violence—violence perpetrated against their bodies, their minds, their communities, their lands, their waters, and their Nations. A violence that with each new day creates ripples of historical trauma that resonate in families. Violence against Native women today is a disease, a disease that if left untreated will continue to haunt communities and halt our progress as Nations. We are facing a global epidemic of violence against Indigenous women that was born as a weapon of war by our colonizers,[69] but there is hope—hope in that each new day we are powerful and strong in our resistance as we journey to decolonize our minds and our legal systems, systems that were held captive for centuries to deny women our birthright and to arrest the hearts of our Nations. Women are the carriers of culture, and therefore it is our centuries-long gendered colonization that has led to the chronic subjugation of our tribal nations. Only when Indigenous women are restored to their rightful place will we begin to see our nations reborn in a generation of prosperity.

NOTES

1. Michael S. Nassaney, "Native American Gender Politics and Material Culture in Seventeenth-Century Southeastern New England," *Journal of Social Anthropology* 4, no. 3 (2004): 338.

2. Bethany Ruth Berger, "After Pocahontas: Indian Women and the Law, 1830 to 1934," *American Indian Law Review* 21, no. 1 (1997): 5.

3. For a discussion of early Dutch trading partnerships with Shinnecock Indians, see John A. Strong, " The Role of Algonquian Women in Land Transactions on Eastern Long Island, 1639–1859," in *Long Island Women: Activists and Innovators*, ed. Natalie Naylor and Maureen O. Murphy (Interlaken, NY: Empire State Books, 1998), 27–42.

4. For a detailed exploration of legal pluralism in early colonial New York, see Simon Middleton, "Legal Change, Economic Culture, and Imperial Authority in New Amsterdam and Early New York City," *American Journal of Legal History* 53, no. 1 (2013): 89–120.

5. For legal pluralism and a review of legal historiography, see Brian Z. Tamanaha, "Understanding Legal Pluralism: Past to Present, Local to Global," Legal Studies Research Paper Series, St. John's University School of Law, paper #07-0080, May 2008.

6. Dorothy H. Bracey, *Exploring Law and Culture* (Long Grove, IL: Waveland Press, 2005), 36.

7. Tamanaha, "Understanding Legal Pluralism."

8. Bracey, *Exploring Law and Culture*, 36.

9. Tamanaha, "Understanding Legal Pluralism," 38.

10. Bracey, *Exploring Law and Culture*, 85.

11. Allen W. Trelease, *Indian Affairs in Colonial New York: The Seventeenth Century* (Ithaca, NY: Cornell University Press, 1960), 189.

12. Jonathan Rabinowitz, "L.I.'s Shinnecock Tribe Considers Giving Women the Vote," *New York Times*, December 26, 1992.

13. Middleton, "Legal Change," 96. The Historical Society of the New York Courts website reproduces this excerpt from Henry Wilson Scott, *The Courts of the State of New York: Their History, Development and*

Jurisdiction (1909) to explain the Court of Burgomasters and Schepens: "In 1650, the Dutch parliament ordered the Dutch West India Company to establish municipal government in New Amsterdam similar to the form of governance in the City of Amsterdam. Elected officers—two burgomasters, five schepens and a schout were to regulate the affairs of New Amsterdam and sit as a court of justice with both civil and criminal jurisdiction." See "The Court of Burgomasters and Schepens, 1650–1660," accessed January 23, 2018, http://www.nycourts.gov/history/legal-history-new-york/legal-history-eras-03/history-era-court-of-schout-burgomasters-and-schepens-1650.html.

14. For more on the Court of Assizes, see https://nycourts.gov/history/legal-history-new-york/other-courts/court-of-assizes.html.

15. Allen W. Trelease, *Indian Affairs in Colonial New York: The Seventeenth Century* (Ithaca, NY: Cornell University Press, 1960), 181.

16. Trelease, *Indian Affairs*, 103.

17. For a description of the types of property a woman could hold under civil law such as separate property, which she owned independently, and community property, in which she had a half-interest jointly with her husband, see W.S. McClanahan, *Community Property Law in the United States* (Rochester, NY: The Lawyer's Cooperative Publishing, 1982). Under the feudal doctrine of coverture, a woman's legal identity was covered by that of her husband upon marriage, and she ceased to have any legal rights. Leo Kanowitz, *Women and the Law: The Unfinished Revolution* (Albuquerque: University of New Mexico Press, 1969), 35–36.

18. Laura A. Otten, *Women's Rights and the Law* (Westport, CT: Praeger, 1980), 43.

19. Dana V. Kaplan, "Women of the West: The Evolution of Marital Property Laws in the Southwestern United States and Their Effect on Mexican-American Women," *Women's Rights Law Reporter* 26, no. 2 (Spring/Summer 2005): 139, 145.

20. Kathleen Bragdon, "Gender as a Social Category in Native Southern New England," in "Native American Women's Responses to Christianity," special issue, *Ethnohistory* 43, no. 4 (Autumn 1996): 577.

21. Bragdon, "Gender as a Social Category," 579.

22. Kelsey T. Leonard, "Performatives of Sovereignty: The Shinnecock Indian Nation" (undergraduate senior honors thesis, Harvard University, 2010), 65.

23. Bragdon, "Gender as a Social Category," 579.

24. John A. Strong, "In Search of Catoneras: Long Island's Pocahontas," *Long Island History Journal* 21, no. 2 (Spring 2010), https://lihj.cc.stonybrook.edu/2010/articles/in-search-of-catoneras-long-island%E2%80%99s-pocahontas/; Roger Williams, *A Key to the Languages of America* (1643; repr., Detroit: Wayne State University Press, 1973).

25. Natalie A. Naylor, *Women in Long Island's Past: A History of Eminent Ladies and Everyday Lives* (Charleston, SC: The History Press, 2012), 15.

26. Strong, " The Role of Algonquian Women," 29; see also Robert Steven Grumet, "Sunksquaws, Shamans, and Tradeswomen: Middle Atlantic Coastal Algonquian Women during the 17th and 18th Centuries," in *Women and Colonization: Anthropological Perspectives*, ed. Mona Etienne and Eleanor Leacock (New York: Praeger, 1980), 43–67.

27. Strong, " The Role of Algonquian Women," 33.

28. Middleton, "Legal Change," 117.

29. Tittum, Simeon, et al., Petition of individual Indians and Squaws belonging to Shinnecock, in Southampton Town Indian Records, June 12, 1765, two handwritten pages; *Southampton Indian Papers 1640–1806*, original manuscript volume, Southampton Town Archives, Southampton, NY.

30. Berger, "After Pocahontas,"1.

31. Rebecca Tsosie, "Indigenous Women and International Human Rights Law: The Challenges of Colonialism, Cultural Survival, and Self-Determination," *UCLA Journal of International Law and Foreign Affairs* 15, no. 187 (2010): 200–01.

32. Oxford Dictionary Online, s.v., "violence," accessed May 2, 2014.

33. Berta Esperanza Hernández-Truyol, "Sex, Culture, and Rights: A Re/Conceptualization of Violence for the Twenty-First Century," *Albany Law Review* 60, no. 607 (1996–1997): 633.

34. For a detailed exploration of forms of violence enacted against women in the modern era and the historical underpinnings for the acceptance of female violability, see Hernández-Truyol, "Sex, Culture, and Rights."

35. US Department of the Interior, Bureau of Indian Affairs, Office of Federal Acknowledgment, *Summary under the Criteria and Evidence for the Proposed Finding for Acknowledgment of the Shinnecock Indian Nation (Petitioner #4)* (2009), https://www.bia.gov/sites/bia.gov/files/assets/as-ia/ofa/petition/004_shinne_NY/004_pf.pdf.

36. Andrea Smith, *Conquest: Sexual Violence and American Indian Genocide* (Cambridge, MA: South End Press, 2005), 10.

37. Sarah Deer, "Sovereignty of the Soul: Exploring the Intersection of Rape Law Reform and Federal Indian Law," *Suffolk University Law Review* 38 (2005): 459.

38. Deer, "Sovereignty of the Soul," 459.

39. Deer, "Sovereignty of the Soul," 459.

40. Smith, *Conquest*, 55.

41. Frantz Fanon, *A Dying Colonialism*, trans. Haakon Chevalier (New York: Grove Press, 1967), 45.

42. Rose Oldfield Hayes, "A Case of Cultural Continuity: The Shinnecock Kinship System," in *The Shinnecock Indians: A Culture History*, ed. Gaynell Stone (Lexington, MA: Ginn Custom Publishing, 1983), 331–35.

43. Deborah A Rosen, *American Indians and State Law: Sovereignty, Race, and Citizenship, 1790–1880* (Lincoln: University of Nebraska Press, 2007), 279.

44. On Shinnecock girls at Carlisle Indian School, see Carlisle Indian School Digital Resource Center, accessed March 8, 2014, http://carlisleindian.dickinson.edu/nation/shinnecock.

45. Strong, "In Search of Catoneras."

46. N.Y. Indian Law § 120 (McKinney).

47. N.Y. Indian Law § 120 (McKinney).

48. On colonization of Southampton and court cases that led to loss of Shinnecock lands, see David Goddard, *Colonizing Southampton: The Transformation of a Long Island Community, 1870–1900* (Albany: State University of New York Press, 2011).

49. Nassaney, "Native American Gender Politics."

50. For a discussion of various strategies employed by newcomers to enhance their prospects in the colonies, including marrying into Indigenous communities, see Middleton, "Legal Change," 89.

51. Deer, "Sovereignty of the Soul," 459.

52. See Susanah Shaw Romney, *New Netherland Connections: Intimate Networks and Atlantic Ties in Seventeenth-Century America* (Chapel Hill: University of North Carolina Press Books, 2014), 181.

53. Toby T. Papageorge, "Records of the Shinnecock Trustees" in *The Shinnecock Indians: A Culture History*, ed. Gaynell Stone (Lexington, MA: Ginn Custom Publishing, 1983), 157.

54. US Department of the Interior, *Summary under the Criteria...* *(Petitioner #4).*

55. US Department of the Interior, *Summary under the Criteria...*
    (Petitioner #4).

56. Jonathan Rabinowitz, "L.I.'s Shinnecock Tribe Considers Giving Women
    the Vote," *New York Times*, December 26, 1992.

57. US Department of the Interior, *Summary under the Criteria...*
    (Petitioner #4).

58. US Department of the Interior, *Summary under the Criteria...*
    (Petitioner #4).

59. Rabinowitz, "L.I.'s Shinnecock Tribe."

60. Strong, "The Role of Algonquian Women," 35.

61. McKinney's Indian Law § 17, NY Indian § 17.

62. US Department of the Interior, *Summary under the Criteria...*
    (Petitioner #4).

63. US Department of the Interior, *Summary under the Criteria...*
    (Petitioner #4).

64. Leonard, "Performatives of Sovereignty," 63.

65. US Department of the Interior, *Summary under the Criteria...*
    (Petitioner #4), 72.

66. US Department of the Interior, *Summary under the Criteria...*
    (Petitioner #4).

67. Strong, "The Role of Algonquian Women," 35.

68. Shinnecock Newsletter, "Voice of the Nation: A Burning Fire to Stop
    Violence against Women," January 2013.

69. For a detailed analysis of sexual violence against Native women as
    "weapon of war" and "tool of colonization," see Deer, "Sovereignty of the
    Soul," 455.

8 | (The Missing Chapter) On Being Missing
From Indian Problem to Indian Problematic

MAYA ODE'AMIK CHACABY

Missing But Not Missed

Dirty Lying No Good Indian was the name given to me by my grandmother—an empty bitter husk of a woman whose spirit went missing in residential school. I went missing when I was thirteen years old. No one came to look for me. No benevolent adults. No mourning family. I was not counted missing and I was not missed.

WAAJIYE, GIWII-BANGI-DIBAAJIM: I am telling a story about missing Indigenous women who do not count in the mournful cries of "missing but not forgotten."[1] I am telling a story about where the ones who are missing *and* forgotten live. It might not be where your family members are, but that is where I lived for a very long time. I lived there longer than I have lived anywhere else. And I am angry and grieving too. So, I am putting on one of those Red Dresses and dancing a ghost dance about that dispossessed, missing and forgotten space.[2] Maybe if that space is noticed, we will see what has been missed and where so much of what is missing can be found. Giinawind, giwanishinimin.

There is a tenuous space *between* Being Missing and Being Murdered. I know. I lived there for over a decade. I remember it like a dream, that hypnagogic space, living in the death world,[3] a spectral Indian ghosting the colonial wastelands, the slums, the seedy piss-filled corners and alcoves between walls and fences. Living between passing out in snow banks (latex boots frozen to skin) and death, between rape and death, drugs and death, cops and death, safe spaces and death, friends and death. Living between the lonely sorrow of being unwanted into non-existence, my spectrality glinting off the eyes of each passerby, and the cold angry adrenaline shock of real fucking death. That space *between* Being Missing and Being Murdered is a borderland, "a narrow strip along a steep edge" where tension "grips the inhabitants…and death is no stranger."[4] A place where the inhabitants are missing, but not missed.

Missing but not missed. We are caught up, hooked in, counted, catalogued, and fixed as objects. Not as sad pictures of missing children on milk cartons though. Fixed instead in the psychic disequilibrium of being a less than human human. Counted as a certain kind of problem: the imperial Indian Problem that fails to adjust to modernity,[5] institutionally transfixed, pinned down by the gaze of arrogant perception. Fixed by this gaze, my missingness becomes part of the pornotropic narrative of Indian girls who just can't be helped, so you can help yourself to us anyway you want. Missing, but certainly not missed.

Manifest Destination

My destination was a place called "anything is better than what I came from." Better to be abused by strangers than family. Better to be cold on the streets than fear death in a warm bed. Better to be unknown and unloved than to be called a Dirty Lying Indian by those who are supposed to love me.

The destination for missing Indigenous women and girls is a diasporic compulsive displacement from selfhood—the privileges of subjectivity and agency—to the objectifying discursive field of "problem" with its colonial classifications of "Indian" and institutionally constrained "solutions." A place where the colonial fixation with the Indian Problem means "mapping it, describing it in all its different manifestations, trying to get rid of it, laying blame for it, talking about it writing newspaper columns about it…researching it, over and over."[6] A place, where I am a series of negations.[7] A negative. I am posters of my dead sisters, empty red dresses and moccasins. I am Missing. I am issues: addictions, suicide, poverty, homelessness. Until I am not. And then I am either dead or rehabilitated: another disappearance.

No matter what, I can only arrive ghosted, where institutions pick up bits and pieces of what they think I am. And that is it. I am only what I am made through institutional responses to the colonial myth that somehow I am responsible for my own demise, that having failed at rehabilitation, my capacity for modern life is tenuous and likely I am already dead.[8]

My destination: a haunting in that space between Being Missing and Being Murdered to be discovered as an object in the one-dimensionality of institutional disappearance. Made manifest.

The Doctrine of Institutional Discovery

I didn't just disappear. I went out with a fight: attempting to kill my pedophilic grade seven teacher, launching a police investigation on my father, and calling C A S to come get my little sister. I thought that maybe, if I fought against all the abuse it would end. It did not. They discovered instead that I was the problem.

Representation of difference, as Homi K. Bhabha explains, "is a discourse at the crossroads of what is known and permissible and that which though known must be kept concealed."[9] What has been discovered and represented in the news, in research reports, and even at the rallies and gatherings is only what is permissible: that there are Indians and that they have problems:

missing and murdered women and girls, alcoholism, poverty, housing, violence. What is not permissible, and therefore something that cannot be discovered, is the underlying fact that the social construction of "problems" faced by Indigenous people are not only historically rooted in a nation-sponsored genocidal regime that began long before residential schools, but that existing contemporary institutions, and their version of solutions are in fact responsible and accountable for continued oppressive practices.

This accountability can be theorized in academia where we can all point our fingers at the phantasmagorical of colonization and cry out for justice at the rallies—a justice predicated on a form of humanness and human rights created by that colonizing beast to begin with. But not actual discovery through comprehensive legislative reviews, institutional ethnographies, discovery of what lies behind the problem/solution dichotomy, and certainly not discovery of social environments and social structures that produce, consume, and subsume us.[10] It is easier to look at the behaviours of individuals as the problem, rather than look at those behaviours as reasonable responses to a horrific situation. The situation itself, and the role that institutions and social environments play in perpetuating it, is left undiscovered, not made accountable for and therefore still missing.

Missing and Murdered Indigenous Women become discovered as a problem through the vulgarity of quantification: a tipping point in public opinion that, after a certain number, it begins to count. However, Missing and Murdered Indigenous Women from a colonial perspective is paradoxically a problem with the Indians that will not go away and therefore remain a legislative burden, a fiduciary duty that slows the resource extraction process, a disruption to the myth of benign nationalism. The Indian Problem from an imperial perspective further consists of "unproductive" bodies who disrupt economic growth by refusing to be human resources. My being a missing Indigenous women is considered then a problem of our failure as Indigenous people to function in civilized society. We can point fingers at who caused these failures, but never debate the legitimacy of what is considered a productive functioning and fully human body. Solutions too are discursively confined within the realm of imperial westernized possibilities.

The underlying social constructions of the problem/solution must be kept concealed (undiscovered) by placing the burden on Indigenous people and their behaviours as the problem and only imagining solutions that do not challenge and instead sustain the status quo. This means that policies, inquests, media attention, and research tend to place the Indian Problem with the individual or community instead of the need for a total upheaval of social structures.[11] If social structures are incriminated, they are either blamed on "bad" individuals within the institution or, if the institution as a whole is to blame, it is safely placed in the past, the unfortunate (but necessary) history of development with the assumption that we have either now progressed or are capable of progressing within the same ideologically saturated institutional systems.[12]

The Human Proclamation

I refused to interact with the kids or teachers at school, I would not speak to humans and refused to speak English. So after failing grade one, they diagnosed me as retarded. A line was drawn. If I wanted to be human, I had to speak English. If I wanted to progress, I had to interact with the humans. And I did. Progress. By grade five I spoke in Shakespearian soliloquies and drew lines with broken beer bottles along my arms. Teased by my classmates for my failed suicide attempts, "Aren't you dead yet?" they'd ask.

Progress? We have progressed further into "Murderous Humanitarianism" where the fabricated version of what it is to be human becomes universal human rights created by the very same thinking that produced, in the name of human progress,

129

MAYA ODE'AMIK CHACABY

mutilated, raped, debilitated, impaired, criminalized black and red bodies.[13] The same thinking that destroys our land and enforces violence amongst us.

Progress? We have inherited (by force and fraud) a colonial legacy that presupposes a natural link between the terms "Indian" and "Problem."[14] This problem, spawned in the seething, disease-filled, impoverished, and war-torn land of excesses, extremes, and degradation, also known as Renaissance Europe, emerged at a time when the very nature of humanness was in question. This occurred soon after the Christian God as Europeans' source of humanness, social structures, and morals died. They killed their own god, and too late realized that the beating god-heart that sustained their morals and social practices could not be revived.[15] Philosophers, politicians, scientists, merchants, and the like rushed forth with constructions of humanness based—not on faith—but on imaginary borders of nationhood with larger military, a whole new economic system, and a bio-medical model of authority to enforce it. An identity born from the bloody killing of their holy father; an identity born of patricide swaddled in the expansive cloth of colonial resource extraction.

This "immense historical rupture" led to an identity based on the "rise of the West" and the "subjugation of the rest of us."[16] The new iteration of human was based on the myth of a civilized polit-ical subject and had as its comparative Other, the uncivilized not quite human humans.[17] To be a civilized human was based on colonial difference—a difference marked along a mythical racial-ized spectrum ranging from complete savagery (not remotely human and therefore natural slaves or beasts of burden) to the noble savage (less than civilized human but human and therefore capable of being uplifted to civilization). The result, as Sylvia Wytner explains, "would be 'the rise of Europe' and its construc-tion of the 'world civilization' on the one hand, and, on the other, African enslavement, Latin American conquest, and Asian subjugation."[18]

Fed with gold, pelts, and pornotropic stories of the savage, the infant colonial human leaves its toy soldiers and forts behind (Pax Britannica, following the collapse of the Napoleonic Revolution and North American War of 1812) mutating into Imperialism. Now instead of a fragile infant version of human kept secure in colonial forts while the Indians run wild and do the resource extraction work, the Imperial Human requires the Indians to be contained (reserves) so the nation-building empire can expand. Cities and towns along its borders, the new imperial nation spreads like acne on pubescent skin.

Gradual Rehabilitation

After missing in Winnipeg I tried to go home and failed. There was no safe home to return to. My failed attempt to go home wasn't noticed but my failed attempt at suicide soon after that was. Then a psych ward, where being served breakfast meant staying in your locked concrete room crying all day. No breakfast means you got electro-shocked, hosed down and left for a day of rehabilitative oblivion. I never tried to go home after that. I was fifteen.

The historical rupture of the Enlightenment required a different course in the treatment of the Indian Problem, away from annihilation towards an ethically (and ethnically) palatable cleansing of the filth of Indianess in order to increase their worth to civilized society.

Through this process, the colonial state and its institutions produce a discursive whitewash that firmly entrenches the Indian Problem as a de facto category of disablement;[19] the "grease and dirt" of the Indian Problem as the "darkest blots" of civilized society, and a new destination: erasure through rehabilitation; for "there is no better way to escape the face of strangeness than by forgetting aberrancy through its dissolution into the social norm."[20]

Dissolution, in the nineteenth century, was the empirical norm of enlightened thinking for the treatment of all the "not quite human humans of undesirable difference" through the institutionalized hegemonic system of assimilative-rehabilitation.[21]

For Anishinaabeg, the empirical norm played out first through an etiologized ensconcement—classified specifications (the Indian Registry, Enfranchisement Act) and safe confinement (reservations and the Indian Act)—to a process of rehabilitation through sanatoriums, residential schools, westernized male-dominated chief and band council governance, children's aid, and myriad policies that, like the smallpox-infected blankets of the past, were disseminated through every institution that Indians came in contact with. All formulated to ensure there would be no Indian Problem; we would all arrive rehabilitated and ready for civilization.

This negation of self through a rehabilitative model based on what is considered a "normal" human is the only legitimate and institutionally actionable doctrine of discovery. My negation: high-school drop out, suicidal, emotionally unstable, underage, homeless, abused, violent. A new negation depending on which institution discovered me. It did not matter if the negations negated themselves; they could and often did contradict. What mattered was how those negations were acted on.

The Missing Act

"Fuck you" was my most common response to social workers who acted all nice and shit. They weren't going to stick around and really help so why give 'em what they want: another participant in some pointless program? Fuck you. I wish I could tell them that I really did want help.

The *fact* of my status as a missing child was not made institutionally actionable through a culturally competent, responsive, caring system. Instead, it was operationalized through a hierarchical system of stigmas. Even if the individuals are caring, their responses are institutionally constrained by who they are allowed to work with, what they are allowed to do, and for how long. What is made institutionally actionable becomes the only reality that is responded to, that people can go to work on—the actualities are subsumed by these forms of representation.[22] Actualities (having no safe and culturally relevant place to consider home) and personal experiences (the fact that I needed a sense of identity beyond homeless, beyond missing, abuse survivor towards something more like belonging in a positive nurturing relationship with the social environment) are based on a medical model of rehabilitation discourse "torn between specification (bordering on exclusion) and nondistinction (which thinks it tends towards integration)."[23]

Non-distinction, the great un-becoming of the Indian Problem, is the default institutional response for dealing with Anishinaabeg. Un-becoming becomes the actuality that subsumes any other, launching a chain reaction of institutional responses towards un-becoming the Indian Problem. Be it mental illness, alcoholism, family violence, intergenerational trauma, autism, or diabetes, the specifications of impairment are usurped by the master status of the Indian Problem, where Indianess is the primary disabling condition.[24] The *fact* of my lived situation was subsumed by the *fact* of being the "discredited Aboriginal subject" undeserving of any supports beyond meagre provisional service, starved out of access to anything but the most basic rationed human services as if anything more would be a waste.[25]

Rehabilitation becomes a slow crawling progression of adjustment to the norm of un-being; an erasure of any beforehand (that my feral refusals were a response to colonial captivity and intergeneration trauma—a cognitive dissonance with colonial reality); an arrival at the gateposts of civilization-cum-technocratic administration "where Aboriginal subjects as deserving of services and of respect, tying in neatly with longstanding racist ideas of Aboriginal people [are treated] as polluted, child-like, and incapable of being modern subjects."[26] No matter the impairment we can only ever

arrive at the margins of civilized society. We can only be the negation: rehabilitation to become the not quite Indian Indian that
forever produces for the whitewashing agents "a supply of docile
human bodies that can be 'subjected, used, transformed, and
improved.'"[27] In other words, by our un-becoming, by our being
the assimilated "success stories," the rehabilitated not quite Indian
Indian, we replicate into perpetuity the institutional doctrine of
discovery of the Indian problem.

Missing or Murdered. For over a decade I haunted those who
would discover me, not as a missing child to be returned to the arms
of her loving family, but instead, I haunted them as *the* Problem.
The doctrine of institutional discovery as the only legitimate form
of recognition strips away everything but the problem.

Their housing. I refused. Why would I live in a concrete slab in
alone and isolated while all my friends are downtown?

Their high schools. I refused. Why would I stay somewhere that
forces me to go to high school with children who have never been
trafficked?

Their therapy. I refused. Why would I talk to a stranger who
can't teach me my language and thinks nothing of culture?[28]

Their treatment centres. I refused.

Their food. I refused.

Their drugs. I refused.

Their psychiatric assessments. I refused them all.

And every time I was discovered, captured, and confined in
their institutions my dear street friends broke me out; jailbreaks
sometimes even when I was still incapacitated, pushing me down
the street in a wheelchair while security guards chased after us.

I was the harsh reminder that their system fails people like me.
Western institutional interventions could not fix me. To those
institutions built entirely on a medical model of rehabilitation
towards a societal "norm" that Indigenous people have never
authored or authorized, not being fixable means not a failure on
their part but a failure on mine. And so, it is far easier to dismiss
me, to miss me from what counts in their performance reports

and practices. To disappear me again and again in their inability to discover how their systems reproduce my missingness. The doctrine of institutional discovery places me at the same dismissed and impermanent status as my ancestors, not able to claim my own selfness, relegated to a justified negation as my ancestors were stripped of homelands and sovereignty. In order to keep the doctrine of institutional discovery alive and well, it is better to act as if I do not exist. It is better to keep missing me.

But I refuse.

From Indian Problem to Indian Problematic

Kinaanaakomininaawaa kakina awiyaa e-wiijiiishiwaaj.

The territory that the Indian problem inhabits is one of unidirectional progress towards deterritorialization (i.e., Gradual Civilization Act, Indian Act, and modern iterations virally dispersed through omnibus bills—the new germ warfare). It is an arborescent process which continuously cuts along a vertical hierarchy marking (debarking) the text-to-work-to-text genealogy from Indian Problem to not quite Indian Indian through reterritorialized rehabilitative pruning.[29]

We are considered rehabilitated and therefore no longer missing when we get nuclear-family-type housing isolated from our communities, get off the street drugs and get on antidepressants, go to Western schools, get a "normal" job, and get our children back from Children's Aid Societies. That is it. That is rehabilitation. What is really missing though—what is made to remain disappeared through the assimilative process of rehabilitation towards a norm that is not ours—is learning how to live well as Anishinaabe. Not some frozen-in-time beads-and-feathers version, but how to live the good life as skilled knowers of our environment even if that environment is the urban Anishinaabe post-apocalypse.[30] Wellness or everyday good living in a contemporary social environment includes our languages, our Clans, our ceremonies, our political practices, our gender roles and responsibilities, our economic practices, our education systems, our Clan kinship ties, our food security practices, our health care system, our social welfare systems, our art, and our technologies. However, these do not count as rehabilitation and are simply disappeared, left under-resourced and delegitimized. That is what is really missing.

Resistance is similarly contained. We can resist by perpetuating the Indian Problem (e.g., deterritorialize through incarceration, tire-burning, disengagement with society via alcoholism, violence, and homelessness), or we can be the rehabilitated not quite Indian Indian, the success stories, the reterritorialized educated middle class, the ones who have cleaned up our acts, overcome our Indian Problems and contribute to civilized society. We become the Indian experts, the ones who are brought in to comment on, diagnose, or intervene with the Indian Problems at the other end of the spectrum. Even the discourse of Indigenous reclamation and reconciliation is often safely confined to ubiquitous free-floating concepts of colonialism (where no one is responsible) or specific instances of injustice, pain, and suffering (the poor Indians and their problems). This containment—the minimizing and suppressing of dissent[31]—is a dynamic conservatism[32] that avoids awareness of the interstitial (rhizomatic) connections between dominating discourse, repressive desublimation,[33] and ruling relations.[34]

To un-become the un-becoming of assimilation we cannot be the Indian Problem: we must be the Indian Problematic. Problems are the issues, revealed experiences, propositions, points of anger, the moans and groans of pain and suffering. The Indian Problematic is an awareness of the spaces where real experience hooks the local to the extra-local and trans-local making the workings of society visible.[35] The Indian Problematic entails a "knowledge of how the structures of everyday activities are routinely produced [enabling] us to tell how we might proceed for the effective production of *desired disturbances*."[36]

I am not a success story.

I am not a rehabilitated Indian.

I am the new story: the Indian Problematic.

Un-settling Society

*Apane babaamosed a'aw Nenabozho gii-pabaamose gii-ayaad
omaa. Mii dash o'ow ani-babaamosed gaa-izhi-miikawaad onow
binesiwan, onow gii-naganaawaad omaamaayiwaa omaa.
Gaa-izhi-gagwejimaad, "Aaniish giinawaa ezhinikaazoyeg," ogii-
kakwejiman a'aw Nenabozho. Mii dash, ogii-nisidotaagoon i'iw
ayaawid. Mii dash, gaawiin ogii-nakwetawaasiigoon onow binewan.
"Gaawiin giwii-pooni'isiinooninim. Aaniish ezhinikaazoyeg?" Mii
dash binesiwag gaa-izhi-inaawaad, "Bine indizhinikaazomin."
"Oon." Inashke niin niizhing indizhinikaaz. Mii i'iw bezhig,
Nenabozho indizhinikaaz. Miinawaa dash Bebaamosed gaye
indizhinikaaz." Oon." Gaawin ogii-nakwetawaasiigoonaan
Nenabozho. "Wiindamawishin ezhinikaasoyan. Niizhing akina
awiiya adayaanaawaa izhinikaazowinan," ogii-inaan Nenabozho.
Mii dash iniw binewan, "Gawigoshko'iweshiinh indizhinikaazomin
gaye niinawind," gii-ikidowag. "Sate! Gaawiin giin. Onzaam sa
go gibi-wiiji'ininim," gii-ikido a'aw Nenabozho. Mii gaa-izhi-
zhaagode'enid gaa-izhi-miiziinaad onow sa binesiwan. Mii dash
gaa-izhi-maajaad a'aw Bebamosed.*[37]

Gawigoshko'iweshiinh, the un-settlers in this story are little
baby partridges who are accosted by Bebamosed and forced to tell
him their name. Bebamosed then proceeds to shit all over them.
The story goes on with Bebamosed continuing along his journey
without another thought for the damage he caused those babies.
And then, at a moment when Bebamosed least expects it, the
mother partridge jumps up and startles him. Bebamosed not only
fails at what he most desires, but ends up falling right off the cliff.

To be the Indian Problematic, we must be the un-settlers. This
is the consciousness of being less powerful in a relationship of

power, but able to make actionable in every space between institutional un-being a "*consciousness of opportunity*, an opening in the situation through which one might intervene and turn matters to one's advantage."[38] An unsettling presence of Indian that disturbs the norm rather than a consignment to failure at achieving the norm. An unsettling presence of Anishinaabe. Not ghosted or reconciled to somehow fit into Western society, to come to terms with being colonized. No. An unsettling presence that brings awareness of relationships that have too long been occupied with erasure.

To be the Indian Problematic we must ask those unsettling questions: What is really missing, who is missing, and what do we need so that they can be found, not as a solution to a problem, but celebrated for their potentialities and protected from the damage on non-distinction?

So what is really missing? A place to come home to. Home is my language and the privilege of subjective agency as well as the necessary resources to find my sense of self in something other than what I have been subsumed by. This includes an unsettling of what we consider being human and having rights. Home is a network of Clan and kinship ties that allow safe passage through multiple spatial and conceptual territorialities; this is the definition of Anishinaabe Nationhood. Home is a social environment where Anishinaabe leadership, gender, life-cycle, and Clan responsibilities are imbued in everyday interactions. Home is the economic infrastructure to fulfill those responsibilities; this is our true measure of wealth. Home is ceremony, upliftment, and rites of passage through every life stage. Home is being celebrated, mentored, welcomed, and wanted. Home is my bundle.

What is missing are the strategies for creating this kind of home in contemporary urban spaces. We are missing the opportunities to behave this way and create these kinds of social environments regardless of funding and policy constraints. Without this kind of home, why would I want to be rehabilitated to fit into a society predicated on the destruction of my people? My missingness was created in a society that has, as its foundation, the need for the disappearance of the Indian. So what does it give me to become a normalized "functional" citizen when the basis of functionality is disappearance through whitewashed education, chemical lobotomization, lonely housing, isolation, lateral violence, consumerism, chronic disease, a cultural void, abuse, and failed relationships? Why would I want to be found when there is no home to return to?

Who is missing? Did you see her? She was here just a moment ago, that twelve-year-old girl with the angry glint in her eyes and cuts along her arms. She is missing right in front of you. And that one too, the mother who can't show up for access visits. And the kids who are missing from school because there is no food for lunch and if the school found out, they'd call C A S. And the quiet boy who has seen too much. He is also missing. The teachers and Elders are missing too. The little kids told me so. The children who tell me how much they want to be taught their culture and language but no one is there to teach them. And the ones missing their names and their Clans. The ones missing their language. The ones living in homes that are missing love and kindness. The girls who wander the streets at night with nothing to do and no safe places to just have fun. The ones who are missing any vision of what they might be in the future, missing connections, missing role models.

To those kids, we are the ones who are missing.

What needs to be found? I need to find a way to speak my language, a way to fulfill my Clan, gender, and life-cycle responsibilities as part of contemporary economic engagement.

To those Beings who gift us Clans, names, language, we are the ones who are missing.

What needs to be found? I need to find a way to be raised up by Elders and taught more than beads and feathers. I need to find a way to be raised without violence.

We are missing. Don't you feel it?

We must create a home worth returning to—for all of us. We must find one another. We must find a home where community behaves resiliently every day, where social environments celebrate life and everyday good living. If we don't find this kind of home, our people will continue to be lost.

I wonder if the plight of missing Indigenous women is worth that kind of effort.

Postscript
Cleaning the Bones of My Ancestors

I went to our ceremonial Ancestors Feast this winter. It is a ceremony where, in a darkened room, the conductor describes the ancestors who have responded to the calling in. Unexpectedly, the conductor described my grandmother. Her features, clearly defined in the dark of ceremony. She was spectral now, not me. I stood, holding my feast plate to her. After all these years that I have been missing, she found me. I spoke to her for the first time in thirty years. I only spoke Anishinaabemowin. She stood there beside the Old Man, beside the lost children. I told her my true name and my struggles since she passed. She opened her arms to me and accepted my offering. She called me by my real name. For the first time I was not *Dirty Lying No Good Indian*, the name she called me my entire childhood. She has been brought back, bones polished. The decay of suffering scrapped from every crevice and carefully rubbed clean. She might be long dead, but she found me. She has returned in and through me to a space before her spirit went missing in residential school. Now, I can carry her home. Now I can carry home all the bones of my ancestors. Now I can carry my pipe and my bundle, my language and my Clan without feeling like something is missing.

AUTHOR'S NOTE

I am thankful to people who found me: Julie who parked her car at the bar in Winnipeg at 3 A.M. and got me away from certain death at age fifteen. Betsy Martin at the Battered Women's Shelter where they let me in at age sixteen even though the rules say a child cannot go to that shelter without their mother. Ma-nee Chacaby who saw me dancing in the fields amongst the ghosts and, along with Betsy, adopted me. It took ten more years before I believed they wanted me. Before I could let them love me. Meanwhile on the streets of Toronto, Phyllis Novak who let me play piano and do art and told me I was amazing every day at the drop-in centre. Then she took us street kids seriously and created a whole new drop-in where we could just do art, no questions asked. My street family (Half-pint and Emmet) who babysat me in constant crisis for most of my youth. Amanda Dale who took me seriously and Cynthia for running talking circles at Sistering's for the worst of us high, drunk, messed-up, angry Anishinaabekwe. Cynthia is the reason I felt Native enough to go get real help: the Elders at the Friendship Centre, Vern Harper and Alex Jacobs, who scraped me off the streets and taught me ceremony and language. And later in life, Alex McKay, Keren Rice, The Old Man, Wilfred Cyr, Gordon Waindubence, Rebecca Martell, Patricia Ningewance, Lilian Pitawankwat, Ed Pitawanakwat, and Doug Williams, who all invested their time and knowledge in me. None of these people were paid to do this. But they are the ones who really found me. I would be dead if they hadn't.

NOTES

1. My condolences to those families who have lost loved ones or who are mourning their missing loved ones. I acknowledge your anger and your grief. Your sorrow and your experiences are valid and valued. This is just a different story. This story may or may not be helpful to you, but it is in no way meant to be disrespectful of your experiences.

2. See the REDress Project website, http://www.theredressproject.

3. Achille Mbembe, *On the Postcolony* (Berkeley: University of California Press, 2001).

4. Gloria Anzaldúa quoted in Julie Avril Minich, "Disabling La Frontera: Disability, Border Subjectivity, and Masculinity in 'Big Jesse, Little Jesse' by Oscar Casares," *MELUS: Multi-Ethnic Literature of the United States* 35, no. 1 (Spring 2010): 37.

5. S.H. Razack, " Timely Deaths: Medicalizing the Deaths of Aboriginal People in Police Custody," *Law, Culture and the Humanities* 9, no. 2 (2011): 352–74.

6. Linda Tuhiwai Smith, *Decolonizing Methodologies: Research and Indigenous Peoples* (London: Zed Books, 1999), 91.

7. W.E.B. Du Bois, *The Souls of Black Folk: Essays and Sketches* (Greenwich, CT: Fawcett Publications, 1961).

8. Razack, "Timely Deaths."

9. Homi K. Bhabha, *The Location of Culture* (London: Routledge, 1994), 128.

10. Jack D. Forbes, *Columbus and Other Cannibals: The Wétiko Disease of Exploitation, Imperialism, and Terrorism* (New York: Seven Stories Press, 2008).

11. Smith, *Decolonizing Methodologies*, 92.

12. For example, rather than acknowledging that the RCMP is an institutionally racist organization in need of system-wide restructuring, former RCMP Commissioner Bob Paulson claims that there are a few racists in the RCMP. This statement was made to a gathering of First Nations Chiefs in December 2015 in discussion about Missing and Murdered Indigenous Women. The RCMP response is a clear example of maintaining oppressive institutional systems by placing the blame on a few individuals, as if getting rid of a few racist individuals would solve the problem.

13. Samuel Beckett and Alan Warren Friedman, *Beckett in Black and Red: The Translations for Nancy Cunard's Negro* (Lexington: University Press of Kentucky, 1999), xxxi.

14. Smith, *Decolonizing Methodologies*, 96.

15. Friedrich Nietzsche, *Thus Spoke Zarathustra: A Book for All and None*, trans. Walter Kaufmann (New York: Modern Library, 1995); Georg Wilhelm Friedrich Hegel, *Phenomenology of Spirit*, trans. Arnold V. Miller and J.N. Findlay (Oxford: Clarendon Press, 1977).

16. Howard Winant, *Racial Conditions: Politics, Theory, Comparisons* (Minneapolis: University of Minnesota Press, 1994) cited in Sylvia Wynter, "Unsettling the Coloniality of Being/Power/Truth/Freedom: Towards the Human, After Man, Its Overrepresentation—An Argument," *CR: The New Centennial Review* 3, no. 3 (2003): 262.

17. Tanya Titchkosky, "Disability Studies: The Old and the New," in *Rethinking Normalcy: A Disability Studies Reader*, ed. Rod Michalko and Tanya Titchkosky (Toronto: Canadian Scholars' Press, 2009), 42–43.

18. Wynter, "Unsettling the Coloniality," 263.

19. Razack, "Timely Deaths."

20. Henri-Jacques Stiker, *A History of Disability*, trans. William Sayers (Ann Arbor: University of Michigan Press, 1999), 136.

21. Titchkosky, "Disability Studies," 42–43.

22. Dorothy E. Smith, *Institutional Ethnography: A Sociology for People* (Walnut Creek, CA: Altamira Press, 2005), 212.

23. Stiker, *History of Disability*, 156.

24. Razack, "Timely Deaths," 372.

25. Jo-Anne Fiske and Annette J. Browne, "Aboriginal Citizen, Discredited Medical Subject: Paradoxical Constructions of Aboriginal Women's Subjectivity in Canadian Health Care Policies," *Policy Sciences* 39, no. 1 (2006): 91–111.

26. Razack, "Timely Deaths," 359.

27. Michel Foucault, *Discipline and Punish: The Birth of the Prison,* trans. Alan Sheridan (New York: Vintage Books, 1995), 136.

28. Michael J. Chandler and Christopher Lalonde, "Cultural Continuity as a Hedge against Suicide in Canada's First Nations," *Transcultural Psychiatry* 35, no. 2 (1998): 191–219.

29. Gilles Deleuze and Félix Guattari, *A Thousand Plateaus: Capitalism and Schizophrenia*, trans. Brian Massumi (Minneapolis: University of Minnesota Press, 1987).

30. Lawrence William Gross, *Anishinaabe Ways of Knowing and Being* (Surrey, UK: Ashgate, 2014).

31. Herbert Marcuse, *One-Dimensional Man: Studies in the Ideology of Advanced Industrial Society* (Boston: Beacon Press, 1964), 11–12.

32. Donald A. Schön, *The Reflective Practitioner: How Professionals Think in Action* (New York: Basic Books, 1983).

33. Marcuse, *One-Dimensional Man.*

34. Smith, *Institutional Ethnography.*

35. Smith, *Institutional Ethnography.*

36. Harold Garfinkel, "Studies of the Routine Grounds of Everyday Activities," *Social Problems* 11, no. 3 (1964): 227, emphasis added.

37. Collins Oakgrove, "Miskwaagamiiwi-zaaga'igan Red Lake," in *Living Our Languages: Ojibwe Tales and Oral Histories*, ed. Anton Treuer (Saint Paul: Minnesota Historical Society Press, 2001), 174–77.

38. Patricia Ewick and Susan Silbey, "Narrating Social Structure: Stories of Resistance to Legal Authority," *American Journal of Sociology* 108, no. 6 (2003): 1336.

III | Challenges

9 | *Violence and Extraction*
Stories from the Oil Fields

HELEN KNOTT

Women's sovereignty is central to Indian sovereignty because nations cannot be free if their Indian women are not free.
—BONNIE CLAIRMONT, Hochunk anti-rape activist[1]

EVERY TIME I SEE A PHOTO of an Indigenous woman or girl who has gone missing, I feel my spirit tighten inside of me. I may not know this woman or girl, I may not know her family, and I may belong to a different tribe or live in a different territory. But I know that we are connected. I know that her family's plight is my plight, that the same blind and blatant dangers that have created this chasm for her to disappear still exist and are real not only for myself, but for my future daughters. They threaten my little cousins who will one day blossom, and await to trap the women that I love. I do not know what it is like to lose someone to this violence, but I know what it is like to lose pieces of myself to it.

I can recall a stage in my life where violence against my body, mind, and spirit seemed to be out of my control. Where an act of rape was no longer objected to and the resulting blame and shame was compressed and stored up only for myself. Years of trauma and childhood sexual abuse had created this space where my body was not my own and I held responsibility for other peoples' actions against me. I believe this acceptance was the end result of the oppression that comes with intergenerational trauma. As Albert Memmi writes, "In order for the colonizer to be the complete master, it is not enough for him to be so in actual fact, he must also believe in its legitimacy. In order for that legitimacy to be complete, it is not enough for the colonized to be a slave, he must also accept his role."[2] As a teenager I was astounded when I met an Indigenous girl my age that had not endured childhood sexual abuse. Up until that point, I thought sexual abuse was a common experience and was an "Indian thing." At a young age I had unconsciously categorized sexual abuse as an event specific to my people and I did not expect the same experience from my non-Indigenous peers. The very events that enabled this categorization also created a vulnerability to repeated exposure to violence and sexual violence. I was aware of the sexually abusive and violent reality of Indigenous females at an early age but did not know how I had inherited it, nor how I could escape it.

Having made it out of this dark realm of racialized and sexualized oppression by reclaiming my power as a Dishinit Sakeh, I wonder how many of our women are still living down there in that darkness. I was fortunate, for as I grew, I was able to deconstruct portions of this reality in regards to my own experiences. I now know that the violence I have experienced is also partially due to the dynamics of the territory in which I live. Liberation comes through that knowledge, through making the connections between land and women, and through healing and finding voice again, as I will discuss in this chapter.

Land and Women

In my traditional homelands, the Northeast region of British Columbia and Treaty Eight territory, we have experienced an oil and gas industry boom, which has translated into an influx of transient workers and—less talked about—high rates of violence against women. The population in my hometown of Fort St. John has more than doubled in the last decade and a half, bringing with it increasing social issues, including multiple forms of violence and drug trafficking. And now, it is terrible to say that, without effort, I can recall the names of ten Indigenous missing and murdered women from our territory. We are not a highly populated region; according to the provincial government, in 2006 the Aboriginal population represented only 12 per cent of the general population.[3] The impact of these losses is tremendous as it ripples out into the families, communities, and territory.

What is the connection between these losses and the assault on our lands? Connie Greyeyes, a grassroots activist who has hosted the Sisters in Spirit vigils in Fort St. John since 2007, has talked about the growth of the resource industry and the consequent levels of violence experienced by Indigenous women:

I fully believe that the huge amount of resource extraction in this area contributes to the violence committed against women. On any given day I talk with women who are actively leaving violent situations—and you have to remember that many of these are unrecorded. I recently spoke with an Indigenous woman who was experiencing financial abuse from a program she was in—in fact, the whole class was from an industry-driven Indigenous organization. I can honestly say that there is more violence directed towards Indigenous people now than ever before. Part of the reason is our commitment to the environment and protecting the land. The levels of racism directed at our people is astronomical and is perpetuated by this belief that we are the reason for financial and tax burdens of non-Indigenous people in this area. I have lived a lot of years in Fort St. John and have been the target of abuse several times. On every occasion I have been dismissed by the police because the events all took place while alcohol was

involved and because I was an Indigenous woman. There
are a high number of transients; men here for work that are
new to the area as a result of the resource extraction;...men
who have no vested interest in Fort St. John as a community,
one that has become known as a town to come to and make
money and leave. It's this attitude that makes Fort St. John
such a dangerous place to live for Indigenous women, and
with the recent announcements for LNG *and the approval of*
the monstrosity Mega Project Site C, *I fear for the worst.*[4]

Like Greyeyes, I have watched individuals who don't care
what happens to the lands move into our territory. They extend
the same mentality to the women, both Indigenous and
non-Indigenous.

Indigenous women particularly fall prey to the mentality that
we are dispensable. A 2014 study done in Fort St. John found that
93 per cent of the Aboriginal participants had experienced some
form of violence, while 73 per cent of their non-Indigenous counterparts had experienced violence—a definite gap.[5] The authors
of the study, Clarice Eckford and Jillian Wagg, suggest that the
"man-camps" that accompany oil and gas projects breed hyper-
masculinity and high rates of substance use, which have been
shown to be a causal factor of violence against women, and the
men in the camps are underserviced in terms of social and health
programs.[6] The ideology that land is solely a resource for profit
enables man-camps, which then foster environments that can
lead to violence against women. While Eckford and Wagg do not
suggest that every man that works in these camps succumbs to
this violent mindset, they do demonstrate that the propensity
for violence exists within this population—a violence that is then
unleashed on the nearby communities. The continued destruction of Indigenous lands has been an essential part of weaving the
narrative that promotes the violence that characterizes Indigenous
women's lives.

This violence to our lands has also disrupted traditional teachings, which are often transmitted on the land where roles and responsibilities are reinforced through active participation. One of my earliest memories is berry picking with my family, and each year I take my son on the land with my Asu (grandmother) to gather berries for the family. Sadly, the saskatoon patches that I have picked since I was six years old now have a pipeline running behind them. Last year I peeked behind the bushes to see the earth dug up in a straight line, running parallel to the saskatoons. This year we decided to look elsewhere, but private property and increased development makes it harder and harder to gather what was once abundant in the north. We did manage to fill our berry bowls, knowing that a pipeline was in near proximity, on an old road forty-five minutes from where we picked. But later, my Asu stared into her bulging bowl of blue silently. When I asked her "What's wrong?" she replied, "Are these berries safe to eat?" I could not say yes without feeling like I would be lying to her. The wells and pipelines encircle us like hungry vultures. They leave us nothing. As we rode home in silence that day, I held my Asu's small brown hand in mine.

This interrupted connection to the land, to harvesting, and fulfilling roles and responsibilities ultimately interferes with the core of who we are as Dane Zaa, Dene, Salteaux, and Nehiyaw people within this territory. I can feel the heaviness in my spirit every time we go to the Peace River Valley, a beautiful area full of cultural heritage sites. It is here that they have begun land clearing to make way for the Site C hydroelectric dam, in spite of strong First Nation and community opposition. The voices are still being ignored, and little is done to take into account how this construction will impact Indigenous women.

Another problem is that the current cost of living in areas that are industry rich is quite high, and this makes finding or taking employment outside of the oil and gas industry difficult. Individuals without post-secondary education often have little choice but to rely on employment in these areas. Kristen Auger, a young Nehiyaw woman, shared her experience of working in the industry and how it impacted her:

> I believe that Indigenous women inherently feel their connection to the land and when the land is being violated they experience that as extremely negative emotions. Having been raised in a city that caters to the oil industry, I feel that the land is completely undervalued in almost every way.
>
> I used to work in the oilfield industry and I've seen and felt that connection to the land be disrupted and severely abused. I've felt tremendous guilt and a deep sadness or gaping hole within myself, which I would try to forget by making myself numb through the consumption of alcohol on a daily basis. When I was out there on the pipeline I honestly felt like what I was doing was morally wrong and that there would be repercussions to pay. There was, and I've paid for them and it was a particularly difficult and painful time in my life, and maybe I am still paying for them in some way.[7]

This high cost of living is created as transient workers enter into the area, making affordable housing nearly unobtainable. Thus the industry becomes a necessity in order to survive in areas that have little other economic development. When this development does cease, we, the original inhabitants, will be left with the bones that have been picked clean.

Presently, the struggle to protect Indigenous lands and Indigenous women are seen as separate, but in examining the early beginnings of the violation of both, it is apparent that the two are intrinsically connected. As Kim Anderson writes, "Native women have historically been equated with the land," therefore "the Euro constructed image of Native women…mirrors Western attitudes towards the earth."[8] The ideology that permits the violation of Indigenous bodies is the same one that perpetuates the violation of Indigenous lands.[9] Historically, Indigenous women held power in several areas of life—politics, family and marriage, ceremonial life, and food distribution.[10] To acquire the power and full ownership over the land, the power that Indigenous women held needed to be undermined and usurped, and this was "the key instigation for Native women's oppression, disempowerment, political demotion, and victimization."[11] Thus, sexism, patriarchy, and sexual violence have been entrenched in colonialism and cannot be separated from the pursuit for sovereignty as "it is impossible to have a truly self-determining nation when its members have been denied self-determination over their own bodies."[12]

Lisa Brunner, White Earth Ojibwe, program specialist from the National Indigenous Women's Resource Center, spoke about the increasing violence against women and girls that is the result of the Keystone Pipeline System. She made the important connection between protecting lands and protecting women at a rally to oppose the pipeline:

> They treat Mother Earth like they treat women…They think they can own us, buy us, sell us, trade us, rent us, poison us, rape us, destroy us, use us as entertainment and kill us. I'm happy to see that we are talking about the level of violence that is occurring against Mother Earth because it equates to us [women]. What happens to her happens to us…We are the creators of life. We carry that water that creates life just as Mother Earth carries the water that maintains our life. So I'm happy to see our men standing here but remind you that when you stand for one, you must stand for the other.[13]

As Brunner points out, addressing violence against the land and violence against women need not be separate in their courses of action and demands for remedies. There are many people in my territory who are vocal and knowledgeable on issues related to land protection, but significantly fewer people who are willing to speak about violence experienced by Indigenous women, and still an even fewer who speak to both. The connection between oil and gas development, loss of identity, and increased susceptibility to violence needs to be further researched so that communities can use the findings when opposing development projects. This will also assist us to advocate for changes on approaches to development on behalf of Indigenous women, youth, and children.

Self-Worth in Indian Country

Taking on the violence brought in by the extraction industry can be daunting, but we can also work within our communities to effect change by lowering risk factors. One risk factor that I have seen go unaddressed is when violence and sexual abuse are first experienced within Indigenous families—no doubt one of the real impacts of residential schools and colonial legacy. These initial experiences normalize violence so it is seen as "just something that happens," and this can place Indigenous women in extremely vulnerable situations. Futhermore, Indigenous women who have been exposed to forms of violence can be met with reactions that halt and hinder any healing process. Clark and Johnson state that "families where violence is common tend to share an unspoken belief that violence is normal and inescapable."[14] Thus, there may be no reactive response to an act of violence from family members or within the larger community. The following excerpt from " The Things We Taught Our Daughters" expresses the silence and generational cycles of violence.

> sometimes we taught them silence
> to let the secrets stay on their lips
> sometimes we taught them to look away
> to forget and not bear witness
>
> we showed them how
> to play hide-and-seek
> with historical afflictions
> to pretend that monsters from the closet

Didn't escape. Quiet Now. That's enough, my girl.
Silence.[15]

Acceptance of violence is not only learned through familial and community-based experiences, but also from the reactions of the local institutions that are put in place to protect. The 2013 Human Rights Watch report *Those Who Take Us Away* examines the relationship between the RCMP and Indigenous women and girls in Northern British Columbia.[16] This report shows how Indigenous women and girls are under-protected by the police and how they have also been the objects of outright police abuse. There are countless cases of Indigenous women who, upon reporting domestic violence events, end up being arrested and questioned as if they instigated and deserved the violence. Thus, several factors create the viable environment for violence to exist (although it is important to note that Indigenous women who have not experienced the normalization of violence are also at risk).

Within our communities, healing and preventing further violence will require understanding the nature of oppression, power, privilege, and the intersection of sexism and racism. Culture and ceremony must also be the centre and heart of these actions, as this will nurture and give grounding to women and girls. Giving voice will also foster self-worth amongst Indigenous women and girls. When community and family responses to violence are characterized by silence and further oppression, they are not an "Indian thing" but are the result of colonization, indoctrination, and historical trauma. Families have silenced their own daughters, preventing them from seeking legal action, and communities have shunned those who have pursued legal recourse. Perpetrators are allowed to freely dominate community spaces, leaving no safe spaces for those who have suffered harm. Furthermore, patriarchal attitudes are still present in our community levels of leadership. The belief that "women are our most sacred resource" is often said, but not always practiced within our communities. The conditions created by "colonization, racism, and oppression all fan the flames of violence."[17]

This is not to state that violence is only created and sustained by us as Indigenous people, which is utterly untrue. But we do have a responsibility to critically examine ourselves, our families, and our communities, and to create safe spaces for our women—spaces where their voices are heard and validated. While we fight for the land, we must also be our own examples of how to restore our women to their rightful place and address the culture of silence and patriarchal remnants within families and communities (both urban and rural). Paulo Freire states that the "humanistic and historical task of the oppressed [is] to liberate themselves and their oppressors as well."[18] To lead the way out of this, we must be taking the steps to help our own people break their cycles and silence.

My answer to silence is to share one of my experiences here, involving an older man from one of the communities near the urban centre where I lived. This man was known to the local RCMP for committing acts of sexual assault, but had always eluded charges. After I had experienced violence at the hands of this man, I moved forward to press charges, but the witnesses claimed they no longer remembered. I personally knew the witnesses and knew how their own sexual assault and abuses were met with silence and inaction. I could not expect more from them—they acted in the only way they knew. And yet this was the first time, after several other sexually violent incidents, that I had tried to do "the right thing" in moving forward with charges—but it did not work out without cooperation of the witnesses. Shortly after this incident, I attended a youth and Elders gathering to spend time visiting Elders and learning how to cut moose meat for drying. This man came to the tables where we were sitting and began to visit, ignoring my presence. The feelings of the incident, still being fresh, caused me to panic. I remember being angry that he was there, and I was even angrier that I was the one who had to leave because he would not.

I know through sitting with other women from communities across Canada that this is not an uncommon experience. How do we reclaim these cultural and community "safe spaces" for those that have a right to them and need them? Furthermore, how do we heal and rehabilitate those that commit the acts of abuse? Communities can come together to take action and develop ways where people are held accountable by other community members and community restorative groups. If possible (and applicable), communities can work closely with Crown Counsel to assure that specific enforceable measures are applied to individuals' release or sentencing conditions. If we look at the alarming numbers and rates at which our women go missing and are murdered, are abused and beaten, we can see that we have no more room for silence and inaction within our own communities. It is time to find our voices.

Raising Consciousness

There are more factors that contribute to violence against Indigenous women; however, I chose to focus on ones that we currently have control over. These are things that are not high-lighted often enough. I believe that the man/woman/leader that stands to speak for the land must be able to stand and speak for the women. Indigenous lands and Indigenous women are woven together and bound to the same destiny, whether we chose to recognize it or not. Furthermore, our women and men should be given opportunity to understand the nature and origin of violence as they experience it, to break free from it and have that space replaced with self-worth and love. As this is happening, commun-ities, families, and individuals need to recognize and break their own cycles surrounding violence and silence to create an environment where girls and boys can grow up to be strong Indigenous people who do not accept the role of violence within their lives. As this raising of consciousness is happening, we will be able to lead the way out of these dark times one girl, one boy, one family, one community at a time. Surely, this will strengthen our capacity to protect our original mother, to become whole again.

NOTES

1. Quoted in Sarah Deer, *The Beginning and End of Rape: Confronting Sexual Violence in Native America* (Minneapolis: University of Minnesota Press, 2015), xvi.

2. Albert Memmi quoted in Waziyatawin Angela Wilson and Michael Yellow Bird, "Beginning Decolonization," in *For Indigenous Eyes Only: A Decolonization Handbook*, ed. Waziyatawin Angela Wilson and Michael Yellow Bird (Santa Fe: School for Advanced Research, 2012), 3.

3. Statistics Canada, "Peace River, British Columbia" (Code5955) (table), 2006 Community Profiles, 2006 Census, Statistics Canada catalogue no. 92-591-XWE, March 13, 2007, http://www12.statcan.ca/census-recensement/2006/dp-pd/prof/92-591/index.cfm?Lang=E.

4. Connie Greyeyes, interview with the author, 2014.

5. Clarice Eckford and Jillian Wagg, *The Peace Project: Gender Based Analysis of Violence against Women and Girls in Fort St. John*, prepared for the Fort St. John Women's Resource Society, 2014, https://thepeaceprojectfsj.files.wordpress.com/2014/03/the_peace_project_gender_based_analysis_amended.pdf.

6. Eckford and Wagg, *The Peace Project*.

7. Kristen Auger, interview with the author, 2014.

8. Kim Anderson, *A Recognition of Being: Reconstructing Native Womanhood* (Toronto: Canadian Scholars' Press, 2016), 100.

9. Andrea Smith, *Conquest: Sexual Violence and American Indian Genocide* (Cambridge, MA: South End Press, 2005), 12.

10. Andrea Stratford, *Racialization of Poverty: Indigenous Women, the Indian Act and Systemic Oppression, Reasons for Resistance* (December 2007), 5, http://www.vsw.ca/Indigenous%20Women_DEC2007FINAL.pdf.

11. Stratford, *Racialization of Poverty*, 5.

12. Sarah Deer, *The Beginning and End of Rape: Confronting Sexual Violence in Native America* (Minneapolis: University of Minnesota Press), xvi.

13. Lisa Brunner quoted in Mary Annette Pember, "Brave Heart Women Fight to Ban Man-Camps, Which Bring Rape and Abuse," *Indian Country*

Today, August 28, 2013, https://indiancountrymedianetwork.com/
news/brave-heart-women-fight-to-ban-man-camps-which-bring-rape-
and-abuse/, ellipsis in original.

14. Rose L. Clark and Carrie L. Johnson, "Overview of Issues Facing Native
    Women," in *Sharing Our Stories of Survival: Native Women Surviving
    Violence*, ed. Sarah Deer, Bonnie Clairmont, Carrie A. Martell, and
    Maureen L. White Eagle (Lanham, MD: Altamira Press, 2008), 93.

15. Helen Knott, "The Things We Taught Our Daughters," in
    #NotYourPrincess: Voices of Native American Women, ed. Lisa Charleyboy
    and Mary Beth Leatherdale (Toronto: Annick Press, 2017), 44–45.

16. Human Rights Watch, *Those Who Take Us Away: Abusive Policing and
    Failures in Protection of Indigenous Women and Girls in Northern British
    Columbia, Canada* (Toronto: Human Rights Watch, 2013), http://www.
    hrw.org/sites/default/files/reports/canada0213webwcover_0.pdf.

17. Hilary Weaver, "The Colonial Context of Violence: Reflections
    on Violence in the Lives of Native American Women," *Journal of
    Interpersonal Violence* 24, no. 9 (2009): 1557.

18. Paulo Freire, *Pedagogy of the Oppressed*, 30th anniversary ed. (New York:
    Continuum, 2000), 44.

10 | *Skirting the Issues*
Indigenous Myths, Misses, and Misogyny

ALEX WILSON

Introduction

Over the past few years, five of my Indigenous trans and two-spirit-identified friends have been murdered. I grieve the violent ends of the lives of my bright spirited sisters.

I grieve, just as deeply, the violence that we know is an all too present threat in the lives of two-spirit people. A recent study showed that, in comparison to the general population, two-spirit women are four times more likely to be sexually or physically assaulted, and they are 50 per cent more likely to be assaulted than Indigenous women who are heterosexual.[1] Nearly half of the trans and two-spirited participants in another study reported that they had been chased, and a similar proportion had been threatened with physical violence because of their sex/gender identity. Perhaps most troubling is the fact that many queer and trans Indigenous youth do not feel supported, welcome, or safe in their own families and communities or in ceremonial spaces. Violence, oppression, and perceived loss of culture all generate societal by-products such as suicide. And, sadly, the suicide rate amongst two-spirit people is ten times higher than that of any other group.

Our communities have witnessed, grieved, and spoken out loudly about our many missing and murdered Indigenous women, and the issue is finally gaining much-needed attention at a national level. A narrative that essentializes women and women's "roles," however, has accompanied this shift. The essentializing narrative, which is rooted in a binary construction of gender, risks further marginalization of two-spirit, trans, and other LGBTQ Indigenous people, and generates confusion about what constitutes tradition.

In this writing, I share an understanding of Swampy Cree traditional law and discuss its contemporary application in relation to gender and sexuality. I offer a brief history of how the sexuality and bodies of Indigenous women and two-spirit and trans people became regulated through governmental and church policy. Through examples, personal observations, experiences, and stories, the meaning and importance of body sovereignty and gender self-determination and expression are presented as necessary aspects of undoing systemic forms of oppression and revisioning as a positive "coming in" process.

Skirting the Issues

Growing up, I cherished the times when my parents' friends and relatives would come over and relay stories about their travels and experiences. These were the times when we got to stay up late, my brothers and I, pyjama-ed, wide-eyed, and hanging on every word. We would resist falling asleep and we would resist waking as the rhythm, nuances, and movements of the stories informed our dreams. It was during these informal circles that we first came to know that eagles could be as large as people, about the clever humour of tricksters, about sasquatches, about constellations and navigation, where the rock paintings were, and many other great mysteries. It was intellectual training that commanded our attention and demanded creativity. They were emotional stories of physical experiences that relied on wonder. Sometimes the stories would start with a joke but usually they would begin in Cree. At times a pipe was brought out and passed to each person, while other times we would pass around a plate of frozen cookies ready to be dunked into hot tea. The smell of the sweetgrass that was burned in our home was as comforting and familiar as that of my mom's homemade bread. It was not unusual to have chunks of roots and plants amongst the empty baking tins, unplucked geese, wax-papered pie dough balls, and horse medication in the "deep-freeze." We played outside and reminded each other of what and how much we knew. In the winter, we would track and set snares for rabbits, ermine, and Bigfoot, and jam sticks into the neighbour's muskrat and beaver traps. Our connection to the land was visceral and political. And, as we spent time with our parents and grand-parents, we were affirmed that what we knew was true. Our ordinary lives were punctuated with extraordinary happenings, circumstance sometimes willed by imagination and at other times not.

When it was time for me to leave our community to go to university, my aunt led the ceremony to see me off. Many family and community members came to show their love and support; some came into the sweat lodge, some prepared food, others tended to the fire and rocks. Nookum, my grandmother, who adamantly opposed my aunt's involvement with the infamously misogynistic "sweathogs," made me a small pouch out of deer hide that she had in her stash. I never opened the pouch but I was told that it contained a small piece of rock from that sweat lodge fire, along with some medicines. I was given a large bundle of sweetgrass, swaddled in bright red broadcloth, each braid tied with crimson wool. Ceremony formalized what I had grown up knowing: that I was loved, that I was a spiritual being, and that I was important to this world.

Skirt Shaming

A few years ago I was asked by a friend to attend a ceremony in a
small community outside of the city. I had been to a quite a few
sweat lodges in my life, taking part either to acknowledge significant events or rites of passage or because someone had asked
for my support, and this time, without question or hesitation, I
honoured my friend's request. When we arrived at the place where
the ceremony would be held, I was glad to see a few familiar faces.
I was introduced to the Elders and others who were standing
around the fire before I was led to the lodge. I changed into my
usual sweat lodge attire of a T-shirt and shorts and awaited instruc-
tion from the hosts. It was then that a (non-Native) woman whom
I had met earlier came out of the change area and stood beside
me. She asked my name again, stating that she had a "government name" and an "Indian name" and told me both. She asked
me what my Indian name was. For the third time, I gave my name,
and then, chuckling, asked where she was from. Wearing a long
flannel nightgown, she suggested that I should change my clothes.
"No," I replied, "this is what I have always worn to sweats." Her
interrogation continued: "Who are your teachers?" She stated that
I would have to go change out of the shorts and T-shirt because
women must wear a dress or skirt for ceremonies. Just then, one of
my friends overheard the exchange and chimed in: "Her parents
are her teachers, and her grandparents." The woman stormed off,
advising me that she was going to tell the Elders.

If a Woman Beats a Drum, Does It Make a Sound?

We are often told that the drum is female and that the drum is
the heartbeat of our earth—and yet we are also told that only
men can beat the drum. This latter assertion (which takes power
from and regulates the bodies of women and two-spirit and trans
people, and simultaneously privileges men) is typically presented
to our children at a very early age and entrenched as a "traditional

teaching" by those in our community who enforce gender-specific protocols at ceremonies and celebrations.

Less than a year after I learned that I was not traditional enough (courtesy of the non-Indigenous woman with an "Indian name"), I helped organize a forum that brought together Indigenous youth to talk about what was important to them and to our communities. Youth were involved in every aspect of the planning, organization, and reporting of the two-day gathering and had invited a drum group comprised of young Indigenous women to open the event. The youth had heard that the drum group had recently been invited to participate in a pow-wow at an American college but, on arriving, had been told that they could not drum because they were women. The youth chose to invite the drum group to our gathering because they were proud of their strength and honoured to have them with us. As the young women brought their drum out at our gathering and set up, a woman who was a schoolteacher and part of the forum audience took it upon herself to ensure that they were adhering to her understandings of protocols relating to the drum. She approached the group and asked, "Have you done what you are supposed to do with the drum?" They had to offer tobacco to the drum, she told them. One of the drum group members had her infant son with her. The teacher took a drumstick from the mother, blessed the young boy, and handed the drumstick to him. Noting that the women wore dress pants, she continued, "And do you know the teachings? You must wear skirts." Conveniently, the teacher had skirts in her minivan, and after the scolding she scurried off to get them. The young drummers pulled the skirts on over their pants and had the honour of performing the opening of the gathering.

Sakihiwawin, Love in Actions

In Swampy Cree there exists a natural law, expressed by the term *sakihiwawin*. It is the natural order of the cosmos, which we, in turn, reflect as love in our actions.

Over a decade ago, a group of two-spirit people was called together by Elder Mae Louise Campbell. I am not too sure what led up to it—perhaps someone had a vision or a dream—but Elder Campbell had put word out that she was inviting two-spirit people to her land so that we could build a two-spirit drum. Word spread fast and soon we were in a convoy of three or four vehicles heading out to her land. When we arrived, she greeted us and said that she was honoured to have us. We were to build what we understood would be the first modern-day two-spirit drum in the region. As she showed us how to prepare the skin and build the drum frame, she told us stories about two-spirit people. When we had finally pieced the drum together, it was time to bless it in a sweat lodge ceremony. When that part of the ceremony was completed, we left the lodge one by one.

As we exited the lodge, I could not believe the Northern Lights. They were brighter than I had ever seen them—bright and multi-coloured, and they seemed to merge and come right down to the ground. It was as though there was a huge spotlight on the lodge and immediate area. I felt the light inside me like an electric charge. In our family lineage, the Northern Lights, *Wawahtao*, are a direct relative.

The experience had been so powerful that, at the feast for the drum that followed, we were all content and silent. After the building ceremony, we held weekly drum group practices and eventually decorated the drum by painting and "dressing" it. Today many two-spirit people have come and gone from the drum group, some passing on to the spirit world, but the drum continues as a reminder of our shared collective power. The drum reminds me that our relations extend beyond interpersonal to spiritual and ancestral connections. While others who present themselves as teachers had enforced "protocols" that attempted to shame and exclude me and other two-spirit or trans people from ceremony, Elder Campbell, by bringing us into ceremony to make and play our drum, had recognized and honoured us as who we are.

Connected to Body, Connected to Land[2]

I am a two-spirit member of the Opaskwayak Cree Nation. My family clan name is Wassenas, which translates as "reflecting light from within." That light is one form of the inextinguishable energy that has been passed to me from my ancestors and through my family and community. In our traditional spirituality, we find guidance in a Great Mystery; that is, that we are connected to everything by spiritual energy, joining us in a limitless circle that encompasses the past, present, and future. Following from this are the Cree principles of kakinow ni wagomakanak (we are in relationship with the land, waters, plants, animals, and other living creatures), a-kha ta neekanenni miso-an (we are all equally important), sakihiwawin (a commitment to act in ways that express love), and mino pimatisiwin (we are responsible to live in conscious connection with the land and living things in a way that creates and sustains balance—or, as my father translates from our dialect, to live beautifully). We understand that the nature of the cosmos is to be in balance and that when balance is disturbed, it must and will return.

Restoring Balance

Two-spirit identity is one way in which balance is being restored to our communities. Throughout the colonial history of the Americas, aggressive assimilation policies have been employed to displace our own understandings, practices, and teachings around sexuality, gender, and positive relationships, and replace them with those of Judeo Christianity.[3] To recognize ourselves as two-spirit is to declare our connection to the traditions of our own people.

The term *two-spirit* first came to a Cree person who was a teacher. She shared it with a gathering of Indigenous LGBTQI people from across North America (held in southern Manitoba in 1990).[4] The term was taken up quickly as a self-identifier, and many two-spirit people understand it to mean that each of us possesses a particular balance of masculinity and femininity or male and female energy. As a self-identifier, *two-spirit* acknowledges and affirms our identity as Indigenous peoples, our connection to the land, and values in our traditional cultures that recognize and accept gender and sexual diversity.

When the term *two-spirit* first appeared, the meaning most often attached to it reflected a binary construction of gender identity. This has changed. As the two-spirit activist Cheyenne Fayant-McLeod states, "Two-spirit means being queer and Indigenous, not that you are half man half woman. Depending on which tribe you're from, who your grandparents are, and what your ancestors have experienced, there are many, many different stories about what being queer means in Indigenous communities."[5] As another observed, our current understandings of the identity of LGBTQI people is "evolving or changing, and the term *two-spirit* is a placeholder until something comes along that more accurately fits the full continuum of who we are in the contemporary context."[6]

The recognition and acceptance of gender and sexual diversity is reflected in the language, spirituality, and culture of our own people. Our Cree dialect does not include gender-distinct pronouns. Rather, our language is "gendered" on the basis of whether or not something is animate (that is, whether or not it has a spiritual purpose and energy). Our creation story takes us back to the stars and the central figure or character Weesageychak, represented by the constellation other people call Orion. A trickster and a teacher, Weesageychak shifts gender, form, and space to playfully teach us about our selves and our connection to the wider universe, land and waters, living things and each other.

Cultural Disruption

When European newcomers first began to explore and settle our lands, they brought with them their commitment (rooted in their own cultures, spirituality and ways of being) to heteropatriarchy and gender binaries. They saw the acceptance of gender and sexual diversity that prevailed in our lands as sinful and threatening. As the Spanish explorer Cabeza de Vaca stated in the early 1500s, it was "a devilish thing."[7] Historic records show that violence on the bodies of Indigenous people who did not conform to the gender and sexual norms of the European newcomers began soon after their arrival. In 1513, forty Indigenous people whom the explorer Balboa had identified as "sodomites" were executed.[8] The imposition of Christianity, Canada's Indian Act, and other laws that apply only to Indigenous peoples, and the residential and boarding school systems imposed by the Canadian and American governments continued the work of Columbus and his fellow explorers. As part of an ongoing effort to assimilate Indigenous peoples, we were forcibly separated from each other and from our traditional cultures, lands, spirituality, languages, and ways of being. Throughout, our bodies, genders, and sexualities have been regulated in a continuum of violence. Penalized and punished for our acceptance of gender and sexual variance, many of us learned that the most certain way to survive was to take these teachings underground, out of sight of the colonizers.

These experiences continue to affect our people, communities, and nations. Today, some of our traditional Elders and spiritual teachers have adopted and introduced understandings and practices that were not part of their own cultures prior to colonization and the imposition of Christianity. This came up in a recent queer pride celebration in a small community. The celebration included a sweat lodge ceremony, and when two-spirit and other participants arrived to take part in the ceremony, the Elder leading the ceremony demanded that some in the group change their clothing to conform to what he perceived their gender to be. He added the warning that if he suspected that they had dressed in a way that did not conform to his assumptions about their gender identity, they would be required to prove that they were female or male. In the face of this direct assault on their body sovereignty and gender self-determination, some people left the ceremony.[9] Others stayed for fear that they would be disrespecting the organizers and the Elder and others, or for fear that they would be punished.

The role of Elders in our communities includes sharing with youth traditional teachings that will help them understand their own experiences, including their expressions of gender identity and sexuality. However, in most of our Indigenous cultures, where gender and sexual diversity were once accepted and valued, our traditional teachings, ways of being, spirituality, and languages were disrupted and displaced through the processes of colonization, Christianization, and assimilation. The result (as the incident described above demonstrates) is that some of our own present-day cultural teachings and practices extend the continuum of violence that two-spirit people have been subject to since colonization began.

In our home communities, two-spirit people are frequently subject to interconnected homophobia, transphobia, and misogyny, and in the larger society they are additionally subject to structural and individual racism and classism. This has had devastating impacts on the two-spirit community. The suicide rate for LGBTQ Indigenous youth is ten times higher than that of any other group in the United States. Thirty-nine per cent of two-spirit women and 21 per cent of two-spirit men have attempted suicide.[10] In a recent study of transgendered and gender non-conforming Indigenous people in the United States, nearly one-quarter lived in extreme poverty; elevated rates of HIV were found among participants, and more than half of respondents (56%) had attempted suicide.[11]

Coming In

There is much work to be done, then, to undo the work that has been done upon us. When we call ourselves two-spirit people, we are proclaiming sovereignty over our bodies, gender expressions, and sexualities. In my own research with Cree and Ojibwe two-spirit people, I heard many stories of "coming in."[12] Coming in does not centre on the declaration of independence that characterizes "coming out" in mainstream depictions of the lives of LGBTQI people. Rather, coming in is an act of returning, fully present in our selves, to resume our place as a valued part of our families, cultures, communities, and lands, in connection with all our relations.

We do not do this work alone. Idle No More is an international grassroots movement that brings Indigenous and non-Indigenous people together to honour the sovereignty of Indigenous people and Nations, and to protect the land and water. Idle No More was organized in resistance to oppressive colonial ideologies and laws, and its activities have included public education on the regulation of sexuality and gender.[13] Another organization doing liberating work is the Native Youth Sexual Health Network. This organization was created by and for Indigenous youth, and works across issues of sexual and reproductive health, rights, and justice throughout Canada and the United States, with activities that include education, advocacy, and outreach with two-spirit and LGBTQ youth.[14]

In both these movements, Indigenous sovereignty over our lands is inseparable from sovereignty over our bodies, sexualities, and gender self-expression. This connection is at the root of the very contemporary understanding of identity held by many two-spirit youth today.

Walking as Sisters

Walking With Our Sisters now includes two-spirit and trans people not legally recognized as women in their discussions of the unreported cases of missing and murdered Indigenous women.[15] The projects No More Silence and It Starts with Us have begun compiling a community-run database that documents the violent deaths of Indigenous, two-spirit, and trans women.[16] Across Canada, communities have drawn on the RED dress Project and mounted their own displays to mark the absence of their loved sisters who are missing or have been murdered, and in many communities, empty red pant suits, T-shirts, or other articles of clothing have been hung alongside red dresses to mark the absence of their two-spirit and trans loved ones and, more generally, to recognize that not all women are most appropriately represented by a dress.

Bringing—and keeping—our two-spirit and trans loved ones into the movement to undo the violence that removes the lives and presence of Indigenous women from our families and communities is a crucial recognition of the fact that, for Indigenous women and two-spirit and trans people, our gender identity has put us at elevated risk of violence, oppression, marginalization, and loss of our place in our culture and community. The hashtag #MMIWG2S is a good start, but we must go further and embrace all of what that means.[17] We must address the interconnections between misogyny, homophobia, transphobia, classism, ablism, and racism. We must name misogyny and homo/transphobia in our own communities. We must acknowledge and protect the bodies and people who have been most impacted by colonial violence and have the courage to stand in the truth of and celebrate our own pre-colonial understandings of gender and sexual diversity. And we must include two-spirit and trans people in every discussion of murdered and missing Indigenous women and the inquiry process.

Generations of our peoples have been forced to march along the long and brutal path of colonization—but we are still here. Still showing up. And still very alive, speaking up for each other and for our missing and murdered loved ones, standing together in grief, anger, ceremony, and love to demand change.

AUTHOR'S NOTE

Portions of this paper have previously been published in Alexandria Wilson, "Two-Spirited People, Body Sovereignty and Gender Self-Determination," *Red Rising Magazine*, last modified September 21, 2015, http://redrisingmagazine.ca/two-spirit-people-body-sovereignty-and-gender-self-determination, and as "Our Coming in Stories: Cree Identity, Body Sovereignty and Gender Self-Determination," *Journal of Global Indigeneity* 1, no. 1 (2015), http://ro.uow.edu.au/jgi/.

NOTES

1. Keren Lehavot, Karina L. Walters, and Jane M. Simoni, "Abuse, Mastery, and Health among Lesbian, Bisexual, and Two-Spirit American Indian and Alaska Native Women," *Cultural Diversity and Ethnic Minority Psychology* 15, no. 3 (2009): 275–84.

2. "Connected to body, connected to land" is one of the many Indigenous teachings shared the Native Youth Sexual Health Network (discussed later in this chapter).

3. Martin Cannon, "The Regulation of First Nations Sexuality," *Canadian Journal of Native Studies* 18, no. 1 (1998): 1–18; Quo-Li Driskill, Chris Finley, Brian Joseph Gilley, and Scott Lauria Morgensen, eds., *Queer Indigenous Studies: Critical Interventions in Theory, Politics, and Literature* (Tucson: University of Arizona Press, 2011); Alex Wilson, "Two-Spirit Identity: Active Resistance to Multiple Oppressions," *Directions: Research and Policy on Eliminating Racism* 5, no. 1 (Spring 2009): 44–46.

4. Albert McLeod, *Two-Spirited People of Manitoba Inc.*, accessed January 24, 2018, https://twospiritmanitoba.ca/we-belong.

5. Fayant-McLeod quoted in Michele Tyndall, "Two Spirit Reclaiming Acceptance through Education," *Regina Leader-Post*, June 17, 2013.

6. Dylan Rose, personal communication, August 2011.

7. Alvar Núñez Cabeza de Vaca, "*Naufragios* de Alvar Núñez Cabeza de Vaca," in *Historiadores primitivos de Indias (Vol. I)*, ed. Enrique de Vedia, trans. Ed Strug (Madrid: M. Rivadeneyra, 1852), 538.

8. Johnathan Goldberg, *Sodometries: Renaissance Texts and Modern Sexualities* (Stanford, CA: Stanford University Press, 1992).

9. Members of this group contacted me directly to tell me of this experience.

10. Karen C. Fieland, Karina L. Walters, and Jane M. Simoni, "Determinants of Health Among Two-Spirit American Indians and Alaska Natives," in *The Health of Sexual Minorities: Public Health Perspectives on Lesbian, Gay, Bisexual and Transgender Populations*, ed. Ilan H. Meyer and Mary E. Northridge (Springer, 2007), 268–300, e-book.

11. National Center for Transgender Equality, *Injustice at Every Turn: American Indian and Alaskan Native respondents in the National*

Transgender Discrimination Survey (Washington, DC: National Center for Transgender Equality, 2012).

12. Alex Wilson, "N'tacimowin inna nah': Our Coming in Stories," *Canadian Woman Studies* 26, no. 3–4 (2008): 193–99; Alex Wilson, "N'tacimowin inna nah': Coming in to Two-Spirit Identities" (PHD diss., Harvard Graduate School of Education, 2007).

13. Idle No More, accessed May 10, 2016, www.idlenomore.ca; Laura Zahody, "Idle No More Organizers Reach Out to Queer Community," in *The Winter We Danced: Voices from the Past, the Future, and the Idle No More Movement*, ed. the Kino-nda-niimi Collective (Winnipeg: ARP Books, 2014), 287–89.

14. "Healthy Sexuality & Fighting Homophobia & Transphobia," Native Youth Sexual Health Network, accessed June 15, 2015, http://www.nativeyouthsexualhealth.com/youthphotoproject.html.

15. "Our Sisters," Walking With Our Sisters, accessed March 21, 2016, http://walkingwithoursisters.ca/about/our-sisters/.

16. *No More Silence* (blog), accessed March 26, 2016, http://nomoresilence-nomoresilence.blogspot.ca/; It Starts with Us website, accessed March 26, 2016, http://www.itstartswithus-mmiw.com/.

17. In the hashtag #MMIWG2S, 2S is understood to refer to both two-spirit and trans people.

11 | *The Moose in the Room*

Indigenous Men and Violence against Women

ROBERT ALEXANDER INNES & KIM ANDERSON

IN THE SUMMER OF 2014, in a third-year Indigenous studies seminar class that one of the authors (Innes) was teaching, students discussed the recently released RCMP report on missing and murdered Indigenous women.[1] Professor Innes asked the students to reflect on the statistic that nearly 90 per cent of the victims knew their killers, which inferred a possibility that the majority, if not the overwhelming majority, of killers were Indigenous men. Every one of the eleven students, all of whom were Indigenous and the majority women, agreed that it was a possibility, and a few noted that, based on their experience, it was very probable. When asked if that was the case, then should we, in the Indigenous community, talk more about this issue, the students unanimously responded by saying, "No, as this would just reinforce negative stereotypes about Indigenous men."

Why are we uneasy within the Indigenous community to discuss the levels of violence Indigenous men inflict upon Indigenous women? As Anishinaabe lawyer Joan Jack stated in an op-ed piece in the *Winnipeg Free Press*, "Aboriginal men kill aboriginal women and girls, rape aboriginal women and girls, beat aboriginal women and girls, and no one is really talking about the moose in our living room."[2] For many, like the students in Innes's classroom, this kind of discussion does reinforce negative stereotypes attached to Indigenous men. Others believe that focusing on violence committed by Indigenous men wrongly shifts attention to them and away from the violence white men inflict on Indigenous women, while others still see it as a means of relieving the government of its responsibility. However, some Indigenous men have begun to acknowledge the level of violence Indigenous men have perpetrated against Indigenous women. This chapter discusses the "moose in the room" as a means of taking on violence within our communities and building healthier families and futures.

Indigenous men have, for the most part, been absent from the discussions about missing and murdered Indigenous women. That changed very quickly in December 2014, when Bernard Valcourt, former minister of (the formerly named) Aboriginal Affairs and Northern Development Canada told the *Ottawa Citizen* that "if we're honest here," it is obvious that "there's a lack of respect for women and girls on reserves…So, you know, if the guys grow up [on the reserve] believing that women have no rights, that's how they are treated."[3] In March 2015, the Aboriginal Peoples Television Network (APTN) news reported that Valcourt had told several chiefs that Indigenous men murdered 70 per cent of the Indigenous women identified in the RCMP report.[4] A month later, APTN reported that the RCMP had corroborated Valcourt's figures.[5] It is possible that Canadians who were against launching a national inquiry accepted the view of Indigenous men as the murderers of Indigenous women; perhaps it allowed them to say that since we know the killers, there is no need for an inquiry. Karyn Pugliese, APTN's director of news and current affairs, outlined the faulty logic of this perception to Jesse Brown of *Canadaland Commons* podcast on December 13, 2015: "if it were Aboriginal men doing it to Aboriginal women it's not really the government's business. There's nothing to see here. But if it is non-Native men doing it to Indigenous women then there is a need for the government to do something."[6]

Exactly how many Indigenous men have murdered Indigenous women is not certain. The RCMP report on missing and murdered Indigenous women does show that over 90 per cent of Indigenous women murdered victims knew their murderers.

Offender-to-Victim Relationship, Female Homicides, 1980–2012

	Aboriginal Victims	Non-Aboriginal Victims
Spousal	29%	41%
Other Family	23%	24%
Intimate Other	10%	9%
Acquaintance	30%	19%
Stranger	8%	7%
Unknown	1%	5%

Source: RCMP, *Missing Aboriginal Women: A National Operational Overview* (Ottawa: Government of Canada, 2014), 12.

The figures in the table suggest that a great proportion of the murderers could have been Indigenous men, though the precise figure is difficult to ascertain. However, the number of spouses who were murderers is significant. Not only is the number of Indigenous women murdered by their spouses lower than it is for non-Indigenous women, but considering that a relatively high number of Indigenous women marry non-Indigenous men, it is very likely that Indigenous male spouses could have been responsible for killing fewer than 29 per cent of Indigenous women.

There are other statistics that indicate that fewer Indigenous women knew their killers than the RCMP reports shows. For example, according to Brzozowski, Taylor-Butts, and Johnson, violent incidents "committed against Aboriginal people were more likely to be perpetrated by someone who was known to the victim (56%), such as a relative, friend, neighbour or acquaintance," and Indigenous people were victimized by a stranger in 25 per cent of all violent incidents.[7] These figures, however, are for all violent crimes and not just murder, and represent both Indigenous women and men. In addition, in their definition of acquaintance, the RCMP included authority figures and business and criminal relationships, which could in fact mean that many of the women's acquaintances were non-Indigenous men. The assumption is that since the women knew their murderers, their murderers were Indigenous. But because there are no race breakdowns of the murderers, there is no way to know with any certainty how many were actually Indigenous. There is enough ambiguity in the statistics to call into question Valcourt's assertion that 70 per cent of the killers of Indigenous women were Indigenous men.

In her *Indian Country Today* exposé about discrepancies in the figures for missing and murdered Indigenous women in Canada and the United States, Lisa J. Ellwood argues that the RCMP narrative explaining their figures was framed in such a way as to point towards Indigenous men as the primary murderers of Indigenous women.[8] Ellwood explains how the compilation of US figures is more exhaustive and considers factors that are absent in the Canadian reporting. For this reason, she sees the US reporting as more relevant than the RCMP's Canadian figures when discussing the context of missing and murdered women. She argues that the figures show non-Indigenous men are overwhelmingly the murderers of Indigenous women. The RCMP, Ellwood concludes, "attempts to make a case for 'MMAW' being the preserve of familial relationships with offenders being known to victims with no consideration for data provided on: (1) actual racial and ethnic diversity in Indigenous families; (2) Indigenous and non-Indigenous interracial relationships and (3) the diversity of residents typically found on and around Reserves."[9] With this analysis, Ellwood raises significant questions about how statistics of missing and murdered Indigenous women are framed within ubiquitous narratives about the criminality of Native men and the seemingly hopeless dysfunction of Indigenous communities.

While acknowledging the veracity of Ellwood's arguments, we cannot lose sight of the multi-faceted nature of violence in our communities. The recent focus has been on the missing and murdered Indigenous women, and rightfully so; however, these are only two forms of violence experienced by Indigenous women. Indigenous women are much more likely to experience physical and sexual violence, a fact that has been overshadowed by the number of murders that have taken place. For example, Brzozowski, Taylor-Butts, and Johnson showed that in 2006 Indigenous peoples were victims of violence three times more than non-Indigenous people. For the most part, the rate reflects the large number of physical assaults, which were "the most frequently occurring violent offence" experienced by Indigenous people.[10] Additional statistics show that domestic violence is the most prevalent form of physical violence that Indigenous women face. Brzozowski, Taylor-Butts, and Johnson noted, for example, that Indigenous women experienced 3.5 times more domestic violence than non-Indigenous women.[11] In addition, a 2004 survey showed that 21 per cent of Indigenous people reported having experienced some form of physical or sexual violence by a spouse.[12] Meanwhile, Shannon Brennan states that "among victims of spousal violence, close to six in ten Aboriginal women reported being injured during the 5 years preceding the survey, compared to four in ten non-Aboriginal women (59% versus 41%)."[13] Also, Brennan reports that more the 34 per cent of Indigenous women report being victimized multiple times in a year.[14]

Katie Scrim notes that Indigenous women consistently report a rate of partner violence much higher than their non-Indigenous counterparts; she cites Douglas Brownridge's 2008 article to demonstrate that whereas "living common law is associated with a 13 per cent greater risk of victimization for non-Aboriginal women, the associated risk for Aboriginal women is 217 per cent higher."[15] According to Brennan, in 2009 almost 67,000

Indigenous women older than 15 "reported being the victim of violence in the previous 12 months. Overall, the rate of self-reported violent victimization among Aboriginal women was almost three times higher than the rate of violent victimization reported by non-Aboriginal women."[16]

In the same way that it is difficult to know how many Indigenous men have murdered Indigenous women, it is difficult to say for certain how many Indigenous men have physically assaulted Indigenous women. However, unlike murder statistics, there are some statistics on domestic violence that focus on reserve communities. For example, a joint report by the Ontario Native Women's Association/Ontario Federation of Indian Friendship Centres (ONWA/OFIFC) noted that in 2007 in some Northern Ontario First Nations communities between 75 and 90 per cent of First Nations women were physically assaulted.[17] In addition, ONWA/OFIFC notes that children witnessed half of the violence that took place in First Nations homes, and that the children were themselves targeted for physical and sexual violence at a very high rate.[18] The violent crime rates on First Nations were reported as being eight times greater then off reserve.[19]

Although it is difficult to know to what degree these rates of domestic violence transfer to the urban context, it is unlikely that Indigenous men's rates of violence towards Indigenous women decreases dramatically, as violence is not simply an issue of location, but is symptomatic of larger issues. Other important and relevant features regarding violence and Indigenous people include the evidence that Indigenous people were more likely to be assaulted near or close to their homes and had a higher likelihood that alcohol and drug use factor in the assaults.[20]

These statistics are in no way definitive. They do not provide explicit evidence of the level of violence directed by Indigenous men towards Indigenous women, children, queer/two-spirit or trans peoples, Elders, or other men. What is certain is that there are multiple risk factors within many Indigenous communities and families, such as poverty, substance abuse, and dysfunctional parenting skills—caused by racism and colonial interventions. These factors have disrupted the social fabric of Indigenous communities and have influenced Indigenous men in negative ways. Government policies and settler racism have fostered internalized racism that has created "the conditions that channel many Indigenous men into situations of despair, dysfunction, and violence."[21] The violence inflicted upon Indigenous men through residential schools and other forms of violent interaction with settler culture has been learned over time and then taught to subsequent generations of young men. Male dominance and heteropatriarchy in Indigenous communities is thus now entrenched through various forms violence.[22] Bopp, Bopp, and Lane explain the way in which domestic violence in Indigenous communities functions:

> There can be little doubt that one of the factors which deter-
> mines the presence, extent and nature of domestic violence and
> abuse is the prevailing belief systems and attitudes in the
> community, particularly: (a) attitudes and beliefs of men
> about women and about male privilege, (b) generally accepted
> beliefs and attitudes related to the treatment of children, and
> (c) generally accepted norms and attitudes related to violence
> and abuse against women and children, and violence in
> general. The extent to which family violence and abuse have
> been "normalized" and taken for granted as "the way it is"
> creates the psychological and social space within where abuse
> can flourish.[23]

Though the exact figures are not known, many Indigenous people agree that male violence in communities is rampant. And whether Indigenous men are responsible for 70 per cent or 30 per cent of Indigenous women's murders, the number is still shockingly high. Thirty per cent represents over three hundred women's lives. This is not a victory in terms of arguments about who are the killers.

Though many Indigenous people would rather not discuss Indigenous male violence, some male leaders are now beginning to talk about it as a means to combat violence against Indigenous women. In 2015, Assembly of First Nations National Chief Perry Bellegarde asserted that "Aboriginal men must address deep-seated issues stemming from the Indian Residential School system, including addiction and cycles of violence," implying a link between violence against Indigenous women and the violent inherited behaviours of some Indigenous men.[24] Some men advocate for change by speaking about their own involvement with violence. Some men, such as the "Crazy Indians" interviewed by Sasha Skye for the Bidwewidam Indigenous Masculinities project, advocate for change by speaking about their own involvement with violence. The Crazy Indians Brotherhood is an organization comprised of former gang members who use the organizational structure of gangs to do positive community work. With chapters in various cities throughout the country, their intentions are to be healthy role models for young men and to guide them away from the allure of gang lifestyles. In a focus group with Skye, many of the participants talked about how they learned to be "men." The following excerpts provide a sense of the violence they learned early on, and how this violence was underpinned by a misogyny that they needed to address as part of their "healing path":

PARTICIPANT 2: *I was never taught how to be a man. I witnessed my mom's drunken boyfriends punch the shit out of her. I saw fights at parties. I accepted that life, the partying life and being surrounded by all that...*[25]

PARTICIPANT 6: *I was also taught that we always had to be superior to women. So I started doing all the stuff that I had seen growing up to my wife. We met when we were young, so I was always that guy. I'd see her crying and instead of showing her love and compassion I would tell her to "quit her fucking*

crying." I was abusive, too. As a man I've learned a lot of
different things over the last eight years that I've been on the
healing path. Now I know we aren't superior to women and
it's actually the other way around. I learned it's okay to take
direction from a woman without questioning her or getting
mad at her for it.[26]

Chris Moyah, also a former gang member who works at
Str8 UP, an organization that helps former gang members adjust
to life outside of the gangs, spoke to the *Saskatoon StarPhoenix*
about the violence of his experiences leading up to joining gangs.
According to the news report, "Moyah grew up in a world filled
with violence. He would see loved ones and friends take abuse
from their partners on a weekly if not daily basis. Hurting people
was just a way of life."[27] Moyah's childhood was thus dominated
by violence and alcohol, which greatly influenced not only his
choice to join a gang but also the way he treated women. He talked
frankly about a violent relationship with a female partner: "It first
started off with accusations. Then it was alienating her, keeping
her from her family to gain control over her. Then it started to get
to be verbal assaults, calling her names. It led to pushing her then it
led to random slaps across the face."[28]

Moyah's reflections, like those offered by the Crazy Indians,
mirror the "prevailing belief systems and attitudes" outlined by
Bopp, Bopp, and Lane for domestic violence. These men eventually
decided that they had to turn their lives around, and one way
for them to do that was by speaking their truths—addressing, in
Joan Jack's words, the "moose in the living room," their violent
behaviours. They were apparently not concerned about whether
they would reinforce the negative stereotypes held by mainstream
society about them; rather, they seemed focused on trying to
become better men to their families and communities. Talking
about their past meant they had be willing to become vulnerable
in ways they were not accustomed to in their former gang lives.
As Jorgina Sunn, an employee at Str8 UP said, "People are masked

behind fear, they are masked behind their shame."[29] The men had to thus face fears of being shamed for their negative behaviours. Faith Eagle, another worker at Str8 UP, added, "When you learn that you can heal—that you don't have to walk in that shame anymore—then it's a whole different point of view."[30] Eagle added that most men would prefer that people did not know about the domestic violence they committed, and pointed to the significance of these men speaking out about their violence.

Some men have begun to show their support through group activity. When the Walking With Our Sisters installation was scheduled for Saskatoon, the organizing committee asked Jeff Baker, a Métis professor at the University of Saskatchewan, and Marcel Petit, a Métis local filmmaker and photographer, to organize a men's subcommittee to find out if there was interest from men in the community to contribute in some way. Baker and Petit organized a meeting where various ideas were discussed. The men decided that they would like to show their support for the missing and murdered Indigenous women and their families by maintaining a sacred fire for the duration of the twenty-three-day exhibit. The idea was presented and approved by the organizing committee. That there were men who wanted to be a part of Walking With Our Sisters in some way was significant, as up to that point few men had participated in the project in other cities. Finding enough men to attend to the fire was difficult, which is perhaps indicative of many men's reluctance to become involved. Nonetheless, the men who did commit, Indigenous, non-Indigenous, and queer/two-spirit peoples, were more than willing to sit by the fire for ten to sixteen hours, which is indicative of commitment and hope.

It is heartening that there are examples of organizational leadership in engaging Indigenous men to end violence against women. The Kizhaay Anishinaabe Niin—I Am a Kind Man program is operated by the OFIFC in twenty-eight communities across Ontario. This is an anti-violence program centred on four objectives:

- To provide education for men to address issues of abuse against women
- To re-establish traditional responsibilities by acknowledging that our teachings have never tolerated violence and abuse towards women
- To inspire men to engage other men to get involved and stop the abuse
- To support Aboriginal men who choose not to use violence.[31]

The program operates from the position that violence against Indigenous women is not a women's issue, but rather an issue where men must assume responsibility through their words and actions to stop the violence. It thus aims to reclaim and revitalize Indigenous cultures and the associated roles and responsibilities of men in building healthy families and communities. It is interesting to note that the OFIFC is now revising Kizhaay curriculum to dismantle heteronormative assumptions, and to address bigger questions around gender binary approaches in this work. Much of their work involves challenging men's notions of masculinity, gender, sexuality, and other aspects that contribute towards men's violence.

Thus far, the Kizhaay program has trained over 150 facilitators to run community-based campaigns, and they are constantly fielding demands for training and opportunities to expand. Kizhaay activities include a twenty-four-week "HIM—Healthy Indigenous Male" course framed around traditional "seven grandfather" teachings and grounded in ceremony, ongoing group meetings, and engaging in community awareness and activism. In many communities, the program is valued for offering men a chance to gather, discuss, and contextualize the violence that has followed them throughout their lives. "Whereas it was once taboo, we see people that are now able to talk about their own cycle of abuse," says Michael White, a trainer with the OFIFC.[32] "Kizhaay addresses the root cause of violence, and often the perpetrators of violence have been victims themselves." The program also appears to enhance the self-esteem and foster a positive sense of identity among many of the men who participate. White points out that men often find a sense of belonging: "men are looking for a place to connect." He reflects on the irony that Kizhaay participants take pride in wearing Kizhaay Anishinaabe Niin sweaters: "It may seem antithetical to advertise that you were once violent against women; but wearing Kizhaay material is more about taking pride in participating in change in the community." For many men, the Kizhaay program is the catalyst for men to take up responsibilities for community wellness. White points out, too, that not all those involved in Kizhaay are past abusers: "Kizhaay is about standing up to make the change in our communities, promoting that violence must end. To that aim, youth, supportive men and women also wear the Kizhaay logo."

Individual Indigenous men have also initiated awareness and activist campaigns. Moyah, a former abuser, decided to raise awareness of violence against women as part of his larger recovery from a dysfunctional lifestyle, and so he embarked on walks of up to ninety kilometres. Though a primary goal of the walks has been to raise awareness of violence, they also provided him time to reflect on this past and think about how he could move forward in a positive way. As he told the CBC, "I used to be so loving and generous. I'm hoping to unlock some of those old things, some of those old habits."[33]

In 2011, Paul Lacerte, who at the time was the executive director of the BC Association of Aboriginal Friendship Centres, went hunting with his youngest daughter, Raven, along Highway 16 in Northern BC. Highway 16 is known as the "Highway of Tears" due to the high number of Indigenous women who have been murdered in that region. Lacerte recalls watching his daughter skin a moose and realizing that Indigenous men had to do more; they had to speak out against the violence.[34] As a result, Lacerte and his daughter came up with the Moose Hide Campaign, where small squares of moose hide could be worn as a symbol of an individual's stance against violence toward Indigenous women.

When Lacerte began wearing the moose hide, people would ask him what it was for. He would respond, "Thank you for asking. I'm speaking out against violence toward Aboriginal women and children." This was a way to challenge more Indigenous men to speak up and speak out, which Lacerte feels is critical: "The level of violence towards women in this country is shocking and totally unacceptable. We need to do more as men to support each other in our healing and also hold each other accountable for our actions. We need to stop taking a backseat on this issue and help drive the change together."[35] The Moose Hide Campaign message is that Indigenous men need to become active, engaged, and prepared to speak out against violence, and it has resonated with many men.

Joan Jack uses "the moose in the living room" as an alternative "elephant in the room" metaphor for Indigenous leaders and individuals who avoid dealing with the issue of violence Indigenous women face from Indigenous men. With the Moose Hide Campaign, this metaphor shifts to that of sustaining and nourishing families and communities in healthy ways. It reminds communities of a time when men had a central role of providing. On Vancouver Island, where Lacerte lives, there are no moose, so they have given it a local character, using deer hide and the slogan "You don't have to hide, dear." Thus the Moose (or deer) Hide Campaign is a reminder to Indigenous men that even though today most men do not, or for a variety of reasons cannot hunt, men can still provide for families and communities by being good husbands, fathers, grandfathers, brothers, cousins, and friends. One of the ways they can do this is by standing up against violence and inequalities within our communities. In doing so, Indigenous men can counteract the disruptive and destructive environment that violence engenders and contribute to strengthening and sustaining positive familiar and community relations.

Conclusion

This chapter took as its launching pointing Jack's metaphor of the moose in the living room. The violence committed by Indigenous men in our communities is not an easy topic to discuss. Victimizers have relatives and friends whose natural inclination may be to protect the victimizers rather than preventing further violence from happening, but this typically means further victimization of women. However, by confronting the moose in the living room, families and communities can begin to openly tackle issues of violence and the shame of victims and victimizers that the violence engenders.

Our examples of men stepping forward to voice their views against violence toward women are few, but those who have spoken out represent a hopeful trend. For these men, the extent to which Indigenous men murder Indigenous women is not their main concern. Nor do they care much about whether their coming out and discussing Indigenous male violence will reinforce the negative perception white people have of them. They are more concerned with acknowledging their complicity in the ongoing violence experienced by Indigenous women. They have decided to refuse to allow their family and friends to enable their violent ways, either by making excuses for their behaviour or simply pretending they have not committed violence. Men who are not violent towards women, like many who volunteered in the Walking With Our Sisters exhibit in Saskatoon, are just now realizing they can no longer remain silent. These men acknowledge that no matter how many women suffer physically at the hands of Indigenous men, it is too many. As Lacerte realized, Indigenous women have been not only been "bearing the burden of abuse, but they also have [had] to bear the burden of advocacy to effect change, and this is a men's problem as much as it is a women's problem."[36] How might men further engage? We would like to close with this invitation to Indigenous men from Rachel Flowers, an Indigenous PHD student in political science at the University of British Columbia:

> *I wonder how an apology to Indigenous women, from Indigenous men who were violent toward women and have since reformed their behavior, might be a powerful and irreplaceable contribution to our desubjectification as objects of patriarchal violence. Whether these women choose to forgive is a separate consideration. However, the move from men to recognize their role in violence and take on the responsibility for change might provide some relief from the crushing weight of the persistent denial of violence within our communities. It is crucial that we shift our mode of thinking away from ownership of community members, toward our own understandings of kin relations, the system of relationships wherefrom we derive our obligations and laws. How might the healing needed in our communities take place differently if men stopped talking about "protecting our women" but rather about "reforming our brothers" and "honoring our sisters, mothers, daughters"?[37]*

NOTES

1. Royal Canadian Mounted Police, *Missing and Murdered Aboriginal Women: A National Operational Overview* (Ottawa: Government of Canada, 2014), http://www.rcmp-grc.gc.ca/en/missing-and-murdered-aboriginal-women-national-operational-overview.

2. Joan Jack, "Excuse Me, There's a Moose in the Room," *Winnipeg Free Press*, December 13, 2014, http://www.winnipegfreepress.com/opinion/analysis/aboriginal-women-fear-their-own-kind-the-most-285701831.html.

3. Mark Kennedy, " Valcourt Urges First Nations, Provinces to Take Action on Murdered and Missing Aboriginal Women, " *Ottawa Citizen*, December 12, 2014, http://ottawacitizen.com/news/national/bernard-valcourt-rejects-inquiry-on-murdered-aboriginal-women.

4. Jorge Barrera, "Valcourt Used Unreleased RCMP Data to Claim Aboriginal Men Responsible for Majority of Murders of Aboriginal Women: Chiefs," *APTN News*, March 25, 2015, http://aptn.ca/news/2015/03/25/ chiefs-say-valcourt-used-unreleased-rcmp-data-claim-indigenous-men-responsible-majority-indigenous-women-murders/.

5. Jorge Barrera, "Top Mountie Breaks with Policy, Says Indigenous Perpetrators Responsible for 70 Per Cent of Solved Indigenous Women Murders," *APTN News*, April 9, 2015, http://aptn.ca/ news/2015/04/09/top-mountie-breaks-policy-says-indigenous-perpetrators-responsible-70-per-cent-solved-indigenous-women-murders/.

6. "Newsworthy Victims: MMIW and the Media," *Canadaland Commons* (podcast), December 13, 2015, http://canadalandshow.com/podcast/ newsworthy-victims-mmiw-and-media.

7. Jodi-Anne Brzozowski, Andrea Taylor-Butts, and Sara Johnson, "Victimization and Offending among the Aboriginal Population in Canada," *Juristat* 26, no. 3, Statistics Canada cat. no. 85-002-XIE (2006): 6.

8. Lisa J. Ellwood, "A Comprehensive Report on MMIW: Different Tales of Violence against Indigenous Women on Both Sides of Turtle Island," *Indian Country Today*, February 10, 2016, https://indiancountrymedianetwork.com/news/ native-news/a-comprehensive-report-on-mmiw-the-curiously-different-tales-of-violence-against-indigenous-women-on-both-sides-of-turtle-island/.

9. Ellwood, "Comprehensive Report."

10. Brzozowski, Taylor-Butts, and Johnson, "Victimization and Offending," 5.

11. Brzozowski, Taylor-Butts, and Johnson, "Victimization and Offending," 5.

12. Brzozowski, Taylor-Butts, and Johnson, "Victimization and Offending," 6.

13. Shannon Brennan, "Violent Victimization of Aboriginal Women in the Canadian Provinces, 2009," *Juristat*, Statistics Canada cat. no. 85-002-X, May 17, 2011, 5, http://www.statcan.gc.ca/pub/85-002-x/2011001/ article/11439-eng.htm#a4.

14. Brennan, "Violent Victimization," 7.

15. Katie Scrim, "Aboriginal Victimization in Canada: A Summary of the Literature," Department of Justice, *Victims of Crimes Research Digest*, no. 3, accessed December 13, 2015, http://www.justice.gc.ca/eng/rp-pr/ cj-jp/victim/rd3-rr3/p3.html.

16. Brennan, "Violent Victimization," 5.

17. Ontario Native Women's Association/Ontario Federation of Indian Friendship Centres (ONWA/OFIFC), "A Strategic Framework to End Violence against Aboriginal Women," September 2007, 3, http://www.oaith.ca/assets/files/Publications/Strategic_Framework_Aboriginal_Women.pdf.

18. ONWA/OFIFC, "Strategic Framework," 3.

19. Brzozowski, Taylor-Butts, and Johnson, "Victimization and Offending," 1.

20. Brzozowski, Taylor-Butts, and Johnson, "Victimization and Offending," 6.

21. Robert Alexander Innes, "Moose of the Loose: Indigenous Men, Violence, and the Colonial Excuse," *Aboriginal Policy Studies* 4, no. 1 (2015): 3.

22. For further discussion on this topic from a number of authors, see Robert Alexander Innes and Kim Anderson, eds., *Indigenous Men and Masculinities: Legacies, Identities, Regeneration* (Winnipeg: University of Manitoba Press, 2015).

23. Michael Bopp, Judie Bopp, and Phil Lane Jr., *Aboriginal Domestic Violence in Canada*, prepared for the Aboriginal Healing Foundation (Cochrane, AB: Four Worlds Centre for Development Learning, 2003), 53–54.

24. Kathryn Blaze Carlson, "AFN Chief Urges Native Men to Help Protect Women," *Globe and Mail*, February 2, 2015, http://www.theglobeandmail.com/news/national/aboriginal-leader-urges-nativemen-to-help-protect-women-in-community/article22755092/.

25. Anonymous participant quoted in Sasha Skye, "A Conversation with Crazy Indians," in *Indigenous Men and Masculinities: Legacies, Identities, Regeneration*, ed. Robert Alexander Innes and Kim Anderson (Winnipeg: University of Manitoba Press, 2015), 268.

26. Skye, "A Conversation with Crazy Indians," 269.

27. Charles Hamilton, "Domestic Abuser Hopes to Spur Change," *Saskatoon StarPhoenix*, September 14, 2015, http://thestarphoenix.com/news/domestic-abuser-hopes-to-spur-change.

28. Hamilton, "Domestic Abuser."

29. Hamilton, "Domestic Abuser."

30. "Former Saskatoon Gang Member Walking to End Domestic Violence: Chris Moyah's Turning Point Came Last Year When He Was Invited to a Ceremony by an Elder," *CBC News*, August 18, 2015, http://www.cbc.ca/news/canada/saskatoon/former-saskatoon-gang-member-walking-to-end-domestic-violence-1.3195564.

31. See the Kizhaay Anishinaabe Niin—I Am a Kind Man website, http://www.iamakindman.ca.

32. Quotes from Michael White are from a personal interview with Kim Anderson, February 3, 2016.

33. "Former Saskatoon Gang Member," CBC News.

34. Joanna Smith, "Moose Hide Campaign Helps Men Address Violence against Aboriginal Women," *Toronto Star*, December 31, 2014, http://www.thestar.com/news/canada/2014/12/31/moose_hide_campaign_helps_men_address_violence_against_aboriginal_women.html.

35. BC Association of Aboriginal Friendship Centres, "Moose Hide Campaign Annual Gathering of Men: Standing Together to End Violence towards Aboriginal Women and Children," *Marketwired*, February 6, 2015, http://www.marketwired.com/press-release/moose-hide-campaign-annual-gathering-of-men-1989619.htm.

36. Smith, "Moose Hide Campaign."

37. Rachel Flowers, "Refusal to Forgive: Indigenous Women's Love and Rage," *Decolonization: Indigeneity, Education & Society* 4, no. 2 (2015): 43–44.

12 | *Considering Wenonah, Considering Us*

WAASEYAA'SIN CHRISTINE SY

Thinking about Ishkode (Fire)

In the context of an Indigenous-inspired movement that persistently addresses violence against Indigenous peoples across Turtle Island, the subject of missing and murdered women is at the forefront of grassroots activism, Indigenous women's research, human rights advocacy, political debate, and social media trends. Within this work, the caption *Missing and Murdered Indigenous Women*, with its associated hashtag #MMIW, is most visible in social media and news. This hashtag has evolved to include two-spirit peoples and girls (#MMIW2SG). Sexual violence against Indigenous women is only latently constructed as connected to the physically violent acts of absencing and murder, despite it being a significant aspect of them. For a brief time, news and research about women in the sex trade was popularized in the form of #MMITW (Missing, Murdered, and Traded Women), yet this acknowledgement of sexual violence as part and parcel of the various forms of violence that make Indigenous females go missing and murdered has since been elided from the popular discourse of #MMIW.[1]

I'm not clear why this elision has occurred. I am clear, though, that the final acts of making a woman go missing or murdered are neither isolated from patterns of violence that lead up to the final act of violence, nor are they spontaneous. As various sources note, women are more likely to experience violence at the hands of people known to them than from strangers. We can suppose, then, that much of the violence we are focused on today—the missing and murdered—is pre-empted by a range of violences that include but are not limited to sexual violence. These acts are the end result of a series of dynamics that infringe on an Indigenous woman's physical life and her well-being. They violate the spiritual assent given for her entry into, and presence in, this physical world. Anishinaabeg philosophy and ontology teaches us that we are first spirit, who, with assent from the spiritual world, enter into the physical realm as a gift to those who bring us here (i.e., our parents).[2]

I advocate attending to a broader range of violence beyond those acts that make a woman missing or dead because women navigate a spectrum of behaviours that are detrimental to our well-being prior to such final acts.[3] In addition to intimate, casual, or random predatory exchanges with others, Indigenous women are immersed in a colonial world that is inherently violent. In this world, we wake up to the structured violence of colonialism that is actualized through human behaviour and attitudes everyday. Where Indigenous peoples are displaced from land and lifeways by violent means generally, a kaleidoscope of intersections including, but not limited to, our Indigeneity and gender further shape our experiences.[4] We need to recognize the everyday violence of colonialism as it occurs throughout all the relationships that women navigate with both non-Indigenous and Indigenous peoples in order to intervene, disrupt, and transform it.

There are many precursors and factors that contribute to the spectrum of colonial and lateral violences. While some are shared by all women, some are specific to Indigenous women. For instance, for Indigenous women, sexual violence can be linked to colonialism.[5] Within the frame of colonialism, Sarah Carter, Janice Acoose, Janice Forsythe, and Kim Anderson have elucidated how settler constructions and portrayals of Indigenous women have contributed to men committing sexual violence against Indigenous women.[6] Others link this violence to the objectification of Indigenous women or the view that Indigenous women are "inherently violable."[7] While acknowledging that it may be considered a form of colonialism, Ruanna Kuokkanen argues that modern globalization creates intensified conditions of racialized and sexualized violence against Indigenous women in Canada and the United States.[8] Within the micro-dynamics of sexual violence, denial of sexual access to our bodies, resistance to sexual advances, or contestation of assault may be precursors to going missing or being murdered. Further, a sense of entitlement to sex and poor ego strength or unwillingness to accept boundaries or hear "no" all contribute to sexual violence against Indigenous women. Misogynistic against all women, these behaviours, beliefs, and attitudes are popularly understood as a rape culture.

The phrase "rape culture" emerged in the 1970s in academic publications and film.[9] Although the meaning of rape culture has shifted across contexts and generations, it generally refers to a culture "that excuses or otherwise tolerate(s) sexual violence."[10] Further, a rape culture can be observed, experienced, or perpetuated in countless ways and exists "where sexual assault, rape and general violence are ignored, trivialized, normalized, or made into jokes."[11] In her monograph on US federal and American Indian law, legal procedures, and ineffectiveness in dealing with rape committed against Indigenous women, Sarah Deer signifies rape as different from what is portrayed in Hollywood, as discernable from domestic violence, as decentred in legal discourse by terms such as "sexual assault," and as a phenomenon instigated by socio-political contexts.[12] For Deer, rape "encompass[es] a constellation of crimes that involves the abuse of sexual power, including child sexual abuse and adult rape, one-time incidents and ongoing abuse, even when not overtly physically violent."[13]

Considering these broader analyses of rape as an act of coloniality, globalization, and North American culture, I focus on how sexual violence occurs against Anishinaabeg women within the Anishinaabeg Nation vis-à-vis Anishinaabeg traditional narrative. My intent in shifting from a generalized discussion of Indigenous women to a more nation-specific focus comes from my desire to contribute to the restoration and regeneration of Anishinaabeg relationalities beyond settler colonial hierarchies of value and domination such as those shaped by patriarchy, heteropatriachy, and capitalism. In particular, I'm interested in gendered relationalities that are based on shared, reciprocal, and/ or complementary power, and relationalities that are supported by broader Indigenous systems. These systems would allow violations of power to be mediated towards restitution/resolution of harms created and restoration of balance in relationship. More foundationally, I wish to contribute to eliminating the practice of seeing and constructing Indigenous women and girls as sexual objects, and as beings from whom all things can be taken—and taken without consequence—including sexual, physical, and spiritual dignity. In focusing on violence against Indigenous women and girls as it exists in Anishinaabe narratives, my intent is to highlight the power and possibility of culture, cultural transmission, and cultural reproduction in perpetuating the very phenomenon Indigenous peoples are presently trying to eradicate. Story provides distance in addressing a difficult, if not triggering, subject that impacts all of us in and beyond our Anishinaabe relationships and communities.[14] The distance a story provides allows breathing room; it allows air to circulate and this is a necessity in making a life-nourishing fire.

Preparing to Make Ishkode
Gathering Tobacco, Birchbark, Wood

For a few years while I lived in Nogojiwanong Peterborough, Ontario, which is a city in Michi Saagiig territory, my daughter and

I attended an Anishinaabe language nest funded and housed in part through space and faculty from the Indigenous Studies program at Trent University. Later, when a co-director of the nest needed to step away, I was invited to co-direct and did so. Language lessons and content were contributed by one main language teacher and various other Indigenous artists, cultural knowers, and language speakers. My co-director and I consulted an Elder on curriculum development. He also occasionally attended the program to teach and guide us in various aspects of Anishinaabe'aadiziwin (culture). During one of our nests, he taught us how to make a sacred fire.[15] Those lessons have stayed with me and my daughter, and we always talk about them when we make our own fire. I think about how to make a fire as I write this chapter—the care and systemic way of doing so, the metaphorical meanings attached to its making, and the need to acknowledge and thank spirit in the making of a fire.

I was first introduced to this person in 2006 by a fellow graduate student, but I had little interaction with him before 2009. I first met him when he was co-teaching a course called Indigenous Knowledges with Dr. Mark Dockstator at Trent University. During the course, my colleagues and I were encouraged to consider what "Indigenous knowledges" meant to us and to identify what we wanted to learn about the topic. I wanted to learn how to snare rabbits, fish, etc. because I was interested in learning about Anishinaabeg subsistence. This Elder had much knowledge about such things, access to land, and the materials needed to facilitate learning. Since then, he has become a significant influence in my life in terms of helping me to learn more deeply and broadly about anishinaabewiziwin—"the elements that make up the Anishinaabe way."[16] One of these elements is Anishinaabe origins, which I learned more about through the stories he told in the community—stories I had the occasion to hear repeatedly in different contexts. Anishinaabeg call these gaawizimaawjisemag—creation and origin stories.[17] One of these stories was about Wenonah—the first breastfeeder, the perpetual nurturer. In all versions that

I've heard or read, Wenonah is constructed as a significant forebearer of the Anishinaabeg in that she birthed four children who became significant in shaping Anishinaabeg ways of being. During one telling—to a group of adults of which I was part—the story included a version of Wenonah's impregnation by a spirit, typically cast as masculine, that implied lack of consent. Some interpret versions of this impregnation as rape. Until I heard this interpretation at that particular telling, I had never considered this story through the lens of rape. Even in my earlier learning of this story in Basil Johnston-ba's *The Manitous: Spiritual World of the Ojibway*, I had not tracked on this theme.[18] The fact is, I had not considered Wenonah's impregnation at all; in all my experiences of the story, it was always the story of her children—her sons— that was emphasized. More specifically, it's Wenonah's fourth son, Waynaboozhoo, who figures greatly in the story of Wenonah and who today is constructed as somewhat of an Anishinaabe celebrity. However, once I considered her impregnation, it became clear that sometimes it was cast as a rape or as sexual violence—even if only implicitly—and I couldn't *not consider* it anymore. I couldn't stop considering how one of our forebears, in some versions of the story, was raped; how Anishinaabe early beginning, in some versions, is based on sexual violence.[19] I couldn't stop thinking about how I had not realized this—someone who, despite lived experienced of sexual violence including rape, formal education, theoretical analyses and praxis, professional experience, and community-based work in anti-violence and sexual violence against women, didn't see this aspect of the narrative. I was disturbed by the naturalization and normalization of sexual violence against Anishinaabe woman—ikawe—one whose body changes or has the ability to change—even within my own consciousness and engagement with our cultural productions.[20]

Through a series of unconnected conversations about Wenonah's story, prompted by fellow Anishinaabeg, I've learned that versions of the story that contain sexual violence raise concerns. For me, the fact that we learn this story in ceremonial contexts or cultural milieus raises additional concerns, and begs a number of questions: How are personal boundaries with Elders or teachers negotiated when versions of this narrative convey sexual violence? Can people leave such spaces without being perceived as disruptive or disrespectful, perceptions that could have consequences in future community relationships and settings? Can these stories be questioned? The emergent pattern of concern, as well as the reflections on the social context this story was being told in, motivate me to attend to the ways gendered sexual violence against Indigenous women and girls exists in some versions of one of our Anishinaabe origin stories. My purpose is not to blame or shame. Every Anishinaabe Elder, ceremonialist, or cultural thinker I know contributes significantly to the persistence of Anishinaabeg thought, values, and practices in a world dominated by non-Anishinaabeg beliefs and false ideas about Anishinaabeg. Most Anishinaabeg I know who teach cultural knowledges do so from within a network of respected and/or recognized network of kinship ties or relationalities. That is to say, they are not transmitting knowledges or interpretations into the world that are disconnected from a deeper web of Anishinaabe ontological, epistemological, and axiological orientations and interests. Wenonah's story, and all its versions, is a community story—it comes from community and therefore the story's reproduction within Anishinaabeg community is shared responsibility between storyteller and audience.

As stated earlier, I did not consciously track on the sexual violence being reproduced in some versions of Wenonah's story, despite my orientation towards reading, critiquing, and developing praxis in anti-violence towards women. This prompts me to consider the power and possibility of our cultural narratives to transmit ideas about who we are without us being conscious of it. It suggests that how we see the world is deeply influenced in subconscious ways. For this reason, we must be open to learning about ourselves and the possibilities for our cultural persistence and regeneration through dialogue with others. It is only through dialogue with others that the theme of sexual violence became evident to me. This said, I do wonder about the purpose and effect of telling such narratives. Perhaps they are told to subdue or socialize certain groups about how to be. The effect of a rape narrative where said rape happens at the hands of a man or a masculine spirit against a woman may support the normalization or naturalization of violence against women, male domination, or in particular, male violence against females. It may also socialize women to expect and accept being violated as a part of nation building and not to expect justice, care, or support. My purpose here is to recognize the impulse of diverse community voices, speaking from their own distinct locations and experiences, that raised concerns about the fact that some versions of Wenonah's story include a rape narrative. My hope is that we can begin to engage it critically in a manner that supports each other to grow our relationships in ways that do not diminish anybody, or at least inculcate practices of competent care that come into play when systems of domination to manifest. In preparing to address this subject, I spoke with the man who taught me and my daughter how to make a sacred fire about the questions and concerns that exist regarding the element of sexual violence in some versions of the Wenonah narrative. He indicated that our conversation made him stop and think about this situation. He said it's important for storytellers to consider the context they are telling their stories in, particularly to consider what in society is shaping how they tell the story. He also indicated that he thought these kinds of stories and subjects need to be discussed more often.[21]

Wenonah's story, according to the version documented in Basil Johnston-ba's *The Manitous*, is actually rendered as a story about four sons—Maudjee-kawiss, Pukawiss, Cheeby-aub-oozhoo, and Nana'b'oozoo.[22] That is, Wenonah's story is embedded marginally within the stories of her boys, which in turn tells of the early ancestral foundations of the Anishinaabeg. Wenonah, who is referred to as a girl (not a woman), figures sporadically in their story. Although she is primarily cast as daughter, bearer of children, mother, object of sexual gratification and retribution, in Johnston's version we do know her briefly as a young and independent girl out in the world—on the land—on her own. During this time of independence, she does something quite out of practical, physical need—she relieves her bladder—and she ends up being "taken" or "ravished" by Ae-pungishimook—the spirit of the west—who is cast as both spirit and father, and therefore male and man: " When Ae-pungishimook saw Winonah's little moss-covered cleft, the coals of lust glowed in his loins, and without prolonged foreplay or the recitation of sweet nothings, he cast his loincloth aside and humped the girl then and there. When his fire had petered out, Ae-pungishimook put his loinclothe back on and staggered away, leaving poor Winonah to manage for herself to face the future alone."[23]

Wenonah becomes pregnant and Ae-pungishimook impreg-nates her three more times, presumably in the same way. She bears four sons in total. In this story, it is suggested that Wenonah is treated as a sexual object within a broader relationality of mistreat-ment by Ae-pungishimook, who ultimately kills her shortly after Nana'boo'zoo, their last son, is born.[24] Growing up with his maternal grandmother, Nokomis, Nana'boo'zoo spends his youth trying to uncover the mystery of what happened to his mother. Nokomis evades the story until he is older. Upon learning about the details of his mother's death, he sets out to seek revenge upon his father, Ae-pungishimook. The two battle, and not being able to outdo each other, the Peace Pipe is bestowed upon them as a way to resolve the conflict.

I retell the story here with a focus on Wenonah, but this summary is distilled from four stories (i.e., chapters) that focus on her sons. Audiences are taught that many Anishinaabeg traditions, practices, and orientations emerge from these four males, and a sense of pride for the gifts these sons give to Anishinaabeg infuses these stories. In my experience of it—both textually and orally—Wenonah's abuse is overlooked for the story of her sons. In considering Wenonah and how her life is told, or not told, orally

and in text, I want to consider us. I want to consider us as we tell
and retell this narrative and as we receive it, as we uphold it as a
source of knowledge about who we are and our history, and as we
embark on its telling as a cultural process of reclamation, persistence, and revitalization. I want us to consider what we are doing
in retelling this narrative and why we are doing it, to think critically about the present context of gendered violence against
Indigenous peoples in which it is being told—woman as victim,
man as savage, and all people who transcend the settler heteronormative gender binary as invisible—and ask ourselves if this
story is helpful. And if it is helpful, to whom? To what end is it
helpful? At the very least, I want us to consider the impacts of
telling this story on audiences. I want us to consider that it's
harmful and consider if we are engaging in a balancing act between
its helpfulness and its harmfulness (i.e., Western ethics). Must the
burden of sexual violence and erasure be borne by girls and women
for the glory of Anishinaabeg as a whole? Must the burden of
brutish, irresponsible, uncontrollably driven, and dehumanizing
decisions veiled and distorted into natural, normal male inclinations be borne by the masculine spirit? Must our extended family
members carry the burden of these dynamics? Our children, the
burden of reconciling parental violence? Must they carry the grief
and loss that ensues from gendered violence? Are violence and
revenge the only methods for our sons to cope with grief and loss?
And what about extended family members and loved ones who
suffer loss due to violence against girls and women as well? And
those who suffer loss when the boys and men they love engage in
violence? Why is Nana'boo'zoo's anger given so much space and
legitimacy but not his mother's? Why is peace between the father
and son worthy of a Peace Pipe but the violence between a male spirit
and a woman not even addressed? Is there another way to tell this
story that does not dehumanize Anishinaabeg girl or woman and
the male spirit? These are just some of the questions that formulate
the premise of this chapter. More deeply and importantly, though,

is the pull and tugging I feel in my belly and heart. I have a need that is stronger than the need for answers to all these questions.

I want to pause and move away from considering us.

I want to pause and consider Wenonah.

I want to talk to her.

Making Ishkode, A Friend

I want to pull on my sugar-bush-stained jeans, throw on a hoodie and hikers, get in my vehicle, and drive to the private property on the rez where I know I can make a fire. I want to go to that place where I don't have to ask permission to make fire, where I'm not afraid to be admonished for making fire. A place where I don't have to apply and pay for a permit ten days in advance of wanting to make a fire, or have a safety certificate indicating I've been trained to do so. This is a place where I can self-determine what makes me feel connected to my body, the spirits, and the land. I want to be in a place where I can experience the kind of community, autonomy, self-determination, and freedom that I imagine millions of Anishinaabeg women ancestors enjoyed for thousands of years: making a fire of their own accord to handle their business.

I want to drive to the sugar bush where trees reach up to anangwan (the star world) and gather mashkiki (medicine) in their roots. See the glow of setting sun through changing and falling leaves: red, orange, yellow; aflame and glowing. This is the place where woman is safe.[25] I want to drive here, pull up, get out, walk around, find the hatchet and make some kindling, shaving the sides with my pocketknife so it'll catch easier, just like that teacher showed me. I want to make several frustrating trips back to daaban to get the mokijiwaniibiish (spring water), mashkodewaashk (sage), lighter. Go back again and pull out the wiigwaas (birchbark) buried with the tire iron and jack and grab the wiingaashk (sweet-grass) from the dashboard. Feel for my asemaa-mashkimodens (tobacco pouch) and get sheshegwan (the shaker). I want all these ones with me.

I want to make fire, put my asemaa (tobacco) down and start with the wiigwaas, anticipating the sound: crackling, sparking, doing what it does for Anishinaabeg. I want to whisper all the steps as I go around building it up and then lighting it, just so I don't forget. I think of the Bodaawedomi women—the Nation whose people keep the fire. I say, "eya" and "amiigawech." I think of the time I kept fire for the men while they went into the lodge for their own healing. I think of their words and gifts to my girl and me as I make this fire now. I say, "eya" and "amiigawech." I crouch, feeling the pull of these old jeans and stretch of toes and babble all the baby-talk Anishinaabemowin words I can to make a prayer. I offer nibi (water). I sing to manidooyag (the spirits), letting them know that I want to move with caution and care as I enter this space.

I want to talk to Wenonah.

I want to do all this in preparation to be with her because a fire is a relative, a friend, a spirit. Ishkode, asemaa, nibi—they all facilitate talking with manidooyag.

I want to but I can't.

| I'm here in an apartment. The kind where the neighbours probably think I'm smoking pot on the daily. Or crystal banging with nidaawe'igan (my drum). I'm away from the places I know where I can go make a fire or where I know the people have land and don't mind if I go there for a little ceremony. It's bizarre how being the descendant of a woman who made this island with support from all of her helpers and a little bit of dirt that I, like so many of us, am without even a little bit of land where I can make a fire so I can talk with my ancestor.

Instead of licking wounds, I go outside, put my asemaa down discreetly beneath the big blue spruce tree at the end of the paved walkway that cuts straight through manicured lawns. I do that and then come back inside never bothering to look to see if a neighbour is watching. I light a candle, smudge, sing a song, and sit towards waabanong (the east).

I want to talk to Wenonah.

I can.

I do.

With Ishkode

Waynaboozhoo Wenonah

Wenonah, waynaboozhoo. makwa n'dodem. name igaye wabidi
n'denawemag. waaseyaa'sin n'dizhnikaaz. baagting n'donjibaa
amiinawaa obiskikaang n'donjibaa. lekwugenwaki migwe n'dodaa.
ndaanis nozhemenhs zhinkaazaa.

Wenonah, amiigawech gaa amiizhyaang. Thank you for everything you've given us. I've said all the words to all the directions
and beings and I've introduced myself in the ways I've been taught.
I've used the language I know the best I can—baby-talk Anishinaabe,
I know. I think of you all the time and wonder about your life.
Skywoman, too. I'm here with this ishkode, my asemaa, and a song
because I want to talk to you about gaawizimaawjisemag. It's a
story about the people of your day but it's also about you and your
life. Actually, the way it's often told, it's more a story about your
sons—Maudjee-kawiss, Pukawiss, Cheeby-aub-oozhoo, and
Nana'boo'zoo—than it is about you. For me, overlooking your life
for the lives of beings constructed as male, even if they are your
children, is part of the problem. I don't know what life was like in
your day, but today we're living in a time when Indigenous peoples
are dealing with huge pressures because other groups of people
want the land and waters we've called home for thousands of years.

The pressures we've been navigating have been ongoing for
a few hundred years. We've been impacted in different ways
based on if we are women, two-spirited or queer people, or men.
Essentially, we've all had something taken from us or put upon
us against our will. There has been and continues to be so much
suffering amongst us in our territory and homes. And yet, in the
distortion of this new, contested, and unsettled order of things, we
can still discern how this violence from a foreign way has impacted
us differently.

Two-spirited people and queer people have been essentially erased from the oral and written record as part of society, constructing a world animated by only men and women. This new falsehood has created a world where only niniwag (men) and ikawewag (women) exist; where only sexual relations occur between niniwag and ikawewag; where families are only built by the pairing of these two groups of people; and where niniwag are literally placed above, inscribed with more power, and are valued more than ikawewag such that life is organized and regenerated according to their wants, visions, dreams, and needs.

I know. Many of us think it's bizarre, including some men. Those men are the ones who recognize that the few privileges they are attributed in this new and contested world come at a much higher cost to their own well-being, their relationships with each other, with women, queer people and with two-spirited people, the spirits, and the land. Through all the convolutions of these difficulties, though, it is the story about you that I want to talk about *with you*.

This gaawizimawjise tells us who we are, where we come from, and who our early people are—and that you are one of our early people. The occurrences in our history over the last few hundred years have destroyed so much of what we know about ourselves that today gaawizimawjisemagag have become vital to our well-being in a way that is not likely the same prior to our lives being dominated by another group. While these stories are vital, it's very possible that the gaawizimawjisemagag we do know about have become distorted, pulled out of a larger context informed through additional stories. Still, we're grateful to have the ones that have persisted and to have people to keep them alive and share them with us. We're grateful that we no longer have to be afraid to share them or to do so in ceremonial settings. In this way, it's difficult to have a problem with any of our stories. None of us wants to question a lifeline that has made it through periods of persecution. None of us wants to be criticized or considered a traitor for doing so either. But the world we're living in today compels me to at least want to talk to you about this story.

Only you and those involved in your story know the truth, but I will talk anyways and hope to find resolution.

The story tells us that you and your sons, your mom, and Epingishmok are significant beings in the early creation, sustenance, and proliferation of Anishinaabeg life. The story also tells us how the conception of your first son with Epingishmok was without your consent. You were angry with Epingshmok for raping you and hoped to never see him again. You were also abandoned by Epingishmok after the fact, and later, when it became apparent you were pregnant, you were shamed and blamed by your mother. Epingishmok returned after the birth of your baby and took part in the child rearing, emphasizing and celebrating all that Maadjiikawiss was because it fit Epingishmok's idea of masculinity. You had three more children with this male spirit and, while the conception of these children are not discussed in detail, it seems that they were also conceived without your consent. The story sounds like you were in an abusive relationship. It implies that you died a violent death at the hands of Epingishmok after the birth of your fourth child, Waynaboozhoo. These days he is mostly known as Nanaboozhoo or Nanabush for short. He is also revered and some question if he is really a he or if he is a she. Some say, your last-born can shapeshift.

Wenonah, it makes me nishkadizi (angry) that you were raped. And that you were treated this way over the course of years. I'm angry that in the story, there is no evidence that you resisted, that you fought back, that you protested. The story erases your entire agency in this experience in order to tell the story of your sons.

It makes me angry that neither your mother nor any other person or being in your world did anything about this; they did nothing in response to the first rape and they did nothing to ensure it would not happen again. In this state, nobody nurtured you in your pain. It makes me angry that you were alone in this and that you were blamed by an Elder woman, a family member.

At least this is how I interpret the story through the sources I have learned it.

If all this violence, silencing, and erasure are true, it makes me sad for you. It makes me concerned for what it suggests life was like in the past for women in our community. This story echoes strongly with what life is like for many Indigenous women today. This alarms me and raises my curiosity. What does it means that one of our origin stories exemplifies the rape culture we live in today? It saddens me to think our Nation may have been complicit in very early forms of violence against women and complicit in very early forms of male brutality and entitlements. I find it confounding that silence in the face of injustice against Indigenous women and silence in the face of male brutality existed back then as well.

So many women are being killed, enduring sexual violence, and being made to go missing today, Wenonah. So many. The sacred humanity of so many Indigenous women and girls is being twisted into objects. If not this, then women's lives and voices are over-looked, diminished, or marginalized. For those women and girls who do find space and relationships that support them as full human beings, we still have to negotiate living in a misogynist society. We are constantly at risk of coming up against negative attitudes towards us. Ikawe (woman) or ishkinii'ikawe (new woman, young woman) as full autonomous, sacred, powerful beings capable of making life are not seen or treated this way by the majority. I wonder if you were ever seen as first and foremost a sacred autonomous being unto yourself and the land before being unto other human beings. Or was your worth always relegated to how you might serve others?

It makes me nauseous that you were made to go missing and murdered, and that your youngest son had to spend so much of his young life dealing with your absence, his loss, and trying to make sense of it. He battled his father to avenge you and your violent death. Is this the legacy Anishinaabeg are supposed to leave our children?

We know hardly anything about you other than these violations and the great sons you birthed. I wonder what you want us to know about your life. What do you want us to know about this story as it is told today? Not knowing what to believe, my asemaa goes into the fire for you regardless of how close or how far away this story is from debwe (truth). It goes into the fire because no matter how close or far away the story is from debwe, it is told as a narrative of violence and erasure against you, and these violations are never attended to in the story with you, only through your son. We need to figure out how we will deal with Epingishmok in our stories, prayers, and ceremonies. We need to figure out how to honour you in our stories, prayers, and ceremonies.

It's getting heavy in here. Let me burn some sage and sing a song to clear the air.

| What if it's not true? What if there was mutual love? Mutual curiosity, interest, or attraction? What if there was just physical, chemical, energetic attraction? Just this between you both and from this your first child was conceived? What about these possible truths? How does this change the course of our history, our present, our future? I want to just spend some time sitting here with you thinking about those possibilities.

| In thinking about all the circles of this story and all the implications for you and for us, your youngest boy comes to mind. The one you never knew. Waynaboozhoo. While many of us have forgotten him, there are many who have worked hard to keep him alive because, as the story goes, he is our greatest teacher. I can't help but wonder if he isn't here with us now operating in some way through this story and through this engagement with it. I wonder what he would think about us having a ceremony for you, about us avenging the violence you endured by acknowledging it and even doing something about it by changing the story.

Yes, I'm sure your son is up to something here.

I have no answers, Wenonah. I do know that since I've started to seriously consider you and us, I pray in a different way. I always include you, your mother, and Giizhigo'ikawe (Sky Woman) in my prayers now. In praying to Epingishmok, I hesitate and allow myself to ponder the possibility of complicated, complex spirits that may have done or do harm. I ask myself if I am supposed to learn to acknowledge dualities: the sacred and the unsacred. What if Epingishmok is both sacred and sick? How are we to deal with this? Do we come out of this unscathed or do we come out with learning how to live with history? Or is this a story for the future? If so, what do we want our descendants to know about how to live well with each other?

In this way, with these hesitant, pondering questions, I cere-mony you. In this way, I ceremony our history and our present and wonder how we are supposed to live into the future with this story. What legacy do we generate for you? Without knowing your truth or the truth of this story, I hold all of the possibilities—those known and not yet known—and I put them in the fire and ceremony you. Nahaaw, mii sa iw. Apidjii nendam, Wenonah. Chi amiigawech gaa miizhyaang. G'zaagin.

Coming Away

It's evening now and the sun has set. Twilight and birds animate the parking lot beyond my window. I recall the kaleidoscope of skies in all the places over the years that I've sat or stood by the fire in ceremony or in camaraderie, all the seasons. I think of all the violence I have witnessed, experienced, or generated with my own words, tone, energy, and actions; stories that have been shared; and resistances that have raged or simmered, constant and slow. I think of all the loving, impassioned, fierce and strategic political, social, and spiritual work that is being done across Turtle Island to stop violence against women and girls. I whisper to this little candle, *let us restore ourselves to ourselves. Let ikawewag be fully recognized again and let there be no fear in recognizing ikawewag again.* I sing a song of thanks, and this time I've had to consider Wenonah and to consider us. I take a drink of mokijiwaniibiish, say my departures to this little ishkode, and go outside to be a part of the life out there, knowing an ember is glowing warmly.

NOTES

1. Nina Koebel, "Domestic Sex Trafficking and Exploitation of Aboriginal Women and Girls: Exploring the Legacy of Colonialism in Canada," (major research paper, University of Ottawa, Graduate School of Public and International Affairs, 2014), www.academia.edu/6922750/ Domestic_Sex_Trafficking_and_Exploitation_of_Aboriginal_Women_ and_Girls_Exploring_the_legacy_of _colonialism_in_Canada; Native Women's Association, *Sexual Exploitation and Trafficking of Aboriginal Women and Girls: Literature Review and Key Informant Interviews*, March 2014, http://canadianwomen.org/sites/canadianwomen.org/files/ NWAC%20Sex%20Trafficking%20Literature%20Review_2.pdf; Sarah Hunt and Julie Kay, "Human Trafficking Research Reveals Canada's Role in Violence Against Aboriginal Women," *Rabble*, September 24, 2014, http://rabble.ca/news/2014/09/human-trafficking-research-reveals-canadas-role-violence-against-aboriginal-women.

2. When the spirit enters woman's physical body, this is called "the quickening" and refers to a particular feeling she experiences in her womb early in pregnancy. James Dumont, personal communication, 1995.

3. The RCMP's 2014 *Missing and Murdered Aboriginal Women* notes a number of offender motives in killing Indigenous women, including argument or quarrel (40%); frustration, anger, or despair (20%); jealousy (12%); sexual violence (10%); no apparent motive (7%); financial gain, settling accounts (6%); and, other (5%). RCMP, *Missing and Murdered Aboriginal Women: A National Operational Overview* Ottawa: Government of Canada, 2014), 14, http://www.rcmp-grc.gc.ca/pubs/ mmaw-faapd-eng.htm.

4. For intersectional analysis, see Kimberlé Crenshaw, "Mapping the Margins: Intersectionality, Identity Politics, and Violence Against Women of Colour," *Stanford Law Review* 43, no. 6 (1991): 1241–99.

5. Andrea Smith, *Conquest: Sexual Violence and American Indian Genocide* (Cambridge, MA: South End Press, 2005); Sarah Deer, "Introduction: Sovereignty of the Soul," in *The Beginning and the End of Rape:*

Confronting Sexual Violence in Native American (Wisconsin: University of Minnesota Press, 2015): x, xiv–xix.

6. Sarah Carter, "Categories and Terrains of Exclusion: Constructing the 'Indian Woman' in the Early Settlement Era in Western Canada," *Great Plains Quarterly* 13, no. 3 (1993): 147–61; Janice Acoose Misko-Kìsikàwihkwè (Red Sky Woman), *Iskwewak Kah'Ki Yaw Ni Wahkomakanak: Neither Indian Princesses nor Easy Squaws* (Toronto: Women's Press, 1995); Janice Forsyth, "After the Fur Trade: First Nations Women in Canadian History, 1850–1950," *Atlantis* 29, no. 2 (2005): 70–71; Kim Anderson, "The Construction of a Negative Identity," in *A Recognition of Being: Reconstructing Native Womanhood,* 2nd ed. (Toronto: Women's Press, 2016), 79–94.

7. Hillary Weaver, "The Colonial Context of Violence: Reflections on Violence in the Lives of Native American Women," *Journal of Interpersonal Violence* 24, no. 9 (2009): 1558, qtd. in Anderson, *A Recognition of Being*, 78; Smith, *Conquest*, 12, 30.

8. Ruanna Kuokkanen, "Globalization as Racialized, Sexualized Violence: The Case of Indigenous Women," *International Feminist Journal of Politics* 10, no. 2 (2008): 216–33.

9. Carrie A. Rentschler, "Rape Culture and the Feminist Politics of Social Media," *Girlhood Studies* 7, no. 1 (2014): 66–67.

10. Shannon Ridgway, "25 Everyday Examples of Rape Culture," *Everyday Feminism* (blog), March 10, 2014, http://everydayfeminism. com/2014/03/examples-of-rape-culture/; Rentschler, "Rape Culture," 67.

11. Ridgway, "25 Everyday Examples."

12. Deer, *The Beginning and End of Rape*, xvii–xix.

13. Deer, *The Beginning and End of Rape*, xix.

14. For Anishinaabeg, story is a sophisticated epistemology. For an edited collection of essays that conveys this, see Jill Doefler, Heidi Kiiwetinepinesiik Stark, and Niiganwewidam James Sinclair, eds., *Centering Anishinaabeg Studies: Understanding the World through Story* (Lansing: Michigan State University, 2013).

15. An earlier representation of this person was approved via phone in 2015. After changes to the chapter, I requested final approval of the revised chapter via email. Unfortunately, as the book went to press, this person had not responded and, therefore, I removed his name.

16. Helen Agger, *Following Nimishoomis: The Trout Lake History of Dedibaayaanimanook Sarah Keesick Olsen* (Penticton, BC: Theytus Books, 2008), 286.

17. The word used here, "gaawizimaawjisemag," is originally spelled as gah-wi-zi-maw-ji-say-muh-guhk in makwa ogimaa (Jerome Fontaine), "ga-mi-ni-go-wi-ni-nan o-gi-ma-wi-win zhigo o-gi-ma-win" (The gifts of traditional leadership and governance) (PHD diss., Trent University, Peterborough, ON, 2013), ii–iii.

18. Basil Johnston, *The Manitous: The Spiritual World of the Ojibway* (Saint Paul: Minnesota Historical Society Press, 2001), 17–60, 247. The suffix "-ba" indicates that the person has passed away.

19. With this new lens, I read more closely for how Wenonah's impregnation is constructed in versions of her story. During the time of writing, I learned of two other versions of this origin story. As a part of a permanent exhibit, it is told in a gentle way where there is no violence portrayed against Wenonah. See Ziibiwing Center of Anishinabe Culture and Lifeways, "Diba Jimooyung: Telling Our Story," http://www.sagchip.org/ziibiwing/exhibits/permanentexhibit.htm. The other source is a story cited as being from Lac Du Flambeau Reservation (Wisconsin, US). In this version, Wenonah is impregnated by a wind that moves up beneath her skirt. While violence is neither implicitly nor explicitly constructed in this story, Wenonah does have a lack of agency or consent and is, in fact, helpless to prevent the wind from moving up her skirt when she tries. That said, I am not sure if or how these concepts of agency or consent apply to Anishinaabeg relationship with the natural world. In Anishinaabeg philosophy, the natural world and its animation through spirit is revered; Anishinaabeg are humbled by the natural and spiritual world because of the gifts both bestow on us and because we recognize we are dependent on both for life. Theorizing this particular story and the implications of how Wenonah is impregnated by a natural element of the land, seemingly against her will, requires more thought. See Victor Barnouw, "The Wenebojo Myth from Lac Du Flambeau," in *Wisconsin Chippewa Myths and Tales: And Their Relation to Chippewa Life* (Madison: University of Wisconsin Press, 1977), 13–14.

20. The word "ikawe" is popularly used amongst contemporary Anishinaabeg to denote or mark gender, specifically woman. The spelling and translation utilized here comes from Helen Roy, Anishinaabe speaker, educator, theorist, and curriculum developer. It is also known as kwe, kawe, ikwe,

qwe, or quay. In trying to relay its meaning, Roy compared it to words like jiibaa'ikawe, binaa'ikawe, and inaa'ikawe—which refer to the changes in food while cooking, autumn leaves while falling, and the sun at midday, respectively. Personal communication, n.d.; Caroline Helen (Roy) Fuhst, *Understanding Anishinaabemowin: Understanding All the Sounds That Are Heard* (Canton, MI: Niish Ishikoden Productions, 2012), 107–09.

21. Personal communication with Elder, April 20, 2015.

22. I use Johnston's spellings here.

23. Johnston, *The Manitous*, 17, 247. Wenonah is spelled "Winonah" in Johnston's story, but to maintain consistency with the previous portion of this text, I use the former spelling. My understanding is "we" refers to continual or repetition, which is commensurate with the translation of Wenonah as continual nurturer.

24. Johnston, *The Manitous*, 59, 247. In a second publication of Johnston's telling of this story, Ae-punighimook kills Wenonah. See Basil Johnston, *Ojibway Heritage* (Lincoln: University of Nebraska Press, 1990), 18.

25. For an Anishinaabeg story about how Nanaboozhoo brought woman (i.e., his grandmother) to the maple grove in the fall to find safety from windigo, see Dorothy M. Reid, "Nanabozho Saves Nokomis," In *Tales of Nanabozho* (Toronto: Oxford University Press, 1963), 65–69. Reid poses an interesting understanding of Indigenous women's relationship with the sugar bush. This story would likely require decolonization as per one method articulated by Wendy Makoons Genuisz, *Our Knowledge Is Not Primitive: Decolonizing Botanical Anishinaabe Teachings* (Syracuse, NY: Syracuse University Press, 2009).

13 | *Centring Resurgence*

Taking on Colonial Gender Violence in Indigenous Nation Building

LEANNE BETASAMOSAKE SIMPSON

FOR THE PAST SEVERAL YEARS I, along with many other Indigenous practitioners and scholars, have been engaged in thinking, writing, and living out ideas of Indigenous resurgence— rebuilding Indigenous nations according to our own political concepts, our own culturally inherent ideas of governance, self- determination, and sovereignty and our own values and ethics. I think the way forward for Indigenous peoples is for us to draw upon the intelligence of our Ancestors in a self-reflective and sometimes critical way, and embody that intelligence on indi- vidual and collective levels as a mechanism for transforming our future relationship with the state. In this way, the idea of resur- gence is not new, it is a concept that comes from within the emergent nature of our ancient teachings and is at the core of Indigenous concepts of time, space, and living relationships. Life was never static for my Ancestors; they lived in a continual state of creation because they carried the responsibility for the continuous rebirth and remaking of healthy and balanced states of being, rela- tionships, and interactions with other beings. So do we.

Land is at the centre of Indigenous resurgence and radical decol-onization. Aki, the earth, is a network of interconnected and interdependent political, social, spiritual, economic, emotional, intellectual, and physical networks including plants, animals, spir-itual beings, lakes and rivers, the sun, moon, and stars, humans; and the land itself provides the context, the inspiration, and the sustenance for this resurgence. The land has presence in the bush, on our reserves, in the cities that sit within our traditional terri-tories and inside of our bodies, and is fully integrated with the spiritual realm. The spiritual world has tremendous influence. Individuals foster a relationship with these elements of creation that is personal and intimate—through lived experience, story, ceremony, dreams, and visions. Spiritual power is considered to be an authentic power, a power that isn't controlled by humans, only influenced by the actions and interactions of humans and non-human beings. This reality made my Ancestors very careful in both their actions and words. It afforded them great respect for individuals and how they chose to carry themselves through their daily lives. It afforded an ethic of non-interference and required an engagement with creation that was committed. It required them to do the emotional and intellectual and spiritual work to understand how to self-actualize within the web of unique interpretations of Nishnaabeg teachings, and it produced societies with tremendous respect for diversity, individual and collective self-determination, and inclusion from the smallest baby to the oldest adult.[1]

In the wake of Loretta Saunders's death, an Inuk university student studying Missing and Murdered Indigenous Women in Halifax, Nova Scotia, and the violent death of Bella Laboucan-McLean, a young Cree woman in Toronto, the *Nations Rising* blog, part of the Indigenous Nationhood Movement, decided to run a series on gender violence. I was supportive of the endeavour because I think it is critically important that we have discussions and act around gender violence in our movement and in our nation-building projects. For me, this issue is at the crux of our collective resurgence as diverse Indigenous peoples. As one of the co-editors of *Nations Rising*, I felt it was important for us to use the blog to highlight diverse and critical voices in our collective discussion. Looking back now, this was the most difficult editorial project that I have ever been a part of because I am emotionally impacted every time I hear about violence directed towards Indigenous peoples. Our writers were writing from this place as well—they were expressing their inner most truths about colonialism, violence, and intimacy. The voices in this series were clear, polemic, and sometimes angry. They were decidedly not nuanced. As co-editors of the It Ends Here series of the *Nations Rising Blog*, we were aware of how difficult this kind of writing is and so we tried to provide as much support to our writers as possible and we tried to edit the pieces in a way that was respectful of individual experience and truth.[2]

When it came time for me to write my own piece, I realized very quickly that I had very rarely been afforded an opportunity to write what I actually thought and felt as an Indigenous woman, because I have found virtually no safe spaces to do so. I was terrified and ashamed. I am fairly established as a scholar and a writer at this point. I have a community of people around me that has my back. So why was telling the truth in this piece so terrifying to share? I think because Indigenous women and queer people have been always been telling our truths, and they are not often heard, validated, or respected because the systemic violence of our lives is so readily normalized within settler colonial misogyny.

The first piece in the series was Cree/Anishinaabe writer Tara Williamson's "Don't Be Tricked." I found her writing bravery inspiring. The tone of the piece was raw, because we were raw. Again. It was angry, because a lot of us were blind with rage. Again. I could personally identify with every word, particularly the line, "The system and most Canadians don't give a shit about you, how strong and talented you are, how hard you've worked, or where you live. If you are an Indigenous woman, you are a prime target for colonial violence."[3] This is something I've felt my whole life and never articulated.

I've never articulated it because I don't want young Indigenous women and queer youth to know that; I want them to feel hopeful and empowered. I've never articulated that because I don't want white Canadians to automatically blame Indigenous men for gender violence. There is a very real risk they will because they've invested a lot of energy into the stereotype of "Indian men" as unfeeling, uncaring, violent savages,[4] and because they've invested even more energy into pretending that they don't benefit from colonial gender violence perpetuated by the state. In fact, they've invested a lot of energy into pretending colonial gender violence perpetuated by the state isn't even a thing. I also don't want Indigenous men to tell me I'm wrong or that this issue doesn't matter or that this all can be solved with women taking self-defence classes, because as much as this is a political issue, this is an intensely painful and personal issue for *anyone* who has survived gender violence, which, if we are honest, is most of us, including Indigenous men. I don't want to have to seek out allies in white feminists, because so many times I have been asked to explain, justify, and rationalize my experience as an Indigenous person in Canada. I want Indigenous men to have my back, even when they feel uncomfortable about what I am saying.[5] And you know what, over the course of the series more than a few of them did, and that was one of the most amazing feelings I have ever had. They emailed support. They checked in. They listened and encouraged. They re-tweeted, posted, wrote, and expressed their outrage.

This is co-resistance. This is community.

White supremacy, rape culture, and the real and symbolic attack on gender, sexual identity and agency are very powerful tools of colonialism, settler colonialism, and capitalism, primarily because they work very efficiently to remove Indigenous peoples from our territories and to prevent reclamation of those territories through mobilization.[6] These forces have the intergenerational staying power to destroy generations of families, as they work to prevent us from intimately connecting to each other. They work to prevent mobilization because communities coping with epidemics of gender violence don't have the physical or emotional capital to organize. They destroy the base of our nations and our political systems because they destroy our relationships to the land and to each other by fostering epidemic levels of anxiety, hopelessness, apathy, distrust, and suicide. They work to destroy the fabric of Indigenous nationhoods by attempting to destroy our relationality by making it difficult to form sustainable, strong relationships with each other.[7]

This is why I think it's in all of our best interests to take on gender violence as a core resurgence project, a core decolonization project, a core of Indigenous nation building, and as the backbone of any Indigenous mobilization. And by gender violence I don't just mean violence against women, I mean *all* gender violence. Resurgence is about both land and bodies. We need to build communities and nations where gender violence is not tolerated. We need to build alternative systems of accountability within our communities and spaces, based on our own legal and healing traditions, and we need to hold the state accountable for the myriad of ways it uses gender violence to control, dispossess, erase, dehumanize, shame, and oppress Indigenous peoples. Because settler colonial misogyny is ubiquitous and functions invisibly to those who do not experience it (and it often goes unnamed for those that do), dismantling this system is both an individual and collective responsibility. Dene scholar Glen Coulthard writes,

> society, including Indigenous society and particularly Indigenous men, [must] stop collectively conducting ourselves in a manner that denigrates, degrades, and devalues the lives and worth of Indigenous women in such a way that epidemic levels of violence are the norm in many of their lives. Of course, this violence must be stopped in its overt forms, but we must also stop practicing it in its more subtle expressions—in our daily relationships and practices in the home, workplaces,

band offices, governance institutions, and, crucially, in our
practices of cultural resurgence. Until this happens we have
reconciled ourselves to defeat.[8]

In this chapter, I begin the discussion around centring Indigenous
resurgence movements in a way that begins to dismantle systems
of colonial gender violence—by continually revealing its existence
and actively working towards building alternative mechanisms
for dealing with the restoration of Indigenous nations in which
gender violence is unthinkable. I hope this chapter continues
the long history of Indigenous resistance to gender violence that
has keep our bodies and spirits alive, and it is my hope that many
others will continue this discussion and work in the coming
months and years.

Re-visioning Quest
Undoing the Colonial Gender Binary

This work begins for me by looking at how gender is conceptual-
ized and actualized within Nishnaabeg thought because colonialism
has imposed an artificial gender binary as a mechanism for controlling Indigenous bodies and identity.[9] This imposed colonial gender
binary sets out two very clear genders: male and female; and it lays
out two very clear sets of rigidly defined roles based on colonial
conceptions of femininity and masculinity.[10]

This doesn't make a lot of sense to me when I think about this
binary from within Nishnaabeg conceptual thought or from within
the reality of so-called "hunting and gathering societies." Nishnaabeg
women hunted, trapped, fished, held leadership positions, and
participated in warfare, as well as engaged in domestic affairs and
looked after children, and they were encouraged to show a broad
range of emotions and to express their gender and sexuality in a
way that was true to their own being, as a matter of *both principle
and survival.* Nishnaabeg men hunted, trapped, fished, held
leadership positions, engaged in warfare, and also knew how to

cook, sew, and look after children. They were encouraged to show a broad range of emotions, express their gender and sexuality in a way that was true to their own being, as a matter of *both principle and survival*. This is true for other genders as well. And while there was often a gendered division of labour, there were also a lot of exceptions based on individual agency. The degree to which individuals engaged in each of these activities depended upon their name, their clan, their extended family, their skill and interest, and most importantly individual self-determination or agency.[11] Agency was valued, honoured, and respected because it produced a diversity of highly self-sufficient individuals, families, and communities. This diversity of highly self-sufficient and self-determining people ensured survival and resilience that enabled the community to withstand difficult circumstances.

Strong communities are born out of a diversity individuals being their best selves. Colonialism recognized this and quickly co-opted Indigenous individuals into colonial gender roles in order to replicate the heteropatriarchy of colonial society. This causes the power and agency of all of genders to shrink, and those that are farthest away from colonial ideals suffered and continue to be targets of harsh colonial violence.

In July 2011, Darrell Dennis hosted an episode of CBC Radio's *ReVision Quest* on the theme of being Indigenous two-spirit, LGBTTQQIA,[12] and gender non-conforming people. I remember pulling over on the side of the highway and listening as he interviewed Anishinaabemowin expert Roger Roulette, Cree scholar Alex Wilson, and many others in his exploration of what it means to be queer and Indigenous. Seven and a half minutes into the episode, Roulette explained the non-judgemental terminology we have in our language regarding queerness: "wiijidaamaagan means s/he cohabitates with a person; wiipemaagan means s/he sleeps with a person and wiijiiwaagan means a friend or companion; according to Roger's uncle…a gay person is described as wiijininiimaagan— a man whose partner is another man; wiijikwemaagan is a woman with a female partner—the word has no judgement in it."[13]

Roulette also explained to the host that gender was not exclusively bound to certain roles in life: "it was determine more by a child's natural inclinations rather than whether baby clothes were pink or blue, and in some places these survived right up into modern times."[14] I felt relieved that Roulette had confirmed something that I had learned from a variety of Elders but that still somehow remains on the margins. Similarly, Anishinaabe historian Anton Treuer writes,

> Sex usually determined one's gender and, therefore one's work, but the Ojibwe accepted variation. Men who chose to function as women were called ikwekaazo meaning "one who endeavors to be like a woman." Women who functioned as men were called ininiikaazo, meaning "one who endeavors to be like a man"... Their mates were not considered ikwekaazo or ininiikaazo, however, because their function in society was still in keeping with their sex [gender]. If widowed, the spouse of an ikwekaazo or ininiikaazo could remarry someone of the opposite sex or another ikwekaazo or ininiikaazo...The ikwekaazowag worked and dressed like women. Ininiikaazowag worked and dressed like men. Both were considered to be strong spiritually, and they were always honored, especially during ceremonies.[15]

In the past, there was a gendered division in Anishinaabeg governance in that men often dealt with international issues and women had a lot of authority in civil governance.[16] There were again, many, many exceptions and examples of women taking on international leadership responsibilities.

One historical example of this division comes from the 1805 negotiations between the British and the Michi Saagiig Nishnaabeg over land between York and the Head of the Lake. Kinewbene, speaking on behalf of the other chiefs of Credit River, said,

> Now Father when Sir John Johnson came up to purchase the Toronto Lands [1787], we gave then without hesitation and we

were told we should always be taken care of, and we made no
bargain for the Land but left it to himself. Now Father you
want another piece of Land—we cannot say no; but we will
explain ourselves before we say any more...I speak for all the
Chiefs & they wish to be under your protections as formerly,
But it is hard for us to give away more Land: The young men
and women have found fault with so much having been sold
before; it is true we are poor & the women say we will be
worse, if we part with anymore; but we will tell you what we
mean to do.[17]

The last sentence is important here because it gestures towards the political power and influence of Michi Saagiig Nishnaabeg women even into the 1800s. During international negotiations, families would travel together to the site of the meetings. Families would camp close by in a community while leaders attending the meetings. There was an expectation that leaders would come back at the end of the day and discuss these issues with the families. Women held influence in these negotiations, and leaders, who were really acting more as spokespeople, had the responsibility for bringing these concerns forward.[18] I see this as a critical aspect of Michi Saagiig Nishnaabeg international governance—having a group of citizens, particularly women but also spiritual leaders, children, youth, and Elders (and at this point it was a large group because colonial authorities were infamous for only recognizing colonial-friendly kinds of male leadership as authority)[19] embedded in what it is important to the community on a daily basis, uninfluenced by the colonial trickery of the negotiations holding those spokespeople accountable within their own families.

Another historical example of the agency and leadership of Michi Saagiig Nishnaabekwewag has been documented by non-Native historian Donald B. Smith. Nahnebahnwequay (Upright Woman)[20] was exposed to the international leadership of Michi Saagiig Nishnaabeg at an early age when her Aunt and Uncle Eliza and Peter Jones took her to Britain with them for a year as Peter was advocating for our land rights in Upper Canada in the early 1800s.[21] At the age of thirty-six, married and pregnant with another child, Nahnebahnwequay travelled to New York and England to continue to advocate for her people, and on June 19, 1860 she met with the Queen. Three weeks later, she gave birth.[22] This is a considerable example of agency self-determination and the fluidity of gender roles, extending into the mid-1800s, in spite of conversion to the Methodist faith by many Michi Saagiig Nishnaabeg, including Nahnebahnwequay and her family.

Louise Erdrich's Two Strikes

A favourite series of books to read aloud in my house is Anishinaabe writer Louise Erdrich's Birchbark House series. This is Erdrich's juvenile fiction series and includes *The Birchbark House*, *The Game of Silence*, *The Porcupine Year*, and *Chickadee*.[23] The series begins in the mid-1800s and follows an Anishinaabeg family living on an island in Lake Superior through three generations of living out an Anishinaabeg existence in an era of increasing settler surveillance and violence. Erdrich has carefully crafted a world that replicates the one so cherished in Anishinaabeg oral tradition, which makes these novels both a gift and a masterpiece.

Erdrich's work is also an important reflection of the relationship between Anishinaabe children and adults, and one that, with a few exceptions, is consistent with my understanding of this relationship coming through the oral tradition.[24] Children were afforded a lot of freedom and agency within their own lives. *The Porcupine Year*, for instance, begins with a story of two children, Pinch and his older sister and main character of the series Omakayas, who at the time is twelve years old, out night hunting for deer in a canoe. This in itself demonstrates a high level of skill (canoeing, firearms, navigation, hunting), self-determination (these two children are the decision makers), and trust from adults in their family. This skill is tested as the children are caught in the confluence of two rivers, whisked over rapids, and forced to use their intelligence to take care of each other and make it back to their family.[25]

Similarly, the character Two Strikes clearly demonstrates that difference and diversity were both valued and fostered within traditional Anishinaabeg culture. Two Strikes, while identified in the novels as a girl, takes up the responsibilities of hunting, trapping, and physically defending the family from a young age, and the family, in fact her extended family and community, not only makes room for her, but they support, nurture, and appreciate the gifts and contributions she makes to their community. She is an excellent shot and without question the best hunter and protector of her generation. She refuses to participate in the culture of women whether its work, ceremonial responsibilities, or political responsibilities. She behaves and lives out the responsibilities of men, and her family and community make room and support her both as a child and as an adult. Rather than coerce or shame her into the responsibilities of women, her family steps back and supports her expression of herself in part because it is Two Strikes's responsibility to figure out how to live authentically in the world and in her family. Two Strikes chooses not to wear skirts, and not to participate in girls' puberty rituals, because her path is different. Her relationship to the spirit world is a powerful relationship in which her family supports her, and is influential, but they also have tremendous respect for her own agency within that relationship.

This idea of supporting an individual's responsibility to self-actualize and find their own path with regards to their life's work, their gender expression, their sexual identity, their relationship orientation, and every other aspect of life is something I have repeatedly experienced within Anishinaabeg society—particularly by those practitioners who are engaged with the complexities of our ancient philosophies, as opposed to people like me, who are very much engaged in a process of reclamation and decolonization. I have also witnessed this in other Indigenous nations—when an individual asserts their identity, it is the community's job to make room and support that assertion. I have also, of course, seen the opposite of this particularly directed towards women and Indigenous two-spirit, LGBTTQQIA, and gender non-conforming people— where rigidity and singular interpretations of protocols and rituals are used to exclude individuals and communities of people. Exclusion has been more common than inclusion, in my experience. I find this extraordinarily problematic and inconsistent with my under-standing of Nishnaabeg teachings. Even if it were consistent with traditional cultures, our collective experience with violence and oppression should tell us that the reproduction of gender oppression and violence has no place within our communities. I think our teachings have to be interpreted within the ancient context of agency, self-determination. and non-interference—in a context where authentic power is in the spiritual realm. I fundamentally don't want to be part of ceremony or nation-building practices that exclude or limit the power and expression of Indigenous bodies. To me, this is not resurgence.

The Skirt

In the years after publishing *Dancing on Our Turtle's Back*, in which I explore Anishinaabe resurgence within our own thought, there is one question that comes up continually: Does Leanne wear a skirt to ceremonies? I purposefully did not answer this question in the book because my point in discussion the reclam-ation of traditions was that we also have to reclaim the context within which those teachings operated—and that context is one of consent, agency, individual self-determination, a celebration of diversity, inclusion, and multiple interpretations of our teachings. Since it's been several years since I published the book, and I'm still getting asked that question, I'd like to take this opportunity to answer it.

To begin with, like most if not all Indigenous women, Indigenous two-spirit, LGBTTQQIA, and gender non-conforming people, I have continually experienced real and symbolic violence throughout my life. That violence is unfortunately part of my experience and part of my context. As a child, I was forced to wear dresses and skirts to church—a place that did not value my Indigeneity or my gender, an organization that actively attacked both. This experience is by no means unique; its message to me was that I was not good enough, not sacred enough, or clean enough in my own right as a young Nishnaabe girl—I had to be wrestled into leotards, plastic shoes, slips, and skirts to give the illusion of worthiness. This was an attempt to make me feel ashamed of who I was as an Indigenous child, and as a girl who was figuring out how to express my deepest truths about my identity growing up in an environment where I didn't have any examples of a positive Native identity. It was an attempt to make me feel ashamed of who I was, and this is by no means a unique experience of Indigenous peoples growing up in the 1970s and 1980s particularly off reserve, in Southern Ontario.

The photo that I grew up with of my great grandma Smoke is one of her and her husband standing in front of their house on the shores of Pimaadashkodeyaang, Rice Lake. My Kokum, who I've never met, is wearing pants. This was significant to me as a kid because all my other Grandmothers—the Michi Saagiig Nishnaabeg ones and the zhaaganash (white) ones—are all wearing skirts or dresses. But my oldest photographed Nishnaabekwe Ancestor is not.

A lot of other people have similar memories and stories about their grandparents and Ancestors from their oral traditions. Tara Williamson, Anishinaabekwe/Nehayowak in her Anishinaabeg family from Gaabishkigamaag, Swan Lake, Manitoba writes,

My kookoo [Kaapiidashiik] was a medicine woman. And she was a good medicine woman. One of those women people travelled miles to see. One of my favourite stories is about how, when my mother told her there was a strange man in the yard, Kaapiidashiik locked up the doors and windows and huddled

in the corner of the house behind a rocking chair with her
granddaughter (my mother) and a loaded shotgun aimed at
the door. My kookoo used to sell red willow baskets to make
extra money for the family. That same red willow was used for
kinnickinick. She harvested her own medicine and used to
make a medicine of a hundred roots that would cure T B.
Although she was a traditional person, I can't imagine that she
checked her snares in a skirt or that she waited for my grand-
father to come home before taking care of her own fire. In fact,
the most beautiful thing my mother remembers about
Kaapiidashiik and Michael (my great-grandfather) was that
they shared their home responsibilities across gender roles. She
remembers their partnership as respectful, loving, and kind.[26]

And so, like our Ancestors, we have to be careful. We have to be careful that our protocols and teachings remain alive in the context of relationships of love, trust, respect, and agency, and that they are not reduced to rules and dogma. We also have an added responsibility, as Tara points out in the same article:

The dilemma for me is that I cannot understand my history in
terms of dogma. Nor can I understand my present in terms of
dogma. Every day, I make decisions that my ancestors never
had to make (where to buy my food, how to give an offering
while I live in a city, etc.), and every day I benefit from deci-
sions that they made. I believe wholeheartedly that the reason
I was lucky enough to grow up with tradition is because my
relatives were clever enough to bend the rules. I believe my
family has the language because they learned to whisper in
school. I believe we still know how to give offerings of asemaa
because we learned to replace natural tobacco with cigarettes.
I believe we still have ceremony because we hid ourselves
so well that nobody noticed. I believe we still believe in Gichi-
manidoo because we understood how much this spirit looked

like G O D. And, so, it is hard for me to condemn those who try
to bend the "rules"—even now.[27]

In our rebuilding of our nations, we have to be careful that we
aren't replicating the oppression we've learned at residential
schools or from Canadian society because gender violence functions so completely in our reality that it informs our struggles for
liberation.[28] In our rebuilding of our nations, I think my Ancestors
would want us to let go of practices and protocols that no longer
open all of our people's hearts to the greater powers and forces that
guide us, or at the very least respect different interpretations of
those teachings. I would certainly want my great, great grandchildren to do that. I think our Ancestors expect us to be intelligent,
critical, and self-reflective to bring the best of their lives and
teachings forward to a new generation. They were after all human,
and not that different from us.

Over the past twenty years, I have learned the teachings behind
skirt wearing and other ceremonial protocols from a group of very
kind and loving ceremonial leaders. I understand the teachings
behind wearing a skirt—they are profound and beautiful. I most
strongly identified with those teachings while pregnant and nursing.
This is part of my identity and it represents a decade of my life. But
it is not by any means my entire identity.

I have always made it a point to ask spiritual leaders in my
community over and over again about these protocols around
menstruation and skirt wearing in the context of our practices.
Two things have been repeatedly told to me: the first is that decisions around these protocols lie in the domain of the women
themselves, and second that if any of these protocols shut down
my ability to open myself up to the spirits during the ceremony,
then I should not uphold the protocol. It is more important to
come into a scared and ceremonial space with an open heart than
to uphold a particular protocol designed to create a space where
individuals are open to the spirit world.

Sometimes I wear a skirt to ceremonies to honour those teachings and to honour Elders who have taught me those teachings. Sometimes that feels good. Other times I do not—particularly if there are women and girls there who are not comfortable wearing skirts (one of whom is often my daughter), or if I do not, for whatever reason, feel in my heart that I can wear the skirt and remain open spiritually. I will not be shamed or forced into wearing a skirt by ceremonial leaders or other women. My identity, spirituality, and my place in the world are far more complex than wearing a skirt, and the decision is ultimately mine to make. While wearing a skirt feels good, not wearing a skirt also feels good. I have had profound spiritual experiences at all times of the month in all different locations and in all different manners of dress. It is important to me that the ceremonies or events I participate in respect my agency around my clothing and my interpretation of our teachings, and I am committed to using my voice to making ceremony and cultural events inclusive of all genders and sexual identities.

Asinkykwe and the Creation Story

In writing *Dancing on Our Turtle's Back,* I wanted to ground the book in a Nishnaabeg Creation stories, because these sacred stories encode so much of our world view and theoretical perspectives. Unable to track down the Elder from whom I needed to get permission to reprint a particular version of a story, I was beginning to worry as each day drew me closer to my publisher's deadline. I was explaining the problem to Edna Manitowabi during the Indigenous Women's Symposium at Trent University, when she offered to share with me her oral version of the story for publication of the book. I was extraordinarily grateful. Over the next weekend, Edna wrote down the story, pen to paper, and dropped it off at my house on the following Sunday night. Over the next few days, I poured over the story, reading and rereading it as it wove it into the text.

Although I had heard her tell this story in traditional teachings and ceremony, I had never read a textual version of the story *told* by a women, and not just told by a woman, but told from a Grandmother's perspective, told by a woman to an audience of women. I suddenly realized that what I had assumed were our Creation stories were really Nishnaabeg male Elder's perspectives on our stories, and although they were beautiful stories, I didn't see or feel my perspectives reflected in them as strongly as I did with Edna's version. Edna's version spoke to me directly—illuminating and validating all of my experiences as Nishnaabekwe.

For me, that was profound. Profoundly sad because I hadn't realized this before and because this perspective is far too rare, and profoundly beautiful because now I had. I felt like new life had been breathed into me.

If the philosophy behind the telling of our sacred stories tells us to insert the very essence of ourselves into the story, why have I not heard our Creation stories told from a transgendered perspective? From lesbian perspectives? How has the heterosexual male perspective become the "objective truth"? Why? How can we reclaim diverse versions and voices that speak our Creation stories to all members of our society? Aren't our stories more powerful when told from a diversity of perspectives?

Nooshenh Knew Exactly What To Do

It was deep in the bboon.
The days were short and cold
and everyone was sick.
their wiigwaaman were full of
blowing and coughing and fever
first it was Binoojiyens
then Mishomis
then Nokomis
then Binoojiinh
then Noos, and
then finally, it was Doodoom.

Soon, the mashkiki had run
right
out.
They were so sick, that they had run
right
out
of mashkiki.

Nokomis sent the strongest runner out to the next
village to get some more from their
Mashkikiiwininiikwe. But the runner took sick
and he collapsed before reaching the lake.

Nooshenh knew what to do.
Nooshenh was the only one healthy.
With all the coughing and sneezing and blowing,
it wouldn't be long before Nooshenh was sick too.
So Nooshenh packed up some food, flint and
all of the brave that would fit into Nooshenh's heart
and set out to the next village.

It was very windy.
It was very, very cold.
Nooshenh walked through the sugar bush,
past the place where they picked wild leeks,
past where the fiddleheads grow,
beside the berry patches
and the Labrador tea,
until Nooshenh got to zaaga'igan.

The ice was thick on the lake
and noodin was fierce and whippy.
But Nooshenh kept walking.

Finally, when Nooshenh was just about to the other side
that old Mashkikiiwininiikwe saw Nooshenh.
and so that old Mashkikiiwininiikwe got her
shkode going big.
She got her niibiishaboo on the fire.
She got ready.
She knew that when Nooshenh got there, they would
be cold, tired and hungry.

Then that old Medicine Woman went and picked them up
and brought them home
wrapped them in warm wabooz blankets
gave them tea and soup
and told them to rest.
"Wabang, we will go together and take the mashkiki to your
family."

It was a good idea, but Nooshenh woke up
in the middle of the night
sick with worry, whispered "Miigwech,"
and slipped out of that old lady's lodge.

The ice was thick on the lake
and noodin was fierce and whippy.
Nooshenh kept walking.
Across zaaga'igan,
past the Labrador tea,
beside the berry patches
past where the fiddleheads grow
past the wild leeks
through the sugar bush
It was very, very cold.
It was very blowy.

Finally, Nooshenh could see the smoke from the family's lodges.
By now, the sun was high in the noonday sky.
The snow was warming up and so of course
one step in that deep snow and they were sunk.

They struggled.
They lost their makizinan.
They lost their patience.
But they didn't lose their fight.

On Nooshenh went, barefoot all the way home to their lodge.
Nooshenh's family was very happy.
They listened to the story.
They drank that mashkiki.
and wrapped Nooshenh's feet in medicine
and warm blankets.

And the next summer
in the exact spot Nooshenh lost the makizinan
grew the most beautiful, pink flowers
anyone had ever seen
Nokomis called them
"Makizinkwe," woman's shoe
in honour of her brave Nooshenh.

But then Nooshenh spoke up
and said that maybe that wasn't exactly
the very most best name for the flower
making Nokomis think, which
is always a good thing to do.
And so Nokomis thought
and agreed and said,
"Makizin Waawaasgoneh," moccasin flower[29]
in honour of her brave and very wise Nooshenh.[30]

The main character in this story is Nooshenh, which means grandchild. There is no gender associated with the term. In other versions of this story, I've used Kwezens (girl) and Giiwezenhsn (boy) as the main character, but since I think about and write about gender a lot, I wanted to be able to tell my children a story in which the main character's gender challenges the colonial gender binary as a matter of fact. I also changed the ending to speak directly to our living generations. Children are teachers with influence, and in our collective decolonization and resurgence, each generation we create should be able to embody our teachings to a greater degree than previous generations. Nokomis recognizes this. She hears Nooshenh and makes a tiny adjustment to her naming that respects, includes, and honours Nooshenh's gender identity, and remains consistent with everything Nokomis embodies.

One of the things I like about this story is that the land recognizes the courage, persistence, and bravery of this young person, and Aki responds by creating another being with agency and self-determination—a moccasin flower. One of the things I like about Walking With Our Sisters and for me I include all of my siblings lost to gender violence, is that it recognizes the courage, persistence, and bravery of Indigenous women and responds by creating another being—a community-based, travelling ceremony of 1,800 makizinan vamps and a series of community conversations about how four centuries of gendered colonial violence has created a situation where there are ever increasing Missing and Murdered Indigenous Women and Girls in Canada. My hope is that collectively we are willing to discuss and address the root causes of colonial gender violence and chart a course for the future that is respectful of both Indigenous land and bodies.

AUTHOR'S NOTE

Revised parts of this chapter were published in Chapters 7 and 8 of *As We Have Always Done: Indigenous Freedom through Radical Resistance* (University of Minnesota Press, 2017).

1. I use the spelling *Nishnaabeg* when I am referring to Mississauga or Odawa Nishnaabeg peoples. I use the term *Anishinaabe* when I am refer to our relatives to the west and the north. These terms reflect the spellings of our different dialects.

2. The series was edited by Siku Allooloo, Jarrett Martineau, Glen Coulthard, and me (although I am no longer working with the Indigenous Nationhood movement). The full series was originally available on the *Nations Rising Blog* of the Indigenous Nationhood Movement website at http://nationsrising.org/itendshere-the-full-series/. The website is no longer maintained.

3. Tara Williamson, "Don't Be Tricked," *Nations Rising Blog*, February 28, 2014, http://nationsrising.org/dont-be-tricked/.

4. Daniel Heath Justice, excerpt of "Fighting Shame through Love— A Conversation with Daniel Heath Justice" from *Masculindians: Conversations about Indigenous Manhood* (Winnipeg: University of Manitoba Press, 2014), interview by Sam McKegney, http://uofmpress. ca/blog/entry/excerpt-from-masculindians-daniel-heath-justice.

5. See the final chapter in Glen Coulthard's *Red Skin, White Masks: Rejecting the Colonial Politics of Recognition* (Minneapolis: University of Minnesota Press, 2014).

6. I'm using the term *symbolic* here to mean rendering the colonial systemic violence and oppression of Indigenous women in their daily lives as invisible, acceptable, and normal.

7. This section is from my piece for the It Ends Here Series, titled "Not Murdered Not Missing," and this chapter is in part based on that initial blog post. It was originally available online at http://nationsrising.org/ not-murdered-and-not-missing/.

8. Glen Coulthard, *Red Skin, White Masks*, 178.

9. Andrea Smith, "Queer Theory and Native Studies: The Heteronormativity of Settler Colonialism," in *Queer Indigenous Studies: Critical Interventions in Theory, Politics, and Literature*, ed. Qwo-Li Driskill, Chris Finley, Brian Joseph Gilley, and Scott Lauria Morgensen (Tuscon: University of Arizona Press, 2011), 43–66.

10. Kiera Ladner, "Women and Blackfoot Nationalism," *Journal of Canadian Studies* 35, no. 2 (2000): 35–60; Chris Finley, "Decolonizing the Queer Native Body (and Recovering the Native Bull-Dyke): 'Bringing Sexy Back' and Out of Native Studies Closet," in *Queer Indigenous Studies: Critical*

Interventions in Theory, Politics, and Literature, ed. Qwo-Li Driskill, Chris Finley, Brian Joseph Gilley, and Scott Lauria Morgensen (Tuscon: University of Arizona Press, 2011), 31–42; Smith, "Queer Theory and Native Studies."

11. Leanne Betasamosake Simpson, "Chapter 3, Gdi-Nweninaa: Our Sound, Our Voice," in *Dancing on Our Turtle's Back: Stories of Nishnaabeg Re-Creation, Resurgence, and a New Emergence* (Winnipeg: ARP Books, 2011), 49–63; Tara Williamson, "Of Dogma and Ceremony," *Decolonization, Indigeneity & Society* (blog), August 16, 2013, http:// decolonization.wordpress.com/2013/08/16/of-dogma-and-ceremony/.

12. *LGBTTQQIA* stands for gay, bisexual, transgender, transsexual, queer, questioning, intersex, asexual. For more information, see the Native Youth Sexual Health Network, http://www.nativeyouthsexualhealth. com/.

13. CBC Radio, *ReVision Quest*, July 20, 2011, starting at 7 min., http://www. cbc.ca/revisionquest/2011/2011/07/20/july-20-21-23-two-spirited-being-glbt-and-aboriginal/. Métis writer Chelsea Vowel has also considered queer Indigeneity in her book *Indigenous Writes: A Guide to First Nations, Inuit and Métis Issues in Canada* in the chapter titled "All My Queer Relations: Language, Culture and Two-Spirit Identity" (Winnipeg: Portage and Main Press, 2016), 106–15. Nishnaabeg two-spirit playwright Waawaate Fobister uses the term *Agokwe* in his play of the same name. I transcribed the Nishnaabemowin words from the recording and then asked language expert and Elder Shirley Williams for help with the spelling. She understood many of Roger Roulette's words and, as an alternative, she suggested "wiichi-ninoonmaagan" or " wiichi-ninoonmaaganimon" for the term *gay* (personal communication, December 12, 2016, Peterborough, ON). I also consulted Anishinaabemowin language expert Patricia Ningewance (through Tara Williamson, on January 22, 2017). Patricia understood Roger's words and added that *wiidigemaagan* means spouse.

14. CBC Radio, *ReVision Quest*, July 20, 2011, starting at 8 min., http://www.cbc.ca/revisionquest/2011/2011/07/20/ july-20-21-23-two-spirited-being-glbt-and-aboriginal/.

15. Anton Treuer, *The Assassination of Hole in the Day* (Saint Paul, MN: Borealis Books, 2011), 27.

16. Treuer, *Assassination of Hole*, 27.

17. Kinewbene (Quinipeno in historical documents, meaning Golden Eagle) is quoted at a meeting with the Mississaugas at the Credit River, 1 August

1805, as quoted in Donald B. Smith, *Sacred Feathers: The Reverend Peter Jones (Kahkewaquonaby) and the Mississauga Indians*, 2nd ed. (Toronto: University of Toronto Press, 2013), 32.

18. Doug Williams, Elder, Curve Lake First Nation, June 15, 2014.

19. Doug Williams, Elder, Curve Lake First Nation, June 15, 2014.

20. Her English name was Catharine Sutton. Donald B. Smith, *Mississauga Portraits: Ojibwe Voices from Nineteenth-Century Canada* (Toronto: University of Toronto Press, 2013), chapter 3, 1, Kobo E-reader version.

21. Smith, *Mississauga Portraits*, 24.

22. Smith, *Mississauga Portraits*, 62–73.

23. Louise Erdrich, *The Birchbark House* (New York: Hyperion, 1999); Louise Erdrich, *The Game of Silence* (New York: HarperCollins, 2005); Louise Erdrich, *The Porcupine Year* (New York: HarperCollins, 2008); Louise Erdrich, *Chickadee* (New York: HarperCollins, 2012).

24. Simpson, *Dancing on Our Turtle's Back*.

25. Erdrich, *The Porcupine Year*, 1–30.

26. Williamson, "Of Dogma and Ceremony."

27. Williamson, "Of Dogma and Ceremony."

28. Bonita Lawrence, *"Real" Indians and Others: Mixed-Blood Urban Native Peoples and Indigenous Nationhood* (Vancouver: UBC Press, 2004), 69.

29. There are several different names for Lady Slipper, including agobizowin (showy Lady's Slipper), makizin (Yellow Lady Slipper), niimiidi makizin (Yellow Lady Slipper), makizinkwe (Pink Lady Slipper), all in *Indinawemaaganidog (All My Relatives) Anishinaabe Guide to Animals, Birds, Fish, Reptiles, Insects, and Plants* (Odanah, WI: Great Lakes Indian Fish and Wildlife Commission, n.d).

30. This is a traditional Anishinaabe story that I have heard and read in both oral and written forms. There is a similar version published in Leanne Simpson, *The Gift Is in the Making: Anishinaabeg Stories* (Winnipeg: Highwater Press, 2013), 25–30, under the title "She Knew Exactly What To Do," and by non-Native authors Lise Lunge-Larsen and Margi Preus in the form of a children's book titled *The Legend of the Lady Slipper (Ojibwe Tale)* (New York: HMH Books for Young Readers, 1999), and Basil Johnson, *Ojibway Heritage* (Toronto: McClelland & Stewart, 1976), 38–39.

Anishinaabemowin: bboon is winter, wiigwaaman are homes or lodges, Binoojiyens (abinoojiyens) is baby, Mishomis is Grandfather, Nokomis is Grandmother, binoojiinh (abinoojiinh) is a child, noos is

Father, doodoom is mama (an older name that a child would call a mother—literally my breastfeeder), mashkiki is medicine, Mashkikiiwininiikwe is Medicine Woman, Nooshenh means grandchild, zaaga'igan is lake, noodin is the wind, shkode is a fire, niibiishaboo (aniibiishaaboo) is tea, Wabooz is rabbit, wabang is tomorrow, and miigwech means thanks, Makizinikwe is one of our names for Lady Slipper, so is Makizin Waawaasgoneh.

IV | Action, Always

14 | *Iskwewuk*
E-wichiwitochik

*Saskatchewan Community Activism to Address Missing
and Murdered Indigenous Women and Girls*

DARLENE R. OKEMAYSIM-SICOTTE,

SUSAN GINGELL & RITA BOUVIER

IN THE EARLY MORNING HOURS of May 19, 2004, a twenty-
five-year-old wife, mother, and fourth-year university student in
education at the University of Saskatchewan went missing from
Saskatoon. She was Daleen (Muskego) Bosse of the Onion Lake
Cree Nation. Bosse's remains would not be found until August
2008, despite a vigorous family search for her in the face of early
months of lax investigation by police.[1] The horrific details of the
case and numerous pretrial and in-process delays, including a
deferred verdict occasioned by a Supreme Court of Canada ruling
on the admissibility of evidence gathered in Mr. Big Stings,[2]
rendered an already acutely painful process all the more draining
and agonizing for those from whom Daleen was so violently torn.

The work with the Muskegos and Bosses done by the
Saskatoon-based activist collective Iskwewuk E-wichiwitochik
(IE)/Women Walking Together[3] is typical of the family-centred
process IE uses to let the families of the missing and murdered

know they are not alone in their grief or in valuing and insisting on remembering the loved ones who have been taken. In testifying to the federal Special Parliamentary Committee on Violence against Indigenous Women, Bernadette Smith, sister of missing Indigenous woman Claudette Osborne, expressly identified that undertaking such work was crucial for others than families of the missing and murdered to do: "there's not enough support out there for these families, and it shouldn't have to always be on us to do that [work]."[4] Quite apart from appreciation from families, IE's work has been recognized as effective and valuable by the City of Saskatoon's Living in Harmony Award and the local Joanna Miller Peace Award, while individual members Darlene Okemaysim-Sicotte, Myrna LaPlante, Pauline Muskego, and Glenda Yuzicappi were honoured with Queen Elizabeth II Diamond Jubilee medals for their outstanding personal contributions to building awareness about and ending the disappearances and murders of Indigenous women in Canada. Additionally, Darlene was one of ten national finalists for the 2014 Samara's Everyday Political Citizen award for her work on missing and murdered Indigenous women and girls;[5] and Darlene and Myrna shared the Saskatchewan First Nations Women's Commission 2017 Leadership and Advocacy Award.

Thus, we believe sharing an account of IE's work has value for those interested in community-based activism in general, but aim especially to give others who are doing, or contemplating doing, grassroots work on the issue of missing and murdered Indigenous women and girls a way to assess whether our model of operating would be applicable and useful in their contexts. We tell IE's story by describing our work with families like Daleen's, the contexts of IE's founding; the collective's values, purposes, and commitment to guarding group autonomy; our activities in our almost twelve-year existence; the larger contexts of our ongoing work; our reflections on our achievements and challenges; and our future plans.

The Daleen (Muskego) Bosse Case and IE

The Bosse case powerfully prompted IE's formation, and Daleen's parents were members of its precursor group. The case has also become a key narrative in the collective's public education and memorial events, not least to help counter the stereotype that the women who go missing or are found murdered are poor, ill-educated, alcoholic or otherwise drug-addicted, and hence deemed throwaway people.[6] One measure of just how much Daleen's disappearance and death have affected members of the group is that Co-Chair Darlene Okemaysim-Sicotte delivered a victim impact statement with ten members of IE present to hear before Daleen's murderer and desecrator, Douglas Hales, was sentenced. Darlene testified that losing the warm, energetic, well-educated young woman, who seemed poised to become a community leader, occasioned anxiety, depression, anguish, and spiritual weakening in Darlene's own life. She also shared feeling deep concern for the impact Daleen's disappearance was having on University of Saskatchewan students and faculty with whom Darlene interacted as administrative assistant in the Native Studies Department (now Indigenous Studies). One woman taken, so many losses sustained.

The larger context of Darlene's own commitment to the founding and work of IE was that "in October 2005, there were over a dozen missing indigenous women and girls in or around the city,"[7] but Daleen's case was the one that motivated Darlene to take on family liaison for IE. That role, she explains, "meant having to know the missing person's family, their heritage, where they resided, the family composite—did they have a partner, husband, boyfriend, common-law? Were they mothers, sisters, nieces, or granddaughters? As part of this role, a person will get to know the last whereabouts of the missing person."[8] Since Darlene accepted this responsibility, much of her life beyond her paid employment and family time has been devoted to this work.

To understand fully the need for and nature of IE's support to Daleen's family, readers require substantial knowledge of the case.

Hales's trial did not begin until ten years (less two weeks) after the day of Daleen's disappearance. Before police took the disappearance seriously, parents Pauline and Herb Muskego searched for their missing daughter across several provinces, hired a private investigator, and contacted the Federation of Saskatchewan Indian Nations' Special Investigation Unit,[9] Child Find, Sisters in Spirit, and Amnesty International to aid in the search. By awareness runs from the Onion Lake Cree Nation on the borderlands of Saskatchewan and Alberta to Saskatoon, and by walks within the city, the Muskegos strove to keep alive in public and police consciousness Daleen's (beloved absense *and* her) unsolved disappearance. By speaking at public events and to the media, family members also sought to draw attention to the larger problem that Daleen's disappearance typified. They waited through the many pretrial delays, and the Muskegos repeatedly drove the nearly 375 kilometres to Saskatoon from their home in Onion Lake to stay in the city to attend the often-recessed trial.

There they sat with the Bosses and other family members, friends, and supporters, including IE members, to listen to often mind-numbing legal arguments from which reference to Daleen would sometimes disappear. All heard undercover-police-recorded evidence of Hales referring in the most dehumanizing racist and sexist ways to the young woman they loved. His having stomped on and burnt her body before secreting the remains beneath an old refrigerator in a field that served as a bush-party site were "details" sprung on the family in court.[10] Thus, they were traumatized anew.

Because IE members have sought at all stages to bear witness to the family's suffering and anger, we are keenly aware of the huge emotional and financial tolls on Daleen's family. IE therefore joined forces with the Muskegos to publicize her disappearance and murder, and to press for justice. IE participated in the awareness walks and runs, and, after Daleen's remains were found, the memorial runs, for which the organization sometimes provided water and other refreshments. Despite the many individuals and organizations that offered support, the family's resources were strained by searching for their loved one, so IE arranged to help feed and pay for accommodations for members of Daleen's family who were in from out-of-town for meetings and the trial. Collective members are further motivated in our work by knowing that a little girl, three at the time of her mother's disappearance in 2004, was, for all her family's attempts to protect and nurture her, growing up grief-stricken and motherless in the shadow of the long search for Daleen and the long uncertainty of the outcome of the Hales trial until its conclusion on December 16, 2014. IE wants to do all it can to ensure that the world she knows as an adult will be a much safer place for her than it was for her mother.

Contexts of Founding of IE/Women Walking Together

While Indigenous women have known for several hundred years that in Canada they face discrimination whose most violent manifestation is abduction and murder, few beyond their circles paid attention. The national context of the 2006 founding of IE includes, first, the Aboriginal Justice Implementation Committee's 1999 release of *The Death of Helen Betty Osborne*, which sparked renewed discussion of the brutal 1971 murder of Osborne; second, wider public attention to the many young Aboriginal women and girls who went missing or were murdered along BC's Highway of Tears before the 2002 disappearance there of white tree-planter Nicole Hoar spiked interest;[11] and third, following a not-guilty plea in January 2006, the much anticipated opening in January 2007 of the trial of Port Coquitlam pig farmer Robert "Willie" Pickton, who often exercised his serial butchery on Indigenous women from Vancouver's Downtown Eastside.[12]

The situation in Saskatchewan was similarly dire. In 1995, Pamela George, a mother of two from the Sakimay reserve, was killed by two young, middle-class, white men, and in the 1997 trial of her two murderers, George, an occasional prostitute, often seemed as much on trial as the men.[13] A similar reversal of blame in a trial in 2003 followed the 2001 sexual assault of a twelve-year-old Saulteaux girl near Tisdale by three young, white males. Both media and court discourse treated the assault as "a one-off occurrence done by 'some of our boys'" while constructing the girl as coming from a people whose representation suggests "violence is who they really are," writes Carol Schick.[14] These outrages followed various criminal matters tied to John Martin Crawford, a white predator on Aboriginal women. After serving his sentence for the largely unremarked 1981 Lethbridge murder of Mary Jane Serloin (35), in 1992 Crawford was charged in Saskatchewan with the rape of thirty-six-year-old Janet Sylvester, who was later found murdered.[15] That killing remains unsolved, as do the contemporaneous disappearances of Shirley Lonethunder and Cynthia Baldhead. Crawford's 1995 conviction for the 1992 murders of Shelley Napope (16), Eva Taysup (30), and Calinda Waterhen (22) nevertheless went so nearly unnoticed at the time Paul Bernardo was on trial for kidnapping, raping, and murdering two Euro-Canadian girls and sexually assaulting others that Saskatchewan Indian Federated College professor Janice Acoose reported "wait[ing] in agonized and frustrated silence for some kind of expression of concern (perhaps even outrage) from members of the community, women's groups, or political organizations."[16]

Nationally, the picture began to change in 2004 when Amnesty International in *Stolen Sisters* called the world's attention to the grossly disproportionate rate at which Indigenous women were going missing and/or being killed relative to their proportion in the Canadian population, especially in cities of the western provinces.[17] The next year, the Native Women's Association of Canada (NWAC) launched its Sisters in Spirit (SIS) initiative in the belief that "over the past 20 years, approximately 500 Aboriginal women have gone missing in communities across Canada. Yet government, the media, and Canadian society continue to remain silent."[18] NWAC would receive $5 million from Status of Women Canada between 2005 and 2010 to "[identify] root causes, trends and circumstances of violence that have led to disappearance [*sic*] and death of Aboriginal women and girls."[19]

In fall 2005, Monica Goulet, then the City of Saskatoon's Cultural Diversity and Race Relations Coordinator, sent out widely to the public, via a listserv, an email calling for people to come together to discuss the level of violence Indigenous women in Canada were facing:

> *Many of us are concerned about the disturbing frequency of missing Aboriginal women. Status of Women Canada issued a news release on May 17th, 2005 about the Sisters in Spirit Initiative. Apparently, the Native Women's Association of Canada has received $5 million in funding over a five-year period to "work in collaboration with other Aboriginal Women's Organizations and the federal government to improve the human rights of and address the violence facing Aboriginal women in Canada."*
>
> *The Cultural Diversity and Race Relations Policy states that "there will be increased awareness and understanding in the community regarding the issues, and acceptance of the various cultures that make up Saskatoon" and "there will be zero tolerance for racism or discrimination in Saskatoon."*
>
> *The Honourable Liza Frulla, Minister of Canadian Heritage and Minister responsible for the Status of Women stated, "We want Canada to be a nation in which Aboriginal women are free from discrimination, fear and violence. We must reduce their marginalization by addressing the root causes that put them in danger."*
>
> *Following Thanksgiving weekend, there will be an opportunity to discuss how we can address this in our communities.*

The initial meeting to address these concerns was held at the White Buffalo Youth Lodge in Saskatoon October 26, 2005, and was attended by approximately seventy-five concerned citizens, about half of them men.[20] Attendees included Indigenous and non-Indigenous academics, politicians, journalists, public service employees, and university students. They represented grass-roots and community organizations, or simply themselves. Their common concern was the outrageous lack of attention and priority given to cases of missing and murdered Indigenous women and girls, particularly in and around Saskatoon, and about the continued threat this indifference posed to a vulnerable segment of the population.

The group decided that something had to be done, and they believed the first step was to create awareness of the issues. A core group of volunteers, chaired by leaders of the City of Saskatoon's Cultural Diversity and Race Relations Committee and the Saskatchewan Human Rights Commission, began meeting on a regular basis to plan a province-wide forum. That forum was held on International Human Rights Day, December 10, 2005, again at White Buffalo. The Organizing Committee invited the Smokeydays, Napopes, and Muskegos, all families of missing Indigenous women; the Saskatchewan Aboriginal Women's Circle Corporation; Premier Lorne Calvert; provincial Justice Minister Frank Quennell, and Elders Maria and Walter Linklater. Empty chairs with blankets and pictures of the current missing Indigenous women of Saskatchewan were set up in the front row of the auditorium to remember and honour the women. The forum attracted a huge turnout from the community, with over 180 participants, and representation from a wide coalition of Saskatoon-based community groups, First Nations and Métis government leaders, activists, academics, and grassroots people, as well as provincial organizations.

Following the successful provincial forum, participants decided that work needed to continue. Meetings under the banner "Missing Aboriginal Women" led to a first round of strategic planning in the spring of 2006 for the group that decided to call itself Iskwewuk E-wichiwitochik (Women Walking Together). Membership included representatives from Amnesty International Canada Chapter 33, the United Way of Saskatoon and Area, the University of Saskatchewan Native Studies Department, the Saskatchewan

Human Rights Commission, Saskatoon's United Church Inner City Ministry, and Catholic Diocese's Justice and Peace Commission. The Cree (nehiyaw) name of the group was chosen to signify female solidarity and for its decolonizing effect in using the dominant Indigenous language both of the territory in which the collective primarily operates and of the ancestors of the majority of IE's members. The name further signifies work across (principally) racialized and class divides. Initially about 10 per cent of the group was male, but IE was conceived of as, and remains, a woman's group. However, members' male partners continue to offer support to our work at key times. The group wished to avoid any hint of wardship and decided its role wasn't to create solutions to what is a national and international problem, but to act locally, walking and working in solidarity with social justice allies to fulfill its vision and purposes.

IE's Vision and Purposes

The depiction of IE's vision statement that follows was created during a strategic planning session. This image represents our taking "respect for all life" as our highest value, our knowledge that overarching macro issues contribute both to violence and to well-being, and our understanding of the factors constituting the environment in which women live. At the outset, we formally recognized a distinction between missing and taken women, but over time came to unify those two categories in our discourse. In practice, however, we remain aware of categorical differences as we monitor media reports and share information about missing persons, male and female, not all of whom stay missing or turn out to be murder victims. Indigenous minors, for example, especially those in state care, are frequently runaways, and Indigenous women are occasionally reported missing when they have chosen, often for reasons of safety, to leave unannounced the situations in which they are living.

Depiction of IE's vision statement.

Respect for Life

macro issues contributing
to violence...to well-being

Missing Aboriginal Women · Murdered Aboriginal Women · Taken Aboriginal Women

Iskwewuk E-wichiwitochik's logo.

The belief that tears shared in the sacred space of a circle are healing explains the ring of tears that is the principal element of our logo. That ring also signifies buffalos' outward-facing protective circle, just as IE believes we must face head-on the challenges of eliminating violence against Indigenous women. The logo further represents the circles in which ayisiyinowak—human beings—live and love, and that each and every Indigenous woman or girl who goes missing is part of such circles, causing the ongoing grief represented by the ring of tears.

Iskwewuk E-wichiwitochik's core purposes are

- to provide moral and direct support to families of missing Indigenous women and girls;
- to call attention to and widen memory of missing and murdered Indigenous women and girls;
- to raise awareness through education and political action of the systemic nature of issues (such as racism and poverty) contributing to violence against women and girls, especially Indigenous females;
- to work with other organizations and programs in the prevention of violence; and
- to network and act with other organizations that are committed to social justice and peace.

The Principles of IE's Autonomous Governance

IE operates on ethical and political principles based on traditional Indigenous philosophy. Our work comes from a non-coercive standpoint and a sense of moral responsibility for the actions needed to support the families of those living in trauma occasioned by the crisis of a missing or murdered loved one. These principles include paying attention to local Indigenous protocols and procedures in the conduct of our work internally and externally; inclusivity; and respecting the wholeness of being as individuals in community, society, and the natural environment. According to founding IE member Christine Smillie, "a key to how we [have] work[ed] together since the beginning" has been non-Indigenous members recognizing "that leadership is provided by our Aboriginal sisters... We support them as much as we can. Our Aboriginal sisters also give us direction for how we work with their elders, the families of the disappeared, etc."

The group functions through learning together as a community of people; consensus decision-making; collective responsibility and leadership; thankfulness for what we have been given;

invocation to kisē Manitou—the Great Spirit, and to some, God—to bring our collective energies together for a greater good; a sense of community in place, mind, and spirit; volunteerism; reflection; and dynamic responsiveness to opportunities that arise for our work. So that IE remains Indigenously centred, it operates with a carefully guarded ideal of autonomy, understood as the freedom to do IE's work the way we want to do it, without manipulating to fit a specified methodology; it's our ways of doing and knowing. This guarding of autonomy is one key to the collective's success, but works in concert with the group's strategy of engaging with allies, including non-governmental and community-based organizations, and those who have provided crucial funding but won't compromise the group's self-governance.

IE does not have an office and receives no government funding. To ensure its autonomy, it has never pursued non-profit status, even when doing so meant we were not eligible for potentially substantial and ongoing financial backing. Thus, we have relied on generous individuals' donations and fundraising by activities such as steak nights and auctions on donated items, and seeking financial donations. More recently, awareness of IE's work and foundational principles has garnered unsolicited donations from various sources. Membership is fluid,[21] and no member has ever been paid for her work in IE, though, for some, regular job activities align with IE's activities. As each member brings different gifts and connections to various communities, members will volunteer or are called upon as necessary to give their time, gifts, and energy to various tasks and requests, including writing this chapter. Work done on a volunteer basis acts as a guarantor of commitment to the cause and has likely contributed to a trust relationship with families and other groups concerned about the missing and murdered because, when members aren't paid for their work, no suspicion of their gaining from others' misery can arise.

IE's Activities

IE has been able to fulfill many of its purposes through a variety of activities. These activities include organizing and hosting vigils, marches, and other public gatherings that honour and memorialize the missing and murdered and that place their families at the centre of the gatherings; holding and supporting other public education and sensitization events; networking with allies; fundraising to support such activities; communicating vigorously both internally and externally; and lobbying all levels of government in Canada, including provincial and national Indigenous ones. The account of activities outlined below is not exhaustive, but is intended to give readers a sense of the range and extent of IE's work to create the kind of systemic change that we seek for Indigenous females and the whole human family.

Supporting Families of the Missing and Murdered

We believe our most important task is to develop and maintain caring connections to the families with a missing or murdered loved one. We assist these families by providing monetary support for their speaking invitations and by group attendance to lend moral support at trials and to enable any necessary responses to media reports of proceedings. Arranging forums for family members to speak publicly about their missing loved ones is our foremost method of doing our family support work, however. IE does not seek out family members of missing and murdered Indigenous women; we only support those families who have gone public and are using media, police, search teams, and/or support groups to assist them during a time of trauma. This practice respects families' right to privacy should they choose it. As of January 2018, IE has provided financial support to twenty-one families, including three from out of province but with connections in Saskatchewan.

IE's sense of the importance of key family members being able to tell their story is exemplified by its support of Carol Wolfe, whose daughter, Karina Beth-Ann Wolfe, went missing from Saskatoon in 2010. Carol is deaf, which has made her search for her daughter and communicating with police and the public more difficult. Victim Services only pays for an interpreter for events they organize, so IE has repeatedly funded this service, which is crucial to Carol's ability to participate in memorial and awareness-raising events. Carol never gave up looking for Karina until police discovered her remains on November 10, 2015, guided by information given by Jerry Constant, the man later convicted of murdering Karina and of offering indignity to her remains by putting her body in a plastic tub along with garbage bags and dumping her in wetlands northwest of Saskatoon.[22] IE members morally supported Carol at the trial, and arranged for her to tell her daughter's story on numerous public occasions, including at Saskatoon's SIS vigils in 2012 and 2013, and in 2014 at the official opening of Jaime Black's REDress installation. When Carol told the riveted university audience the heartbreaking story of Karina's disappearance and her family's determined search for her, Carol left her listeners with a clear sense of the agony of having a missing loved one for years, thus helping IE realize its goal to increase empathy for families of the missing and murdered.[23]

Creating Awareness of the Missing and Murdered

To succeed in raising awareness about the missing and murdered, we have learned the importance of being involved with non-Indigenous as well as Indigenous society in a variety of activities, including hosting and/or participation in searches, vigils, memorial and awareness walks, family healing gatherings, conferences and workshops; contributing to plans to bring art installations to our city; creating other kinds of memorials; and engaging with and through the media. We thus keep society and the general public informed about the ongoing nature and scale of the atrocity, provide analysis of root causes, share strategies for addressing the crisis, and prompt others to be on the lookout for any leads that may assist the families, police services, and search units in locating a missing loved one.

In Saskatoon and surrounding areas, IE has either led co-ordination or been asked to participate in numerous awareness actions. A sample of actions indicates the breadth of IE's involvement. Some events such as the annual December 6 Take Back the Night Walk were broadly concerned with violence against women. Others, such as parades through city streets or public gatherings carrying banners and pictures of the missing and murdered (e.g., Walk for Justice and its successor, the Tears for Justice Walk; Honouring Our Sisters Walk held in conjunction with the Wanuskewin Powwow; the Prince Albert Grand Council Annual Walk), and the NWAC Family Healing Gathering held in Saskatoon in 2007, had a more specific focus on Aboriginal women.

We have participated in or presented at local, national, and international conferences and led workshops. Local conferences include the Cutting Edge: Saskatchewan Provincial Restorative Justice Conference, aimed at greater justice for Aboriginal people; the Missing Women's Conference, University of Regina, which had strong participation from Mexico; the Awâsis Aboriginal Education Conference; the Amnesty International Saskatchewan Fall Regional conference; and the Our Way Conference hosted by the University of Saskatchewan Native Law Centre and College of Law Ariel F. Sallows Chair in Human Rights, with Oskayak High School. We also prepared and hosted a workshop for a Federation of Saskatchewan Indian Nations Youth Leadership event, Supporting the Way Forward. Participation in national conferences includes organizing and facilitating an education event "Sharing Stories of Missing and Murdered Indigenous Women in Saskatchewan: Not Invisible" for a National Anglican Church Women's Presidents' conference in Saskatoon, our subtitle being a rejoinder to the House of Commons' *Invisible Women: A Call to Action: A Report on Missing and Murdered Indigenous Women in Canada*. As a follow-up to this event, IE created a list of resources to be posted to diocesan websites to help session attendees learn more about the roots, nature, and scale of the problem. The Healing Our Spirits Worldwide Conference in Hawaii in 2010 provided IE's first opportunity to send a representative abroad to share its strategies for addressing violence against Indigenous women and learn about others' work in the field, and, at the North American Indigenous Studies Association conference hosted by the University of Saskatchewan in 2013, Okemaysim-Sicotte presented "Missing Indigenous Women: Remembrance, Awareness, and Support" in a panel that also featured US and Swedish presenters.

IE believes that public memorials to missing and murdered Indigenous women and girls counter erasure from public space and history of both the painful issue and specific women and girls. We share Adrian Stimson's vision that memorials can "transform an ending into a beginning"[24] because they honour those whom perpetrators of violence have so dishonoured and show a new valuing of Indigenous women and girls that can also help families heal. Members have therefore participated on the committee led by the Saskatoon Tribal Council, the Saskatoon Police Service, and the City of Saskatoon to establish a memorial for missing and murdered Indigenous women and girls. We participated in the unveiling of *Wicanhpi Duta Win, or Red Star Woman*, in front of the Saskatoon Police Service building on May 5, 2017.[25] Honouring and memorializing MMIWG, the monument also teaches present and future generations about the uncivil war against Indigenous females. As a kind of "resistant remembering" of the violence,[26] it will also be a means of provoking change. Like other memorials to murdered women across Canada, it will "[tell] two stories,"[27] the horrific one of unrelenting violence against women and girls, and the more hopeful one of women and men working together to end that violence.

Art installations can be a powerful way of raising awareness of an issue, moving new people to action to eliminate violence against Indigenous women and girls, and re-energizing the struggle-worn. IE's support for such installations and its own organizing of an art show also come from the desire to humanize the statistics on the missing and murdered. As Elizabeth Matheson writes, "creative gestures…have the possibility of restoring the human element to a part of twenty-first-century life that is often depersonalized."[28] Thus, IE participated in bridging work between families and the organizers of a University of Saskatchewan 2014 project to bring Jaime Black's REDress memorial installation to the campus and to a site serving Saskatoon's core neighbourhoods. Collective members also contributed to the planning and acted as family liaison for Walking With Our Sisters, Saskatoon, a ceremonial installation of moccasin vamps (decorated tops), lovingly executed by over 1,700 artists to honour the missing and murdered.[29]

Raising awareness is a constant activity, and IE is generally highly receptive to any opportunities that arise. However, we have learned to make strategic choices given our limited resources and our knowledge of those issuing invitations. Thus, when the regional appointee to the Canadian government's Special Parliamentary Committee on Violence against Indigenous Women extended an invitation to meet with us, we declined to participate because we lacked confidence in the appointee's ability (based on previous handling of other files) to represent the serious and critical matter with which the committee was charged. We did, however, meet with Status of Women Minister Kellie Leitch in May 2014, before the release of the Government of Canada's *Action Plan to Address Family Violence and Violent Crimes against Aboriginal Women and Girls*, and were distressed to see the report's privileging of the tough-on-crime stance and lack of new money to address the social determinants of violence.

(Net)Working with Social Justice Organizations
Building relationships and networking with organizations that are committed to social justice, peace, and eliminating violence is an ongoing activity that requires constant communication and

responsiveness to national and local developments. In this regard, IE has worked most closely with Amnesty International through founding IE member Helen Smith-McIntyre. Okemaysim-Sicotte did an interview for the tenth anniversary of Amnesty's *Stolen Sisters* report[30] and acted as workshop leader for Amnesty Saskatchewan's 2014 conference, Getting Active with Amnesty. IE has also networked significantly with NWAC, sharing information, hosting annual SIS vigils in Saskatoon since 2006, and contributing squares for the SIS memorial quilt. IE also maintains relationships with police forces, developing an increasingly strong relationship with former Chief of Saskatoon Police Services (2006–2017) and past President of the Canadian Association of Chiefs of Police (2014–2016) Clive Weighill.

Communications

In addition to monitoring news stories about Indigenous women and girls who go missing or are found alive or murdered, related legal proceedings, and political responses to the crisis, IE also actively seeks opportunities to participate in various media. We make presentations about the missing and murdered and our work to programs on national television networks and both Aboriginal and non-Aboriginal radio stations. We give interviews to reporters from the *Regina Leader-Post*, *Saskatoon StarPhoenix*, and 650 CKOM-AM. We participate in podcasts, write letters to newspaper editors, and offer opinion pieces both in and outside the province when mistaken or misleading constructions of events or situations call us to challenge discourse that diminishes Indigenous women's and girls' lives. We think that affirming journalists when they report respectfully on the lives and deaths of the missing and murdered is important, too; Jeremy Warren's *StarPhoenix* 2014 article "Waiting for Daleen" is a case in point.[31]

Collective members stay in touch between meetings and events, often daily, and usually weekly, most often by emails, sharing news about positive events and information about specific cases of the missing and murdered and alerts provided by our police and other contacts about dangerous offenders in our vicinity. Posts on the collective's Facebook page form a running history of reports of new missing and murdered Indigenous women and girls or violent assaults on them, the progress of cases under investigation, and political and artistic work to press communities and governments for meaningful action on the issue.[32]

Lobbying

By providing information and feedback to IE member and Canadian Senator Lillian Dyck, speaking with provincial politicians and Saskatoon city councillors, and at meetings of the Federation of Saskatchewan Indian Nations and the Assembly of First Nations, IE seeks to influence policy related to missing and murdered Indigenous women and girls, and to prompt action. Our focus in lobbying is to get politicians to recognize the scale and urgency of the problem, to draw on the painfully won knowledge of families with a missing or murdered loved one to make Canadian institutions' responses to those victimized by such trauma more humane, and to help find solutions that don't oversimplify the interrelated problems at the heart of the issue.

The Saskatchewan Contexts of IE's Ongoing and Future Work

Since IE was founded, the social and political landscape in Saskatoon, as elsewhere, has shifted. The pre-IE provincial forum in 2005 was used as a launch of the Saskatchewan Provincial Partnership Committee on Missing Persons, whose members were "to work towards a future that ensures that when people go missing there is a full response that mobilizes all necessary participants and that recognizes the equal value of every life."[33] The committee's mandate and vision were not specifically focused on Aboriginal women, and IE was not offered a seat on the committee. The Saskatchewan government invested nearly $2 million over the next three years to solve historical and current cases of missing persons in Saskatchewan, and to enhance police and community responses to cases of missing persons. According to the committee's final report, a Provincial Cold Case Investigators Association (PCCIA) had been formed in 2003 with representatives from the RCMP and Saskatchewan's large municipal police services.[34] It meets at least every six months to "share information, expertise, and...resources...to try to find missing persons," and other provinces' investigators are also beneficiaries of PCCIA's information sharing.[35] The PCCIA played a key role in the development of the Saskatchewan Missing Persons website, which was launched in April 2006 and makes missing persons data readily available to both general public and police services.[36] After the first sixteen months of operation, the PCCIA reported that investigators had found five long-term missing persons, all deceased and all female, in Saskatchewan, three of which resulted in homicide investigations.[37] In the Victoria Nashacappo case, the Saskatchewan Association of Chiefs of Police website reported that Brian Casement was convicted of first-degree murder in Saskatoon on January 21, 2010.[38] The Saskatchewan Association of Chiefs of Police is the only policing body to present detailed statistics on missing persons in their jurisdiction.[39] At the end of December 2014, the Saskatchewan Association of Chiefs of Police website reported that 18 of 33, or 54.5 per cent, of missing women in the province were of Aboriginal ancestry.[40]

Among the key findings of the 2010 SIS report were the linking of missing and murdered Aboriginal women and girls and fetal alcohol spectrum disorder, hitchhiking, gangs, mobility from reserve setting to urban areas and within the city of residence, and jurisdictional issues.[41] In working with families in Saskatchewan, IE has learned that the province's missing and murdered Indigenous females come from diverse backgrounds, thus defying the stereotypes propagated and perpetuated by the media. Among those reported missing and murdered in Saskatchewan, some were unluckily in a place and at a time that a predator was present; some were university students; another was a senior living alone on her property; and others young women walking home in an urban area.

Achievements, Challenges, and Future Plans

After over twelve years, Iskwewuk E-wichiwitochik continues to function and thrive, with an ever-renewing membership. As of January 2018, IE Co-Chairs are LaPlante and Okemaysim-Sicotte; Keepers of Records are any Keepers of the Circle (core members); and the Keeper of Communications (Facebook) is Okemaysim-Sicotte. In calling attention to the problem of missing and murdered Indigenous women and girls, IE has found practical ways to engage ordinary citizens as well as societal leaders. In the eleven years the group has been working on raising awareness of missing and murdered Indigenous women through the SIS vigils and like gatherings, about 1,650 people have attended our events. We have developed a methodology that involves bringing together resources from diverse social justice communities and some individuals to enable us to provide forums in which we and others can hear the families' stories, and simultaneously educate ourselves and the broader public about the human loss and pain behind what can be dehumanizing rehearsals of statistics, indifference, or walls of ignorance or denial about the problem. And increasingly, we have been called on to support other groups in their quest to learn more about the issue or raise awareness of the problem.

We have met approximately 145 times, averaging a meeting per month, and participated in over 150 actions. IE has also set annual dates to create awareness and remembrance activities. In addition to the October 4th national SIS vigils, we mark the December 6th National Day for Remembrance and Action on Violence Against Women, December 10th International Human Rights Day, March 8th International Women's Day, February 14th Annual Women's Memorial March, and March 21st International Day of Elimination of Racial Discrimination. We have an informational brochure, a banner, and a growing Facebook group, and we have been successful locally in building wider awareness of the scale and urgency of the problem. One small measure of that success is that when Aboriginal women or girls are officially reported missing or when their bodies are found, the news now most often appears on the first to third pages of the *Saskatoon StarPhoenix*, rather than on the back page.

Despite the group's successes, the number of missing and murdered Indigenous women and girls in Saskatchewan and Canada has, sadly, continued to grow.[42] By 2009, NWAC recorded 520 cases of missing and murdered Aboriginal women and girls, the majority of the disappearances and deaths occurring in the western provinces and among women under the age of thirty-one, many of whom are mothers who leave children behind.[43] This number doubled to 1,181 in the RCMP's 2014 national overview, which covered 1980 to 2012.[44] The issue, these profoundly distressing realities demonstrate, are systemic, deeply and complexly embedded throughout Canadian societal structures. Where, then, do we go from here?

We expect that IE's work will continue to be primarily family focused, and that we will keep on learning from the stories families tell of their missing or murdered loved ones. No doubt our work with the media will continue through interviews and writing, and will form part of the larger project of public education. Education about the issue is key to solving it. Therefore, IE plans to work with existing institutions and programs designed to prevent violence and to enhance decision-making skills of youth in schools and communities.

Believing that Canada's National Inquiry into MMIWG2S will have an educative role as well as serve IE's other purposes, we are supporting the inquiry in a variety of ways. For example, we met with Ministers Bennett and Wilson-Raybould during the pre-inquiry; Okemaysim-Sicotte actively participated in planning the inquiry launch for August 2016, and accepted the invitation to attend (LaPlante also attended); before and after the launch, we spoke with

Prime Minister Justin Trudeau on a number of occasions about the need for a national inquiry; we've helped family members to register to testify at hearings; and we hosted and participated in Saskatoon hearings November 20–24, 2017. In 2018, we are on the schedule of those with standing at the inquiry and expect to attend or participate in an expert panel. Our Co-Chairs have been particularly active as volunteers—Okeymaysim-Sicotte on the Saskatchewan Community Lead Team and LaPlante as part of the National Family Advisory Circle—and, having missing family members, in a family capacity as well.

We will continue to hope that Canada's National Inquiry into MMIWG2S will spur justice in this context. Until the racism, sexism, and homophobia that underlie the disappearances and murders have been comprehensively and effectively addressed, IE will continue the critical work of envisioning an end to this national atrocity, doing what we can within our strategically limited goals to contribute to realizing it, and easing the pain along the way for those with loved ones for whom that ending did not come soon enough.

265

AUTHOR'S NOTE

IE would like to thank the many individuals, institutions, organizations, and businesses, too numerous to mention by name, for their past and present support. We could not have done the work we have for the past twelve years without their help.

NOTES

1. Pauline Muskego and Herb Muskego, "The Story of the Disappearance of Daleen Kay Bosse (Muskego)," in *Torn from Our Midst: Voices of Grief, Healing and Action from the Missing Indigenous Women Conference, 2008*, ed. A. Brenda Anderson, Wendee Kubik, and Mary Rucklos Hampton (Regina: University of Regina Press, 2010), 36; Holly A McKenzie, "'She Was Not Into Drugs and Partying. She Was a Wife and Mother': Media Representations and (Re)presentations of Daleen Kay Bosse (Muskego)," in *Torn from Our Midst*, 148.

2. The ruling was made July 31, 2014 in the context of the Nelson Lyle Hart case, *R. v. Hart*, 2014, SCC 52. The Crown had appealed the Court of Appeal for Newfoundland and Labrador's overturning of Hart's 2007 conviction on two counts of murder in the drowning deaths of his three-year-old twin daughters, Karen and Krista, and the ordering of a new trial.

3. The English name is a metaphorical translation of the Cree for "women working together."

4. Canada, House of Commons, Special Committee on Violence against Indigenous Women, *Invisible Women: A Call to Action: A Report on Missing and Murdered Indigenous Women in Canada*, 41st Parliament, First Session (March 2014), 56, http://publications.gc.ca/collections/collection_2014/parl/xc2-411/XC2-411-2-1-1-eng.pdf.

5. For more information about the Everyday Political Citizen award, see the Samara Canada website at www.samaracanada.com/everyday-political-citizen.

6. No matter the life course of the woman or girl who goes missing, that person has innate value as a human being and is embedded in networks of friends and relations. No person is justly viewed as a throwaway, then. However, Daleen defied the cruel and misleading stereotype of the missing or murdered Indigenous woman. Hers was a family in which the parents, who are teachers, consciously broadened the children's horizons, and Daleen was highly active in extracurricular activities as both a child and teenager, travelled within Canada and abroad, secured her first job at thirteen, and was successful both academically and socially. See Muskego and Muskego, "The Story of the Disappearance of Daleen," 35–36.

7. Darlene Okemaysim-Sicotte, Victim impact statement at Douglas Hales Trial, December 16, 2014, (unpublished), 2.

8. Okemaysim-Sicotte, Victim impact statement.

9. Muskego and Muskego, "The Story of the Disappearance of Daleen," 148. The Federation of Saskatchewan Indian Nations (now called the Federation of Sovereign Indigenous Nations) established the Justice Secretariat's Special Investigations Unit in February 2000 to call for a justice inquiry because of widespread perception among First Nations people of "abuse by police officers and other personnel within institutions of justice." Federation of Saskatchewan Indian Nations, accessed December 28, 2014, http://fsin.com/index.php/special-investigations-unit.html. Furthermore, "On March 1, 2000 the Federation established a Toll-Free Help Line to receive calls regarding abuse by police officers and

other personnel within institutions of justice in Saskatchewan." Federation of Sovereign Indigenous Nations, Special Investigations Unit, accessed January 2, 2018, http://www.fsin.com/justice/special-investigations-unit/.

10. Daleen's family apparently only learned during the courtroom reading of the charges against Hales that he had set Daleen's body on fire. He later admitted under questioning he couldn't be sure she was dead when he did so.

11. Reported numbers vary widely according to distance from the notorious Highway 16 stretch between Prince George and Prince Rupert, BC, but the RCMP Project E-PANA has, according to its website, investigated eighteen cases of missing and murdered women along Highways 16, 5, and 97, as of January 2018 (accessed January 2, 2018, http://bc.cb.rcmp-grc.gc.ca/ViewPage.action?siteNodeId=1525). The Carrier Sekani Tribal Council's Highway of Tears Initiative's website reports that, of the nine young women who went missing or were found murdered along Highway 16 between 1989 and 2006, "all but one…were Aboriginal." The website also reports that of women who have gone missing in Northern BC, "many people living in the north believe that the number exceeds 30" (accessed January 31, 2015, http://www.highwayoftears.ca/about-us/highway-of-tears).

12. D. Kim Rossmo, *Criminal Investigative Failures* (Boca Raton, FL: CRC Press, 2008), 29, 33.

13. Sherene Razack, "Gendered Racial Violence and Spatialized Justice: The Murder of Pamela George," in *Race, Space, and the Law: Unmapping a White Settler Society*, ed. Sherene Razack (Toronto: Between the Lines, 2002), 123, 126.

14. Carol Schick, "Media: A Canadian Response," in *Torn from Our Midst*, 135, 136, 140.

15. Warren Goulding, *Just Another Indian: A Serial Killer and Canada's Indifference* (Saskatoon: Fifth House, 2001), xiv.

16. Janice Acoose (Misko-Kìsikàwihkwè), *Iskwewak—Kah' Ki Yaw Ni Wahkomakanak: Neither Indian Princesses nor Easy Squaws* (Toronto: Women's Press, 1995), 86.

17. Amnesty International, *Stolen Sisters: A Human Rights Response to Discrimination and Violence against Indigenous Women in Canada* (Ottawa: Amnesty International, 2004), 3, http://amnesty.ca/sites/default/files/amr200032004enstolensisters.pdf; Native Women's

Association of Canada, *What Their Stories Tell Us: Research Findings from the Sisters in Spirit Initiative* (Ottawa: Native Women's Association of Canada, 2010), 2, https://nwac.ca/wp-content/uploads/2015/07/2010-What-Their-Stories-Tell-Us-Research-Findings-SIS-Initiative.pdf.

18. NWAC, *Voices of Our Sisters in Spirit: A Research and Policy Report to Families and Communities* (Ottawa: NWAC, November 2008), accessed December 27, 2014, http://www.nwac-hq.org/en/sisresearch.html.

19. Canada, House of Commons, Standing Committee on the Status of Women, *Ending Violence against Aboriginal Women and Girls: Empowerment— A New Beginning*, 41st Parliament, 1st Session (December 2011), 11, http://publications.gc.ca/collections/collection_2011/parl/XC71-1-411-01-eng.pdf.

20. White Buffalo Youth Lodge is "dedicated to improv[ing] the quality of life and health for children, youth, young adults and their families in the inner city through integrated, holistic support services." It is "a multipurpose centre used during the day for educational classes, functions, meetings, etc., and in the late afternoon/evening it serves as a [fee-free] youth recreational facility." "White Buffalo Youth Lodge, Description of Program," Saskatoon Tribal Council, accessed November 11, 2014, http://www.sktc.sk.ca/programs-services/family-community-services/community-supports/white-buffalo-youth-lodge/.

21. Founding members were Val Arnault-Pelletier, Mary-Ann Assailly,* Rita Bouvier, Darlene Desmarais, Lillian Dyck, Monica Goulet, Kit Loewen, Shannon Louttit, the late Patricia Monture, Pauline Muskego, Darlene Okemaysim (now Okemaysim-Sicotte),* Lorraine Pura,* Marlee Ritchie, Rose Roberts, Priscilla Settee, Christine Smillie, Rajesh Saxena, Helen Smith-McIntyre,* Carol Thomas, Colleen Thomas, and Glenda Yuzicappi. As of January 2018, in addition to the names asterisked above, the most active members include Louise Clarke, Rachel Fiddler, Susan Gingell, Myrna LaPlante, and Kathie Pruden.

22. Bre McAdam, "'What You Did Shattered My Heart': Karina Wolf's Mother Tells Murderer," *Saskatoon StarPhoenix*, June 17, 2016, http://thestarphoenix.com/news/crime/karina-wolfe-jerry-constant-pleads-guilty-murder-life-sentence2.

23. CTV News employee and filmmaker Grace Smith, who made the documentary *My Only Daughter* (2016) to tell Karina's story, explains in the film's "Production Notes" online, "I was watching our newscast, and saw a story about the Red Dress project display at the University of

Saskatchewan. It moved me, because it helped me understand the gravity of the situation. I wanted to do something and since I knew Carol personally, approached her and asked if she wanted a documentary made on her daughter Karina." See https://gracesmithdocumentary.com/my-only-daughter/.

24. Adrian Stimson, "Bison Sentinels: A Living Memorial to Murdered Missing and Aboriginal Women," in *Torn from Our Midst*, 117. Stimson was writing specifically of living memorials, but we believe the idea holds for other kinds of memorials.

25. Saskatoon Police Service, "Missing and Murdered Indigenous Women and Girls Monument Unveiling – SPS HQ," news release, May 5, 2017, https://saskatoonpolice.ca/events/227.

26. Cultural Memory Group (Christine Bold, Sly Castaldi, Ric Knowles, Jodie McConnell, and Lisa Shincariol), *Remembering Women Murdered by Men: Memorials across Canada* (Toronto: Sumach Press, 2006), 23.

27. Cultural Memory Group, *Remembering Women*, 18.

28. Elizabeth Matheson, "Missing and Taken," in *Torn from Our Midst*, 114.

29. For more about the REDress Project, see www.theredressproject.org/; for more on Walking With Our Sisters, see http://walkingwithoursisters.ca/.

30. Okemaysim-Sicotte, "Women Walking Together: A Conversation with Darlene R. Okemaysim-Sicotte," interview by Jacqueline Hansen, *Amnesty Canada* (blog), accessed December 19, 2017, http://amnesty.ca/blog/women-walking-together-conversation-with-darlene-r-okemaysim-sicotte.

31. Jeremy Warren, "Waiting for Daleen: How a Family Never Gave Up Their Search for Justice," *Saskatoon StarPhoenix*, December 20, 2014, http://thestarphoenix.com/news/local-news/waiting-for-daleen-how-a-family-never-gave-up-their-search-for-justice.

32. Iskwewuk E-wichiwitochik Facebook page, https://www.facebook.com/groups/5646182010/.

33. Betty Ann Potruff, "Presentation of the Provincial Partnership Committee on Missing Persons," in *Torn from Our Midst*, 106.

34. Provincial Partnership Committee on Missing Persons, *Final Report of the Provincial Partnership Committee on Missing Persons* (Saskatchewan Government Publications, October 2007), 39, http://publications.gov.sk.ca/documents/9/30559-missing-persons-final.pdf.

35. Provincial Partnership Committee on Missing Persons, *Final Report*, 39.

36. The missing persons list is on the Saskatchewan Association of Chiefs of Police's homepage at www.sacp.ca.

37. Provincial Partnership Committee on Missing Persons, *Final Report*, 39.

38. "Victoria Jane Nashacappo," Saskatchewan Association of Chiefs of Police, accessed December 28, 2014, https://sacp.ca/missing/details. php?id=74.

39. NWAC, *What Their Stories Tell Us*, 16.

40. Saskatchewan Association of Chiefs of Police, "Saskatchewan Missing Persons, 1940–2014, Female Victim's Race," accessed December 27, 2014, http://sacp.ca/missing/pdf/20141210/Female_Race.pdf.

41. NWAC, *What Their Stories Tell Us*, ii.

42. Not counting cases of suspicious death and unknown ethnicity, Pearce records the following numbers from 2007, the year after IE was founded, to 2013: Missing: 2007, 2; 2008, 2; 2009, 1; 2010, 1; 2011, 0; 2012, 1; 2013, 3, and murdered: 2007, 1; 2008, 1; 2009, 0; 2010, 4; 2011, 3; 2012, 3; 2013, 2. IE members know of one additional person who went missing in 2011, and 1 murdered in 2011, 2 in 2012, 2 in 2013, and 1 in 2014. In January 2015 alone IE knows, at the time of writing, of 4 deaths of Indigenous women and girls being investigated as homicides. See Maryanne Pearce, "An Awkward Silence: Missing and Murdered Vulnerable Women and the Canadian Justice System" (LLD thesis, University of Ottawa, 2013), http://ruor.uottawa.ca/ handle/10393/26299.

43. NWAC, *What Their Stories Tell Us*, 18, ii.

44. Royal Canadian Mounted Police, *Missing and Murdered Aboriginal Women: A National Operational Overview* (Ottawa: Government of Canada, 2014), 3, http://www.rcmp-grc.gc.ca/pubs/ mmaw-faapd-eng.htm.

Iskwewuk E-wichiwitochik

15 | *Woman Sacred*

PAHAN PTE SAN WIN

Introduction

Imagine a world where each girl child anticipates her own woman-hood with excitement, knowing her community will celebrate and honour her when she reaches this rite of passage. Imagine a world where woman's sacred responsibility as the life giver to the next generation is revered and cherished. Imagine a time where woman's gifts of strength, nurturance, and sensitivity are valued and recognized as critical to the well-being of the community, where her wisdom is sought on critical matters affecting the tribe. This is a world in which the teaching of Woman Sacred is known and practiced, the world view of many tribal societies and the way of life lived by my First Nation grandmothers, my ancestors.

Through the teaching of Woman Sacred we learn that Creator put woman on Mother Earth as the vessel for the creation of new life. With this role came great responsibility for which she was also given the gifts of courage and a heart to love. The teaching of Woman Sacred reminds us that woman is sacred and to be respected, protected, and honoured at all times.

The reality for an Aboriginal woman living today is worlds away
from that of my grandmothers. Instead we can expect a life in
.which we are devalued, silenced and where a raging storm of
violence is directed towards us, and from which we must seek
shelter and, yet still too often, endure. According to a report
released in 2009 by Statistics Canada, Aboriginal women are three
times more likely to be the victim of a violent crime than non-
Aboriginal women. The report adds, " This was true regardless if
the violence occurred between strangers or acquaintances, or
within a spousal relationship."[1]

Over a twenty-year period as a social worker and therapeutic
counsellor, I have worked with hundreds of Aboriginal women
who were victims of trauma, abuse, and assault at the hands of
men. Two of these women were Betsy and Joan.

After a night of drinking and years of fighting off abuse, Betsy
hung herself while her husband watched. When her six-year-
old son awoke, he found her hanging from the shower curtain
rod. Joan went to bed beside her boyfriend after another evening
of enduring his beatings. She never woke up. She died of a brain
hemorrhage from a blow to the head. She left behind an eight-
year-old son and a newborn baby.

The horrific events women experience and the intense
suffering that carries on for so long afterwards speaks to woman's
perseverance, resiliency, and, for some, her capacity to heal. During
my career as a counsellor, I found it inspiring to witness a woman
moving beyond her pain and breaking through the blame and
judgement that followed the abuse. Yet, on a personal level, I also
found myself feeling disgust and anger towards the perpetrator.
Sometimes, at the end of a difficult day of listening to a woman
share an incident of abuse, I would make that journey down the
sidewalk from my office to my home, the weight of her story
bearing down on me. My mind would be filled with images of
what happened to her, my heart heavy from witnessing her intense

suffering. As my feet pounded the pavement, I would feel the anger rise up in me and I would think, "I hope the man who did this to her is found, locked up, and never released to harm another person again."

The Men

What happened to crush our knowledge and practice of Woman Sacred? What is it about Aboriginal women today that is so threatening to some men that they feel the need to use violence to keep us down and silent? Who are these men?

After many years of working with Aboriginal women, I found myself working as an Elder in a federal prison for men. Each day I came face to face with men who had committed heinous crimes.

My first day at work I was very surprised to learn that my counselling office had a large window in the wall and another window in the door. It was built like that for safety. In the event that there was a critical incident, the correctional officers would be able to see into my office and this would help them to resolve the situation in the safest way possible. Men in prison, just like everyone else, do not want anyone to see them when they are in a counselling session. For this reason, they learn to sit in the chair with their back to the window so that no one can see their face.

The other safety feature in my office that I was unaccustomed to was a panic button. I was to position my chair so that I could hit that red button if I ever felt threatened or in danger. One bang and a throng of officers would come running.

In my role as Elder, I met with the men for counselling and in ceremony and immediately saw there was a great need for healing and support. In time, trust grew and one by one they began to share their stories with me. I heard what had happened in their lives that had eventually led them to prison, and a profound realization came to me. These men were the sons of the women that I had worked with. They were hiding under the bed, trembling and afraid while she was being attacked. When they were small children, they were neglected, abused, and had witnessed terrible things. To my surprise, as they told their stories, the man sitting before me transformed into the innocent, vulnerable, perfect child he once was. I could see that boy was full of hope and potential and that he needed what all children need—love, food, shelter, and protection.

Sadly, this is not what happened. We as a community had failed him. We had not protected him. We had forgotten him. As a boy, he was hurt and wounded. When he grew, his hurt turned into anger. Later as a man, his anger turned into hurting others and hurting himself. That was when we found him, locked him up away from the rest of society with the rest of the unwanted—the throwaway people—hoping that he would never be released to harm another person again—just as I had hoped for on my walks home, years before. In my time working in the prison, I heard the worst stories of abuse of my entire career.

Perpetrators and Prison

Violence towards Aboriginal women is a terrible thing that robs our communities of the potential for health, for a promising future. Although we think of women as the victims of abuse and we are, the truth is we all suffer because of violence towards women. And although we think of men as the persistent perpetrators of abuse, the truth is that they too have been victims first.

Perpetrators of violence must be held accountable for these acts, and it is right and good to protect the vulnerable from those who would harm. However, punishing, blaming, hating, and locking our men away in prison is not sufficient to promote change. If it were, this problem would have been eradicated long ago. It is a temporary solution to an enduring problem. For a time, our communities feel safer; however, the absence of our men within the community robs us of the positive contribution they could make if only they could heal from the trauma they experienced and learn new ways of solving problems and interacting with others. We gain nothing when we vilify men, who in reality are our husbands, brothers, uncles, nephews, grandsons, and even grandfathers.

Prison is not a place to learn to interact in a healthy manner. Violence towards women attempts to utilize power and control as a way to deal with conflicts, differing needs and wants. Prisons use the same approach to dealing with offenders—power and control. Imprisonment reinforces an erroneous belief system that perpetuates the problem. How can we expect our men to approach others with respect when they have not even learned to respect themselves? Yet that is exactly what is needed to become a person who can contribute to the community in a positive way. A new approach that supports men to heal from the trauma they experienced followed by a re-parenting that provides them with the tools to interact in healthier ways is desperately needed. Still, treating men who offend is only one prong in a three-pronged effort to eradicate violence directed towards Aboriginal women.

Change Efforts

The second prong is healing for women. It is not enough to raise awareness of the violence, and to lock the perpetrators away and invite them to find healing. To produce lasting societal change that prevents future violence we require more. Change efforts must include women too. We need to heal from incidents of abuse and from living in an unsafe and hostile environment.

In our healing efforts we bandage the wounds, repair the damage caused from the emotional trauma, and replace the self-limiting beliefs that occur as a result of mistreatment. As victims, we often respond to abuse in ways that we later regret. Women need to heal our own self-image and sense of self-worth and forgive ourselves for our response to the abuse and violence we experience. As one victim of violence told me, "Bones mend, bruises heal but the emotional abuse, the hurts you can't see, those are the ones that are the hardest to live with. After a while

I believed all the terrible things he said about me. I felt I deserved what happened to me because I was such a bad person." One of the great tragedies of violence towards Aboriginal women, and there are many, is that over time victims of abuse begin to believe that we have no value, that we deserve the abuse. It is a fact—violence and abuse erode self-worth. Over time we believe the messages that we are not valuable.

To heal we must recognize where we have internalized negative beliefs about ourselves as Aboriginal women. Only then can we work to extinguish the message in our mind, free ourselves from its power, and replace it with a positive and truthful representation of ourselves. This is critical to living the best life possible and one in which we are safe and violence free.

Healing from the physical, emotional, and mental wounds caused by violence gives us the capacity to take the necessary steps to create a positive and healthy life. We cannot always avoid abuse, but a healthy self-image protects us with a better insight to avoid potentially violent situations and the courage and strength to stand up for ourselves when we can.

Racial Stereotypes and Gender-Based Violence

The third prong in our efforts to eradicate violence towards Aboriginal women must be directed at changing the beliefs that those outside of the Aboriginal community have about Aboriginal women. We are harmed by racial stereotypes that perpetuate the mistaken belief that Aboriginal people are somehow inferior to other nations. Misogyny is a potent fuel that ignites violence towards women.

The influence of all forms of media cannot be understated for its role in shaping public perceptions and either reinforcing or dispelling common stereotypes. Now is the time to use the power of media to mould a new positive and true image of Aboriginal women. Imagine the impact a national publicity campaign could have to offer Canadians an alternative understanding of Aboriginal women and to replace the common negative stereotypes?

Conclusion

Years ago when I was an eager university graduate, fresh from social work school, I attended all the marches to raise awareness of violence towards women. We were a small group of feminists hitting the streets with a mega horn shouting out, "Hey, hey, ho, ho. Yes means yes. No means no. Hey, hey, ho, ho, violence towards women has got to go!" Our social activism was going to change the world, intoxicating. I was thrilled to be a part of it. As a community, we had not yet awoken to the fact that Aboriginal women were so overrepresented in this group of victims that a unique and sickening phenomenon was taking place.

Now, twenty-five years later, after working with hundreds of victims, my hair is grey and I rarely march. Somewhere along the road I stopped wanting to raise awareness of the violence and began wanting to promote the teaching of Woman Sacred. I have come to believe that violence towards women is a symptom of a much bigger problem. Hate. Hate for women. Hate for Aboriginal people. Hate for ourselves.

Yet still I believe in the possibility of returning to the days of my grandmothers, where the teaching of Woman Sacred is known and honoured. I have hope that my granddaughters can live in a world where they are proud to grow into women, where they feel safe in their own homes and communities. I see that we possess the power to create significant change in this area; however, it requires that we try innovative approaches. A three-prong effort that includes healing of perpetrators as well as victims is needed. A focus on changing societal attitudes and stereotypes nation-wide is necessary to eliminate the hatred that fuels and allows the violence to continue.

Out of our collective pain for the Missing and Murdered Indigenous Women, a great demonstration of love has emerged. The Walking With Our Sisters campaign is a true example of an outpouring of love that flows to heal the wound caused by this hate. It has united concerned families and citizens within and outside of our Aboriginal communities. This is our Sisters' gift to us, as in spirit they show us the true nature of our hearts and our community. This is also the path that leads to a community where women are honoured, a path littered with demonstrations of love. That is path that I would be happy to march. I look forward to a new wave of efforts that use the demonstration of love to revive the teaching of Woman Sacred and with that change our world.

NOTE

1.   Shannon Brennan, "Violent Victimization of Aboriginal Women in the Canadian Provinces, 2009," *Juristat*, May 17, 2011, 7, www.statcan. gc.ca/pub/85-002-x/2011001/article/11439-eng.htm. This figure does not include violence against women in the North, in Yukon, Northwest Territories, and Nunavut, where the majority of Inuit women live.

16 | *Leading with Our Hearts*
Anti-Violence Action and Beadwork Circles as Colonial Resistance

LAURA HARJO, JENELL NAVARRO &

KIMBERLY ROBERTSON

Action starts at our kitchen tables, backyards, on the street,
in community spaces, and with families.
    —NATIVE YOUTH SEXUAL HEALTH NETWORK, "Supporting
    the Resurgence of Community-Based Responses to Violence"

Introduction

Sexual and gendered violence has been, and continues to be, an
integral component of settler colonialism in the United States and
Canada. Because the Indigenous anti-violence movements that
have arisen in response to this violence are composed of activists,
scholars, and survivors from literally hundreds of Indigenous
communities, the scope and focus of these movements are hetero-
geneous. Likewise, they employ a wide range of ever-evolving,
anti-violence strategies. Three of the most prominent Indigenous
anti-violence movements in the contemporary moment are Idle

No More, the movement to address missing and murdered Indigenous women and girls (MMIWG) in Canada, and the movement to address violence against Native women in the United States. Each of these interrelated movements executes impactful and captivating community-centred strategies that animate Indigenous knowledges, world views, and cosmologies to invoke community belonging and culture. Examples of such strategies include, but are not limited to, theatrical productions, commemorative art installations, ceremonial gatherings, flash mobs, musical events, information and communication technologies, beading circles, and community feeds. The community-centred projects each movement has developed and implemented have marshalled the creativity and specificity of the local Indigenous place, while still mapping onto the larger scale of the international Indigenous community.[1]

The large-scale and collaboratively developed commemorative art installation Walking With Our Sisters (WWOS) is a powerful example of the community-centred approaches to Indigenous anti-violence organizing. While firmly rooted in the local communities that host the installation, WWOS also transcends settler colonially imposed borders and has ignited multiple sites of community building and resistance. WWOS has prompted Indigenous action on multiple scales and the dialectic of the local/global social movement building, and is precisely what has compelled us, as three US Indigenous women, to join in solidarity in the writing of this piece. Individually, and collectively, the work we do both inside and outside of the academy employs Native feminist analytics to address the sexual and gendered violences, among others, that plague our communities. Although we have not participated directly in WWOS, we have felt its impact personally, politically, and intellectually. Thus, in support of WWOS, and in further commemoration of the missing and murdered Indigenous women that WWOS honours, this chapter aims to analyze the role that WWOS plays in the movement to eradicate violence against Indigenous women.

Specifically, we argue that WWOS operationalizes Indigenous knowledges, world views, and cosmologies as modes of decolonial struggle against the settler colonial imperative to violate and eliminate Indigenous women in two ways: (1) through the mobilization of community, and (2) through the practice of beading. We begin with a brief overview of violence against Indigenous women in the United States and Canada, as well as the contemporary Indigenous anti-violence movement of which WWOS is a part. The chapter then narrows into a more nuanced discussion of the role WWOS plays within this context, focusing specifically on the ways in which WWOS mobilizes community and positions the practice of beading as sacred in order to break the settler vow of silence that seeks to eliminate Indigenous women and render said elimination invisible. Lastly, we argue that the concretized form of decolonization that WWOS enacts is, perhaps, the most essential component of efforts to restore justice to our communities and eradicate violence against Indigenous women and girls.

The Violence of Settler Colonialism and Heteropatriarchy

It is actually gender violence that marks the evisceration of Indigenous Nations.

—DIAN MILLION, *Therapeutic Nations: Healing in an Age of Indigenous Human Rights*

The relatively recent development of settler colonial studies as a discipline confirms what Indigenous peoples have known intimately for several centuries: in colonial contexts where the settler has come to stay, like the United States and Canada, land is paramount. Settlers want land, both as a resource to profit from and as "territory" upon which to construct settler nations. As sovereign peoples with prior relationships to the land that settlers want, Indigenous peoples thwart the insatiable appetite of settler colonialism and threaten the legitimacy of settler colonial nationhood. The organizing logic of settler colonialism, therefore, is the elimination of the Native. As long as Native peoples (political structures, epistemologies, relationships to land, etc.) have not yet been entirely disappeared, the project of settler colonialism is incomplete and practices of elimination must be reasserted daily.

Sexual and gendered violence has always been, and continues to be, an integral component of this process. In the United States and Canada, violence against Native women, girls, Two Spirit, and lesbian, gay, bisexual, transgender, transsexual, queer, questioning intersex, and asexual (LGBTTQQIA, an acronym we adopt from the Native Youth Sexual Health Network) peoples has been employed to establish settler claims to land since the earliest moments of colonization. When European nations arrived to the Indigenous lands that the United States and Canada would eventually claim as their own, Native nations had complex structures of kinship and governance wherein Native women and LGBTTQQIA peoples held highly respected positions of social, cultural, political, economic, and spiritual authority. European nations, on the other hand, were organized around the heteropatriarchal subordination of women and LGBTTQQIA peoples. This meant that only heterosexual men had access to power within European social formations. Colonizers understood that the subjugation of Indigenous peoples would require the imposition of heteropatriarchal logics that disempowered Native women and girls; demonized (and disappeared) Two Spirit and LGBTTQQIA peoples; and eliminated Indigenous conceptualizations of gender, sexuality, and kinship altogether. Inflicting pervasive and relentless violence against Native women, girls, Two Spirit, and LGBTTQQIA peoples became a central component of this process.[2]

Native women, it has been argued, pose a particular threat to the settler colonial project because of their abilities to *reproduce* Native peoples, Native nations, and, by extension, Native land epistemologies.[3] It may come as no surprise then that violence against Indigenous women is as prevalent in the present as it has been for the last five centuries. *Maintenance of the settler state necessitates the ongoing assault against Native women.* The ideologies, policies, and practices of settler colonialism make it difficult to ascertain the exact degree and the full range of violence to which Indigenous women are subjected, but even the limited evidence that does exist demonstrates this claim. In the United States, for example, Native women are battered, raped, stalked, and trafficked at far greater rates than any other group of women.[4] In Canada, Indigenous women face higher rates of spousal assault, family violence, and homicide than non-Indigenous women.[5] In fact, the rate of violence committed against Native women in the United States and Canada is so alarming that Amnesty International has denounced both countries' failure to ensure the safety of Indigenous women and has published multiple reports characterizing the situation as a blatant violation of human rights.[6]

One of the most prominent and egregious contemporary examples of this violence involves the MMIWG in Canada. After Amnesty International released its scathing report *Stolen Sisters: A Human Rights Response to Discrimination and Violence against Indigenous Women in Canada* in 2004, the National Women's Association of Canada (NWAC) was awarded federal funding to support Sisters in Spirit—a research, education, and policy initiative aimed at raising awareness about the ongoing persecution of Native women. The funding for the initiative only lasted until 2010 but it allowed NWAC to establish a database of the Indigenous women and girls who had been disappeared or murdered between 1990 and 2010. As of March 31, 2010, 582 cases had been entered into the Sisters in Spirit database.[7] Although the Sisters in Spirit initiative ended, concern for Indigenous women and girls did not. Individuals and communities began to develop databases of their own and to demand a national inquiry. The federal government refused to cooperate but in 2013 the Commissioner of the Royal Canadian Mounted Police launched an investigation of their own. In 2014, their findings were released: according to police records, 1,181 Indigenous women and girls had been disappeared or murdered in Canada between 1980 and 2012. The significance of this number cannot be overstated. Although Indigenous women and girls only account for 4.3 per cent of the overall female population in Canada, they represent 11.3 per cent of the females who have been disappeared and 16 per cent of the females who have been murdered.[8]

Indigenous Responses to Sexual and Gendered Violence

We are... family members who are affected by disappearances, murders and violent deaths, as well as community organizers who have seen the harms of state-led interventions. We call attention back to ourselves: we have the answers and solutions. We always have.

—NATIVE YOUTH SEXUAL HEALTH NETWORK, *"Supporting the Resurgence of Community-Based Responses to Violence"*

Although the specific practices, policies, and ideologies that enable violence against Native women differ between Canada and the United States, the settler colonial logic (of elimination) that necessitates said violence is one and the same. In other words, while there are notable differences between, for example, the specific forms of violence Indigenous women experience as a result of the Indian Act of 1876 in Canada or the General Allotment Act of 1887 in the United States, the fact that Native women are targeted for violence in efforts to eliminate Indigeneity remains constant. As a result, the histories and contexts of Indigenous anti-violence organizing in Canada and the United States frequently converge.

Despite the fact that the prevailing narrative of anti-violence mobilization in the United States and Canada locates the emergence of anti-violence activism in the 1970s and 1980s when (predominantly white) women began to publicly denounce the violence they experienced in their lives, Native women have mounted resistance against the violence of settler colonialism and heteropatriarchy for centuries. Indeed, when mainstream anti-violence movements did begin to develop, Native women employed their experiences resisting domination to help shape the mainstream movements. Unfortunately, however, the presence and participation of Native women in these spaces did not prevent the movements from marginalizing, and even compounding, the violence Indigenous women experience.[9] Thus, Native women in the United States and Canada have continued to develop decidedly *Indigenous* anti-violence movements—movements that address the specificities of violence against Native women, including colonialism, tribal sovereignty, tribal traditions, etc.

Because these movements are composed of activists, scholars, and survivors from literally hundreds of different Indigenous communities, each of which have distinct circumstances and needs, and because Indigenous women theorize sexual and gendered violence in relation to capitalism, the dispossession of Indigenous lands, and the elimination of Indigeneity, the foci of Native anti-violence activism are extremely wide. Incarceration, reproductive rights, interpersonal violence, human trafficking, boarding schools, the Sixties Scoop, cultural appropriation, poverty, spiritual appropriation, and environmental injustice are only a handful of the issues centralized in Indigenous anti-violence movements.

Likewise, Indigenous anti-violence movements employ a wide range of ever-evolving anti-violence strategies. Current strategies in operation can be divided into at least the following categories:

- *Efforts directed toward the settler state.* These strategies appeal to settler colonial institutions and governmental bodies to reform the practices and policies that cause sexual and gendered violence and to allocate resources for preventing and responding to violence.
- *Efforts directed toward Indigenous nations and tribal governments.* These strategies focus on identifying and critiquing forms of tribal sovereignty that replicate the sexual and gendered violences of settler colonialism.
- *Efforts directed toward Indigenous communities.* These community-centred strategies aim to empower and mobilize Indigenous communities to resist sexual and gendered violence at the grassroots level.

- *Efforts directed toward the international Indigenous community.* These strategies focus on creating awareness of sexual and gendered violence outside of national contexts in an attempt to build a global community of Indigenous peoples, allies, and potential allies.

Our attempt to identify the predominant approaches taken by Indigenous anti-violence activists and scholars in the contemporary moment is not intended to be prescriptive, hierarchical, or exclusionary. Rather, it is meant to help us evaluate current strategies, refine them when necessary, and even imagine entirely new ones.

For example, let us return to the investigations of MMIWG in Canada. The findings of the Royal Canadian Mounted Police intensified the demand for a national inquiry into the disproportionate disappearance and murder of Indigenous women and girls. Native anti-violence activists provided testimonies to Canadian governmental bodies in both 2011 and 2013. In 2014 they also participated in meetings with the United Nations Committee for the Elimination of Discrimination against Women and the United Nations Special Rapporteur on the Rights of Indigenous People.[10] Unfortunately, these actions did not result in any meaningful changes. The federal government, under Conservative leader Stephen Harper, held fast to its refusal to look deeper into the situation. In fact, in December of 2014, Harper publicly declared that a national inquiry into MMIWG "isn't really high on our [the Canadian government's] radar, to be honest."[11] We do not recount Harper's words here because we find them shocking. We do not. As we have already argued, maintenance of the settler state necessitates the ongoing assault against Native women. Rather, we recall his words to remind ourselves, to remind all Indigenous anti-violence activists and scholars, the depths of soullessness we are dealing with when we employ state-centred strategies to redress sexual and gendered violence against Indigenous peoples. We recall his words because they fuel our conviction that community-centred approaches are absolutely crucial to Indigenous anti-violence mobilization and projects of decolonization.[12]

WWOS and Operationalizing Community-Centred, Indigenous Practices

Counterstories are powerful forms of resistance which are repeated and shared across diverse Indigenous communities.
  —LINDA TUHIWAI SMITH, *Decolonizing Methodologies: Research and Indigenous Peoples*

When contending with a settler state, the difficulty is that settler colonial logics are normalized across institutions and agencies, which are complicit in maintaining structural racism and violence against Indigenous peoples, especially Indigenous women. This complicity makes it difficult to appeal to the state with grievances because such appeals are direct challenges to the status quo. For example, in " The Unspeakability of Racism," Sheila Gill writes of Cree Member of Parliament Oscar Lathlin who was sanctioned and expelled from Manitoba's provincial parliament for characterizing Canada's practices towards Indigenous communities as racist.[13] This incident illustrates governmental sentiments towards Indigenous concerns and elucidates a violent gesture of silencing Lathlin for not assimilating properly in respectable space. Although less violent than MMIWG, the government's treatment of Lathlin nonetheless shows how deeply entrenched racism and violence towards Indigenous peoples remain. However, the anti-violence movement has garnered international attention and support, which is hopeful. It is no longer only Indigenous peoples in critique of their home nations. Instead, recent efforts have drawn the attention of an international community of Indigenous peoples, allies, and potential allies. Although Indigenous community demands are being made to and within a settler state, Indigenous groups have managed to carry out community organizing that is decolonizing in its methods and resonates with many Indigenous communities.

Art, events, projects, protests, and flash mobs are a few examples of movement building and are sites for raising political consciousness within a community, which is important in building a broad base of support. Individuals can gain a deeper understanding and awareness of issues through engaging with survivors, and with families of lost loved ones, which raises the level of consciousness across the community. Cultivating the political consciousness of many individuals translates into a broad base of support that carries impact and pressure when mobilizing toward a desired result, such as demanding action from decision makers in the form of a deeper and wider investigation of MMIWG. The MMIWG movement has brought international attention to an issue that Canada has failed to respond to appropriately. This international attention is a result of the multitude of local movements and their responses, and it has a social media presence within Indigenous Twitter, Instagram, and Facebook.

Indigenous nations are subjected to settler colonial logics on a daily basis that foreclose on what the community and the ancestors would have wanted for their respective communities; however, WWOS is an example of decolonizing community organizing and re-centring Indigenous values.[14] Namely, WWOS displaces logics that force communities to disavow their cosmologies and teachings and make settler colonial logics appear "natural."[15] The unique element of movements within Indigenous communities is that the cosmological aspect of Indigeneity is often front and centre in the movement and related events. This is in itself a form of protest and fighting. Specifically, to keep singing, to keep making art, to keep dancing is fighting, but it is more than that. It is also thriving and continuing on despite the disappearance and murder of Indigenous sisters.

Indigenous movement building that animates Indigenous knowledge, world views, and cosmologies enacts emancipatory actions while honouring Indigenous ways of knowing that do "double duty." First, they sustain and protect communities while transmitting cultures and, second, they dismantle the dominant narrative that reduces Indigenous women to dehumanized stereotypes such as "the prostitute" or "the addict." Within the MMIWG movement, the WWOS installation has provided a powerful and loving presentation of MMIWG and the people who care about them. Similar Indigenous community-centred approaches have been employed within the US anti-violence movement and land rights organizing in Canada. Examples of these efforts include the plays *The Frybread Queen*, by Carolyn Dunn, and *Sliver of a Full Moon*, by Mary Kathryn Nagle, and the Idle No More movement. These examples are also demonstrative of the possibility for Indigenous grassroots efforts to communicate messages and expand power.

The MMIWG movement has many grassroots responses, but in this section we will focus on WWOS and on information and communications technology (ICT-) based strategies. We chose to focus on the WWOS installation as it has provided a platform from which familial and community loss can be conveyed, while seeking action from the Canadian government to address the MMIWG human rights crises. The WWOS installation also provides insight for informing constituencies at many scales, going from local to global and vice versa. In this section, we consider WWOS in terms of community organizing. Community-driven action related to MMIWG, and land rights, has been sustained precisely because these are deep wounds on the everyday lives of Indigenous people and communities, and this is a familial response. Movements are important for information and communication across a community.

Much of the information received related to WWOS in the United States has emerged from the internet, and social media has served as a venue for the transfer of information. Currently the WWOS Public Facebook Group has over twenty-one thousand followers,[16] and there are several community specific sites, such as "Walking With Our Sisters—Akwesasne." As the bundle travels, there is an intentional effort to honour the host community's cultural practices. Akwesasne used their Facebook page as a venue for communicating information and providing local co-ordination to receive the bundle. According to their promotional materials, they organized their process into five major stages: (1) planning efforts, (2) volunteer orientation, (3) Elder meetings and other volunteer organized events, (4) installation of the bundle, and (5) opening ceremony.[17] However, different communities may have distinctive configurations and protocols; there are many aspects that develop when organizing the event that reflects the interests and ideas of the community—there is no singular way to host the installation. Community feeds, singing, drumming, and providing video of community testimony are a few of the practices involved. Collaborating across many interests and perspectives is important to create a culturally relevant approach to caring for the bundle.[18] Moreover, one community organizer indicated that while there are skirts and smudging materials available for women who want to use them; they are not required. There was a controversy in news related to the wearing of skirts; however, engaging many viewpoints provides an opportunity early in the installation process to address any concerns or issues that may arise to ensure a safe and welcoming installation space.

The Akwesasne community identified twenty specific roles of the planning committee. It was of paramount importance to engage many sectors of the community, including those deemed dissident. The Akwesasne community demonstrated how to fully represent all sectors of the community in ways that engender dialogue, produce knowledge, and strengthen social networks.[19] Building on the information in the manual provided by wwos, the constituencies and tasks outlined with the Akwesasne community include the following roles:

- Elders
- Keepers
- Keepers Helpers
- Lead coordinators

- Media relations
- Social media "butterflies"
- Volunteer coordinators
- Fundraising and finance
- Family liaison
- Community outreach
- Promotion (optional)
- Youth programming
- School tours organizer
- Men's leadership and programming (optional)
- Two-spirit programming (optional)
- Community conversation organizers
- Security (as needed)
- Meals and hospitality (as needed)
- Counselling and Elder scheduling
- Additional Events coordinators[20]

When we pause and conduct a headcount for the WWOS installation, it shows that it takes a community commitment— there are upwards of forty individuals needed to receive, care for, and present the bundle, as well as attend to additional events. In essence, the bundle represents missing and murdered sisters, and the community must organize as a family with love and intention to receive this bundle, as it embodies the lives of many relatives. In terms of community development, the community conversations created by WWOS have been significant. These conversations place the community in dialogue about MMIWG. Fundraising is also needed for the installation and related activities, and communities have been creative in this aspect. Akwesasne held a mukluk drive, similar to boot drives firefighters hold to raise money, and the Parry Sound community presented at organizations and received donations.

Linda Tuhiwai Smith outlines several community projects as possible examples of decolonization, including storytelling, bearing witness, rereading, claiming, and connecting, and Dian

Million considers the production of felt knowledge crucial to decolonization.[21] In activating Smith and Million's frameworks of decolonization, Indigenous community organizing is grounded in the cultural relevance of the local community; the act of organizing produces "networks of relational meaning-making" that produce and transmit distinct knowledges about the community.[22] The community hosting WWOS is engaged in rereading who the MMIWG are, claiming space and place, and connecting through art rendered by many Indigenous places and cultures. Community organizing can have tactical results, but those involved in WWOS are cultural workers who are actually shifting the paradigm of missing and murdered sisters away from narratives of essentialism and dehumanization—which is an act of decolonization.[23] Similarly, the beadwork art of the installation also offers a practice of decolonization because it too incites the community to reclaim and love our Indigenous sisters.

WWOS and the Sacred Ontology of Beadwork

Walking With Our Sisters actuates a moving glyph focusing on the embodied sovereignty of Indigenous women.
—KARYN RECOLLET, "Glyphing Decolonial Love through Urban Flash Mobbing and *Walking With Our Sisters*"

WWOS honours MMIWG through the art of beadwork. The use of beadwork in this memorial is significant because it renders visible the lives of missing and murdered women, and the pain their families and loved ones still endure, without putting their faces and bodies on display. Instead, the over 1,700 beaded moccasin tops use the ceremony of the beadwork and the spirit of the beads to speak to the absence of these women and girls. Importantly, Indigenous peoples have used beadwork as storytelling, ceremony, and honour for thousands of years. Prior to colonization, many Indigenous communities used shells, quills, or turquoise to create beadwork, and many continue this practice. Even with the onset of settler colonialism, Indigenous peoples turned to beadwork to narrate important agreements.

For example, the Two Row Wampum Belt is a historical record of the 1613 treaty between the Haudenosaunee and the Dutch settlers. This treaty was outlined with the use of purple and white Wampum shell beads. As a part of renewing the promises of the belt in 2013, Onondaga Nation Chief Irving Powless Jr. described the meaning of the beads in this way:

> We use these beads for identification, as carriers of messages, and as records of events…We then informed the Dutch people that we would put our record of this event in a wampum belt.
>
> We think that in the future, there will come a time when you will not have your piece of paper, but we will still have our belt…
>
> The Two Row Wampum belt is made of white and purple beads. The white beads denote truth. Our record says that one purple row of beads represents a sailboat. In the sailboat are the Europeans, their leaders, their government, and their religion. The other purple row of beads represents a canoe. In the canoe are the Native Americans, their leaders, their governments, and their Way of Life, or religion as you say it. We shall travel down the road of life, parallel to each other and never merging with each other…
>
> The Haudenosaunee have never violated this treaty…
>
> We have never passed a law telling you how to live…
>
> You and your ancestors, on the other hand, have passed laws that continually try to change who I am, what I am, and how I shall conduct my spiritual, political and everyday life.[24]

In this example alone it is clear that beadwork has served multiple storytelling purposes of resistance for centuries in Indigenous communities. However, much of the Indigenous beadwork created today is made with glass beads and the import lies in the pattern, use of colour, and meaning established in the artwork. Similar to the Two Row Wampum Belt, the beaded moccasin tops, referred to as vamps, in WWOS narrate a particular story that must be heard. While the story is one of loss and absence of MMIWG (thus the incomplete moccasins), it is also a story of resilience and resistance.

The beadwork in WWOS acknowledges the settler colonial history of violence against Indigenous women that has been taking place for over five hundred years. A variety of different patterns sewn onto the vamps reflect this recognition of violence. For example, there are tops with silhouettes of Indigenous women with their children, eyes of women sewn above police tape that reads "police line, do not cross," floral designs, rose patterns, rainbows, landscapes, and animal/bird life. While the tops are all unique, they share the spirit of the beads in order to give life where it has been taken. In many ways, it is necessary to think of the actual beads as having an ontology—a sense of being or life. For instance, the beadwork on the vamps intervenes in colonial power and violence by speaking life into a different narrative—one that does not assume racialized and gendered violence must be the script for Indigenous women and girls. As a result, the beadwork in WWOS is a decolonial aesthetic that works to unearth abusive settler practices against Indigenous women and simultaneously call attention to the need for this violence to end.

The ontological life of the beads used for these vamps under-scores the juxtaposition of silence/invisibility versus voice/visibility. Namely, the life-giving potential of beadwork in this memorial is rooted in the ceremonial positioning of the installation and the sacredness of the beads. Arguably, beadwork has a sense of life by helping to maintain community, and acting as a transmitter of culture and knowledge. In regards to the maintenance of community, the WWOS installation has created over sixty-five beading groups where people gathered to answer the call for artwork.[25] Beading in community allows for multigenerational dialogue, a space for storytelling, and a practice that can be ceremonial. Those of us who bead know that when we gather it is a special time around someone's kitchen table, in a community centre, or another space set aside for this practice. Moreover, when communities gather to bead, it opens a space for cultural and knowledge transmission to take place as a sacred practice. As Kim Anderson has noted in *Life Stages and Native Women: Memory, Teachings, and Story Medicine*, there is a "spiritual nature to knowledge transfer, as this kind of sharing involves work that I can only describe as unlocking the space between the teller and listener so the story can enter."[26] With the WWOS installation, there is a sacred transfer that takes place both in beading together in community and when viewers *listen* to the stories told by the moccasin vamps.

Importantly, there are many stories told by the numerous chosen patterns on the moccasin vamps, and we would suggest that a single design narrates multiple stories. For example, there are several pairs of vamps with hummingbird designs. The hummingbird has often stood for hope, or the bird that announces good news in Indigenous communities. If taken in the context of our MMIWG, this is a powerful message of resistance—that we can still have hope in the face of horrendous violence. Furthermore, different Indigenous groups deem hummingbirds sacred because of their great resiliency, given their small size, the distances they travel, and their ability to fly forwards and backwards. Thus, the hummingbird vamps represent a symbol of resiliency and strength in regards to Indigenous women and girls. The hummingbird designs in WWOS underscore a relentless hope that this violence will end and our women and girls will one day be afforded the bodily integrity and safety they all deserve.

Additionally, the WWOS website has posted each pair of vamps along with the artist's name and the artist's statement (if they submitted one when they mailed in their vamps). While most of the narration is short, it is very powerful. For example, Caitlin Morrison's vamps depict an Indigenous woman with a radiant heart and all the cycles of the moon. Morrison's statement about this pair of vamps reads, "I wanted to capture the pure radiance and beauty of Indigenous women's spirits. I have included the four

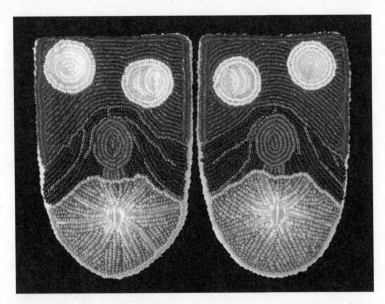

Grandmother Moon vamps beaded by Caitlin Morrison for the Walking With Our Sisters commemoration.

phases of the moon, our Grandmother, and a blue background for water/sky; symbols of our femininity and responsibilities."[27] The beadwork and colour choice in this beautiful design faces the devastation of MMIWG with a hopeful and sacred posture by calling on *la luna* for protection of our women and girls, representing them with full hearts, and using the blue background to centralize life instead of death through the life-giving nature of the water and sky. Therefore, the decolonial aesthetic of Morrison's vamps can be located in the continued existence of Indigenous women and girls along with the reliance upon Grandmother Moon to protect these lives.

Another story of resistance narrated through the beadwork in WWOS can be heard in the multiple pairs of vamps with butterfly designs. While the butterfly is the utmost symbol of transformation, it also represents a migration from our physical life to our spiritual life. In this way, MMIWG are honoured beyond this life. For example, the butterfly vamps beaded by Regina Meyer-Eastman are "in memory of Lucy, a 3 yr. old girl from Portland OR, who died after

*Butterfly vamps made by Regina Meyer-Eastman for the Walking With Our
Sisters commemoration to honour a three-year-old Indigenous girl.*

being raped while in foster care."[28] The colourful beadwork on
these vamps denotes a childlike presence and playfulness against
the trauma of Lucy's life. These vamps celebrate Lucy and her short
life by inciting a decolonial love—an affect that seeks to rupture
colonial power and violence in the act of relationship building.
Moreover, the art and act of beadwork by Meyer-Eastman illustrates
one way to lovingly respond to this violence. As Karyn Recollet's
recent work on WWOS argues, "each vamp enacts a radical pedagogy
of love."[29] If taken further, this means the life force of the beadwork
is to teach us something. Perhaps in this case the beadwork artists
are storytellers who are asserting agency and a sovereign presence
in regards to MMIWG. The sovereign space needed here is located
on land and body alike since the settler state needs both to oper-
ationalize its violent and abusive practices of elimination where
Indigenous women and girls have always been targeted.

In *Islands of Decolonial Love* Leanne Betasamosake Simpson
writes, "the skill set you need to survive is not the same skill set
you need to love and be loved. and while all those white mothers
were holding their babies and stroking their heads and singing

them songs, i'd like to say our brown mamas were doing the same but they weren't afforded the luxury. yes. luxury. they were targeted and they knew we'd be targeted."[30] Therefore, we know Indigenous women have never been able to seek protection from the settler state and the beadwork in wwos creatively narrates *both* a genealogy of violence against Indigenous women and girls and a genealogy of resistance to this violence. The power of storytelling via beadwork maintains a cultural legacy that settlers have not been able to eliminate. Specifically, as Maria Campbell (the Elder and advisor on traditional protocol for wwos) states, "[stories] give us a sense of place, a sense of safety, courage, and vision…They make us laugh and teach us to be better people, families, and community."[31] Thus, the stories told through the wwos beaded vamps offer healing, medicine, and resurgence.

Conclusion

If we don't decolonize our bodies, minds and relationships
to each other, when we do get our land back, all we will do is
destroy ourselves on it.
   —LEANNE BETASAMOSAKE SIMPSON referencing Daniel
   Heath Justice, *Islands of Decolonial Love*

In her recent work, Sarah Deer situates sovereignty as both political and personal. Most importantly, she argues that defining sovereignty as self-determination is a critical move for the anti-violence move-ment. She writes, "Self-governance or self-determination necessarily implies the development of concrete solutions to problems."[32] While formulating solutions to end all forms of violence (domestic violence, sexual violence, murder, and disappearance) against Indigenous women and girls is no small task, we support the work of wwos because it aims to concretize recuperation. The specific goals of wwos are

• to honour the lives of missing and murdered Indigenous women of Canada and the United States;

- to acknowledge the grief and torment families of these
  women continue to suffer;
- to raise awareness of this issue; and
- to create opportunity for broad community-based dialogue
  on the issue.[33]

Because WWOS makes these goals material through the "story
medicine" of moccasin vamps,[34] it draws on some of the most
significant forms of recuperation. As Deer argues in regards to
ending rape of Native women, " The most important sources for
the process of recuperation are oral traditions, stories, and traditional belief systems, as well as statutes and contemporary tribal
appellate case law that sometimes encompass the traditional
belief system."[35] In this way, the work of WWOS moves beyond
the metaphorization of decolonization to enact visibility around
MMIWG and establish healing through the ceremony of the
bundled installation as it travels.[36] Thus, WWOS is decolonial
in its aesthetics by liberating our senses in art spaces and in its
commitment to ceremony and colonial resistance. In short, this
form of decolonization furthers our awareness and knowledge
about MMIWG as deeply historical and traumatic. However,
WWOS simultaneously gives us hope, like that announced in the
various hummingbird vamps, that the multiple strategies of anti-
violence work surrounding MMIWG will eviscerate the expected
vow of silence and all Indigenous women and girls will be afforded
the justice and human dignity they deserve.

LAURA HARJO, JENELL NAVARRO & KIMBERLY ROBERTSON

NOTES

1. Manuel Pastor Jr., Chris Benner, and Martha Matsuoka, *This Could Be the
   Start of Something Big: How Social Movements for Regional Equity Are
   Reshaping Metropolitan America* (Ithaca, NY: Cornell University Press,
   2009).

2. Paula Gunn Allen, *The Sacred Hoop: Recovering the Feminine in American
   Indian Traditions* (Boston: Beacon Press, 1986); Andrea Smith, *Conquest:
   Sexual Violence and American Indian Genocide* (Cambridge, MA: South

End Press, 2005); Quo-Li Driskill, Chris Finley, Brian Joseph Gilley, and Scott Lauria Morgensen, eds., *Queer Indigenous Studies: Critical Interventions in Theory, Politics, and Literature* (Tucson: University of Arizona Press, 2011).

3. Inés Hernández-Ávila, "In Praise of Insubordination, or What Makes a Good Woman Go Bad?" in *Transforming a Rape Culture*, ed. Emilie Buchwald, Pamela Fletcher, and Martha Roth (Minneapolis: Milkweed, 1993), 375–92; Katsi Cook, "Women Are the First Environment," *Native Americas* 24, no. 3 (1997): 58.

4. Sarah Deer, Bonnie Clairmont, Carrie Martell, and Maureen White Eagle, *Sharing Our Stories of Survival: Native Women Surviving Violence* (Lanham, MD: Altamira Press, 2007).

5. Native Women's Association of Canada, *What Their Stories Tell Us: Research Findings from the Sisters in Spirit Initiative* (Ottawa: Native Women's Association of Canada, 2010), https://nwac.ca/wp-content/uploads/2015/07/2010-What-Their-Stories-Tell-Us-Research-Findings-SIS-Initiative.pdf.

6. Amnesty International, *Stolen Sisters: A Human Rights Response to Discrimination and Violence against Indigenous Women in Canada* (London: Amnesty International Publications, 2004); Amnesty International, *No More Stolen Sisters: The Need for a Comprehensive Response to Discrimination and Violence against Indigenous Women in Canada* (London: Amnesty International Publications, 2009); Amnesty International, *Maze of Injustice: The Failure to Protect Indigenous Women from Sexual Violence in the USA* (New York: Amnesty International USA, 2007); Amnesty International, *Maze of Injustice: The Failure to Protect Indigenous Women from Sexual Violence in the USA: One Year Update* (New York: Amnesty International USA, 2008).

7. Native Women's Association of Canada, *What Their Stories Tell Us*.

8. Royal Canadian Mounted Police, *Missing and Murdered Aboriginal Women: A National Operational Overview* (Ottawa: Government of Canada, 2014), http://www.rcmp-grc.gc.ca/en/missing-and-murdered-aboriginal-women-national-operational-overview.

9. Kimberly Robertson, "Righting the Historical Record: Violence against Native Women and the South Dakota Coalition against Domestic Violence and Sexual Assault," *Wicazo Sa Review* 27 no. 2 (2012): 21–47.

10. Native Youth Sexual Health Network, "Supporting the Resurgence of Community-Based Responses to Violence," press release, March 14, 2014, http://www.nativeyouthsexualhealth.com/march142014.pdf.

11.   Tanya Kappo, "Stephen Harper's Comments on Missing, Murdered Aboriginal Women Show 'Lack of Respect,'" CBC *News—Indigenous*, December 19, 2014, http://www.cbc.ca/news/aboriginal/stephen-harper-s-comments-on-missing-murdered-aboriginal-women-show-lack-of-respect-1.2879154.

12.   Moreover, since the election of Justin Trudeau the Canadian administration has agreed to conduct a national inquiry on MMIWG. While we agree that this is a necessary step, we do not think this action should be solely relied upon to end the violence taking place against Indigenous women and girls. We assert that Indigenous communities and Indigenous anti-violence strategists should be afforded the resources necessary to be leaders in this work. Since there are many who are already engaged in ending violence *now*, we caution against a national or local dependence on the government inquiry as it may take many years to complete, and past inquiries have not been successful. See Sarah Hunt's interview, "Do We Need an Inquiry to End Violence against Indigenous Women?" *The 180*, CBC Radio November 1, 2015, http://www.cbc.ca/radio/the180/mmiw-inquiry-debunking-electoral-reform-and-what-is-the-west-1.3295363/do-we-need-an-inquiry-to-end-violence-against-indigenous-women-1.3295403.

13.   Sheila Dawn Gill, " The Unspeakability of Racism: Mapping Law's Complicity in Manitoba's Racialized Spaces," *Canadian Journal of Law and Society* 15, no. 2 (2000): 131–62.

14.   Taiaiake Alfred, *Peace, Power, Righteousness: An Indigenous Manifesto* (Oxford: Oxford University Press, 2009); Laura Lea Harjo, "Muscogee (Creek) Nation: Blueprint for a Seven Generation Plan" (PHD diss., University of Southern California, 2012), http://gradworks.umi.com/35/13/3513774.html.

15.   Kerry L. Prosper, Jane McMillan, Anthony Davis, and Morgan Moffitt, "Returning to Netukulimk: Mi'kmaq Cultural and Spiritual Connections with Resource Stewardship and Self-Governance," *The International Indigenous Policy Journal* 2, no. 4 (2011), doi: 10.18584/iipj.2011.2.4.7.

16.   Walking With Our Sisters Public Facebook Group, accessed December 19, 2017, https://www.facebook.com/groups/walkingwithoursisters/about/.

17.   WWOS – Akwesasne Facebook page, accessed November 30, 2015, https://www.facebook.com/wwosAkwesasne.

18. Derek Okubo, "Community Visioning and Strategic Planning," in *An Introduction to Community Development*, ed. Rhonda Phillips and Robert Pittman (New York: Routledge, 2009), 77–103.

19. Laura L. Harjo, *Spiral to the Stars: Mvskoke Tools of Futurity* (Tucson: University of Arizona Press, forthcoming).

20. "Roles for Planning Committee Members," Walking With Our Sisters – Akwesasne Facebook Page, October 6, 2015, https://www.facebook.com/wwosAkwesasne/photos/a.990807430933414.1073741828.990802757600548/1204557072891781/?type=3&theater.

21. Linda Tuhiwai Smith, *Decolonizing Methodologies: Research and Indigenous Peoples* (London: Zed Books, 1999); Dian Million, *Therapeutic Nations: Healing in an Age of Indigenous Human Rights* (Tucson: University of Arizona Press, 2013).

22. Sarah Hunt, "Ontologies of Indigeneity: The Politics of Embodying a Concept," *Cultural Geographies* 21, no. 1 (2014): 27–32.

23. Million, *Therapeutic Nations*.

24. Chief Irving Powless Jr., "Two Row History," Two Row Wampum Renewal Campaign, 2013, accessed December 19, 2017, http://honorthetworow.org/learn-more/history/.

25. "Beading Groups," WWOS, accessed January 17, 2018, http://walkingwithoursisters.ca/artwork/beading-groups/.

26. Kim Anderson, *Life Stages and Native Women: Memory, Teachings, and Story Medicine* (Winnipeg: University of Manitoba Press, 2011), 25.

27. "Moccasin 'Vamps,'" Walking With Our Sisters, accessed October 19, 2015, http://walkingwithoursisters.ca/artwork/moccasin-vamps/.

28. "Moccasin 'Vamps,'" Walking With Our Sisters, accessed October 19, 2015, http://walkingwithoursisters.ca/artwork/moccasin-vamps/.

29. Karyn Recollet, "Glyphing Decolonial Love through Urban Flash Mobbing and *Walking With Our Sisters*," *Curriculum Inquiry* 45, no. 1 (2015): 134.

30. Leanne Betasamosake Simpson, *Islands of Decolonial Love* (Winnipeg: Arbeiter Ring Publishing, 2013), 86.

31. Anderson, *Life Stages*, xviii.

32. Sarah Deer, *The Beginning and End of Rape: Confronting Sexual Violence in Native America* (Minneapolis: University of Minnesota Press, 2015), xv.

33. "The Project," Walking With Our Sisters, accessed October 22, 2015, http://walkingwithoursisters.ca/about/the-project/.

34. Anderson, *Life Stages*.

35. Deer, *Beginning and End of Rape*, xv.

36. Eve Tuck and K. Wayne Yang, "Decolonization Is Not a Metaphor," *Decolonization: Indigeneity, Education & Society* 1, no. 1 (2012): 1–40.

303

Epilogue

Sitting in with Sisters

Facilitation and editing: KIM ANDERSON

Participant sisters: TRACY BEAR, CHRISTI BELCOURT,

MARIA CAMPBELL, MAYA ODE'AMIK CHACABY,

TANYA KAPPO, TARA KAPPO, LYLA KINOSHAMEG,

JO-ANNE LAWLESS, BRENDA MACDOUGALL,

SYLVIA MARACLE, RAMONA REECE,

MADELEINE KÉTÉSKWEW DION STOUT

Support: BELLA LAFONTAINE, MICHAEL WHITE

KEETSAHNAK was put together as a companion piece to Walking With Our Sisters (WWOS) as a means of further commemoration, honouring, and education. As we moved to finalizing the book, we realized that there were gaps in the types of discussions it represented or might encourage, and we wanted to see what women associated with the national WWOS and friends of the collective might say about it. And so we booked a weekend in January 2016, and brought together a number of sisters to reflect on the articles in *Keetsahnak* and the issue of missing and murdered women on the whole. The dialogue was hosted by the Ontario Federation of

Indian Friendship Centres, where Sylvia Maracle works as the executive director.

This epilogue offers portions of a very rich weekend of conversation, organized according to some of the themes we touched on.

Starting with Stories

We began the weekend by remembering women in our family histories who had shown strength of spirit. We offer a few of those stories here to show the reader how we brought the humour, resilience, power, and poetry of Indigenous women into the room with us as we engaged in the work of walking with our sisters.

Sylvia's Story: Auntie Eva

The one who is with me really strong today is Yotsi'tsi:son, Sky Woman—that Woman who came first in our Creation Story. *She* came; with a child, who was the first-born here—a female. So that first-born is important. It's always been a great responsibility. And so there is great comfort in the community when your first-born is female. Can you imagine growing up in a society where there's great joy if the first-born is a female?

It's because Creation continues.

My Aunt Eva was the eldest in her family. She never referred to herself as a strong woman or any of those concepts. She used to say, "I'm a Wild Woman" [Laughter]. Auntie Eva was born in 1922, and went overseas in 1942 with the Women's Army Corps as an active recruit. She had a job driving military brass around, both in England and in France. She was very close to front lines.

I used to talk to her as I was growing up about *People who believe in a Great Peace*—asking her, "What made you go to war?" She would say, "I always knew I was a Wild Woman." And then, "My girl, I think you're going to be a Wild Woman. Pay attention."

She explained that the church had come to the community and so we were restricted in what we could do. "So I joined the military," she said, "because I wanted smoke cigarettes and wear pants" [Laughter].

I said, "Really?" And she said, "Yes. No one knows you or knows your family. They just know we're here, and we're going to be at war. I'm either going to save your ass because I'm a good driver or not. And if it's 'not,' it doesn't matter because we're all going. I'm not going to stand there alone saying 'It's too bad the back blew up.'"

She told me that she had two best friends. One was an Ojibwe woman; for us that was like Russian—so different to who we were. The other friend she met was Mi'kmaw. These three—they were called Indian women in the old days—found each other in war in the middle of a bind. They would get a bottle of liquor and they would go and have a bath. Water was rationed. We all come from communities where there is lots of water—and it was really hard. They understood the teachings of water being a female element, and it was rationed. But they found a way.

These three women were "Onkwehonwe-istas,"[1] she used to say.

"We would light up our cigarettes, have a drink, and fill the tub up and lay there." Nobody is around. Nobody there rationing. She said, "Oh, it was nice. It was a good friendship" [Laughter].

One day a bomb went off too close and "boom!" All the bathtubs went and there are these three brown women running around with this little washcloth, in downtown London [Laughter]. I just shook my head [Laughter].

Then I asked Auntie Eva what it was like when she came back, and she talked about freedom—being free to be who she was. She said, "I came home for a couple of weeks and I couldn't stand them clucking around me and I couldn't go back to the way they wanted me to be. So I dyed my hair red and I went to Toronto" [Laughter]. She said, "You know I've been married four times. I was always widowed. I could never find a man who could keep up with me."

I remember at one of her later weddings she called me over and said, "My leg is bad. We want you and your partner to do the first dance for us." This is at home in the community—at the community centre on the Rez. I looked at her. She had accepted me, no ifs, ands, or buts. At a matter of fact, when I went home to "come out" and to tell her—I said, "I like wearing pants." She laughed and said, "You're a Wild Woman."

So here's this very old woman in the community having me and another woman dance the wedding dance for her and this old man [Laughter]. She got up and danced after that. I said, "I thought your leg was sore." She said, "It was sore, but I'm still a Wild Woman and I'm still here to protect you, my girl."

I said, "I can't thank you enough Auntie."

I always hoped a little bit, with the exception of smoking and drinking, that I would grow up to be a "Wild Woman." That is who is here with me today. She had a good time. She made no apologies to anybody, and lived her life to the fullest.

That's my wish for the first-born in our next generation—my niece who's now eleven. She was with me in the holidays and she asked me, "What do you think I'm going to be when I grow up?" I said, "I think you're going to be a Wild Woman." And so she heard the story of her Great Aunt.

Auntie Eva, that dyed, red-headed Mohawk warrior, in her own way is who I am. I hold her in high esteem. She who taught me, showed me with her behaviour what freedom was like, and not to fear. Nya weh.

Maya's Story: Nokomis

Waaciye, Ode'amik nintishinikaas, Amik nitootem. Kaministiquia nitoonji.

I'm very happy to be here today. I want to first say I've been identified as working here at the Federation (Ontario Federation of Indigenous Friendship Centres). But with you, my sisters, I want to say that I was a Missing Indigenous Woman. That's why I'm happy to be here today. I went missing when I was thirteen and I stayed missing until I was in my early twenties.

I hear all of the stories today, and I see these beautiful families that are talking about their loved ones who are missing—these sisters, aunties, and these parents. I didn't have anyone who would go look for me. It was the Friendship Centre that found me.

Alex Jacobs and Vern Harper. Yeah—Vern. He didn't care if I was high, if I had my backpack and had not bathed. It didn't matter to him. He took me in. He gave me my first teachings about being Two-Spirited, when I was a kid.

Who I was thinking about today—this might seem strange—she was one of the main people who caused me to be missing. That was my grandmother. I've been thinking about her quite a lot these days. I can't say she was a residential school survivor. She did not survive. She was an angry, bitter, empty husk.

I was the whitest in the family, but to her, when I was a child, I must have failed to be white. I don't know what it was about me—I wouldn't speak English. I wouldn't speak to any humans, so they called me retarded. My grandmother was trying to raise me the way she was raised in residential school. Horrible, horrible things. Anything I did that looked Anishinaabeg would result in serious abuse. All of that abuse as a child led me to eventually to run away on the streets.

She is who I'm thinking of as being the inspiring one today.

She passed on when I was eleven, and everybody blamed me for it. I caused her death, they said, with my thinking. I always resisted all that stuff. I was always Anishinaabeg, no matter what. So they blamed me for that.

So, I met her again two months ago—three months ago now, in the Ancestor Feast. If you don't know—the Ancestor Feast—in the city, the way they do it is in a dark room. No light. Everyone brings their own feast plate. It's just for women. Everything is covered up—all of the windows. We face the West. Everyone sits there with their own plate and in their own time. The Conductor will describe the people who come into the room. I hadn't had anyone in mind. I always go and pay my respects, because there are so many people who have helped me in my life. This Conductor—the first person she described was my grandmother.

My grandmother had dyed red hair, pulled back in a bun. There aren't too many Anishinaabeg who look like that, so I knew when she was describing this woman that it was her. So I stood up. I stood up in that dark room with my feast plate in my hand. I haven't seen her since she passed when I was eleven years old. That was a long time ago. I'm forty. It was the first time I've spoken to my grandmother, and we had a very good talk. I told her my real name. Ode'amik. I told her everything that has come about in my life to bring me here—to be the person I am today. I asked for her to have compassion for me.

She said " Thank you" to me. She said, " Thank you for continuing to do what you were born to do." Even though she couldn't do it at that time. She said it was okay—that she is happy—and that she is proud today.

All these years of struggle, and being alone on the streets, and having no one looking for me, having no home and no family—it was because of what she went through. And she walked with me all that time. All of that pain and hurt. Hers. I carried.

It's very beautiful now that she's walking with me without that pain. We're walking this journey together as I enter a new stage of my life and she's right there with me.

I have to acknowledge her today. It's my responsibility to carry her forward. Miigwetch.

Ramona's Story: Mercy D
My ancestral lands are in Karankawa (Auia) and Caddo territories, also known as Houston, of the Texas Gulf Coast region. Some of my ancestors also came from Africa.

Just this week, my young cousin, Irene, contacted me to ask for photos of my father's sister, Mercy D, for a photo exhibit she is creating. I sent Irene about twenty-five photographs. Among them is a photograph of Mercy D, flanked by my father and her first husband, Leo.

The three of them were standing in front of Leo's fancy car. Irene thanked me for the photos, and also asked me about the jazzy, black man in that particular photo (Leo). Mercy D and Leo split up long before Irene was born, so she knew little, if nothing of him. This is the family story that goes with that photograph.

One day, Mercy D, a schoolteacher at the time, took a different route home from work. Her drive took her through one of wealthier neighbourhoods of Houston. As she hugged the curves of a tree-lined boulevard, she spotted a car that looked exactly like her husband Leo's car, parked in a driveway at a house unfamiliar to Mercy D. She wasn't entirely sure it was his car. Not saying anything to Leo about it that evening, she jotted down his licence plate number.

A week later, at the same time of day as before, she drove by the mysterious house and found the car parked there again. It was definitely Leo's car, and as it turned out, he was definitely cheating on her. So she parked nearby and waited.

Leo eventually emerged from the house, and Mercy D watched him get into his car and start the motor. Just as he backed out of the driveway and onto the street, Mercy D shot the back tires of his car. She then floored the accelerator and fish-tailed her car right in front of him—making sure he knew it was her. She went home, gathered a bunch of her clothes and possessions, and drove to my grandparents' home.

My grandparents lived in the country, about forty-five minutes north of Houston. Leo wisely gave her a wide birth to let her cool down. After a few days, he screwed up his courage and drove to my grandparents place at a time of day Mercy D would be working.

He approached my grandfather, who was headed to the wood-pile. Leo told my grandfather he was sorry, that he knew he messed up, and begged him to tell Mercy D that he missed her, and to please give him another chance. My grandfather said, " Tell her yourself." To that, Leo replied, "I'm scared of her! She tried to kill me!" My grandfather assured Leo that Mercy D had not tried to kill him—otherwise, he wouldn't be there to have that conversation.

Mercy D, like her four older brothers, had to hunt in order to eat. She was a capable woman, able look after herself—that was how she was raised. It is also how she helped raise us, her nieces. She was an elegant, intelligent, and independent woman—a strong woman. Haw'wih.

Christi's Story: Grandmother Artists

The thing I think about is my grandma—her name was Matilda—my dad's mom. I think about what she went through. I also think about her mom, and her mother. So I think about my grandmothers going all the way up, and what they had to go through in the communities where they lived. Violence was part and parcel of life in Lac Ste. Anne. It just was.

I think about how the women in that community didn't even have the power to say no. There was no choice back then. You had to put up with it. I'm so grateful that my daughters now have that choice and don't have to put up with it. So things are changing.

Madeleine [Kétéskwew Dion Stout] and I were talking and she asked me, "Which artists do you admire?" I said that we don't even know the names of a lot of the artists I really like. When I look at the basketwork, or the beadwork—the really old things—the things that were made to allow us to survive, that's the kind of artwork I admire most. I think about all of the generations and generations and generations—thousands of years of stitch work, beadwork, or quillwork, inscribing on birch—of all of those things that were done out of love and creativity by women. How they really held the communities together and held their families together. How they married, birthed, and buried the people. How we fed people. How we tended the fire. How we did everything, and how we still are doing the same thing. Hai hai.

Account-ability, Response-ability

Over the weekend we discussed how the book might be read by different audiences, and pondered our hopes for how it might contribute to ending violence against women.

SYLVIA: When I read through the book, somewhere about the middle of the articles, I thought, "Okay, so I'm reading who we are, and where we've come from." So, logically, I'm going to read next where we're going, and the last question is " What's my responsibility for this?" So it's not just about saying, " This is how we got to this point historically. Here's the trauma." And it's not just what are we responsible for as individuals, but what is it that people expect to see now as the change?

MADELEINE: I think we have to help the readers change the narrative. We have to engage the bystanders and see what are the takeaways from it.

TANYA: How do we make it " Yes, this is our harsh history but that doesn't mean that's who we are"? Maybe talk about some of the things to celebrate, some of the movements. We're these resilient people who suffered this and yes, we still suffer this, but *this* is where we come from.

I think the quote that stuck out in my mind was from the piece by Knott: "Every time I see a photo of an Indigenous woman or girl who has gone missing, I feel my spirit tighten inside of me." I think that's really important because I feel the same. So again, it goes back to that place of "How do we protect us in the midst of putting this truth out this way?"

MADELEINE: I think you raise some very important points, because that quote you just spoke to is the one I was trying to find—because I feel my spirit tighten in me. I was also thinking about how difficult it is for Indigenous women.

A couple of the writers talk about accountability, and we've mentioned responsibility here, and can add to that another word like "answer-ability." I heard a woman get up and talk recently about how difficult it is for her, having had the experiences she had in her home community. She was very much violated there, and she couldn't talk to the Chief about it, because he was also a perpetrator. So when you break down that word, "accountability," to two words, you have the account, but you don't have the ability to share it because of the repercussions, and you're really putting yourself forward to be re-traumatized. And the same thing with "responsibility;" when we think about readers, what is their ability to see the depths we're trying to communicate? And, you know, the same thing with "answerability"; how will they answer to all of this when they don't have the ability, they don't have the capacity, they don't have the openness of mind, they don't have the understanding? It's always that tension, right, about how do you educate people in a way that's transformative for women, that's really transformative? We want it as a protective factor for Indigenous women.

BRENDA: I read it with the lens of teaching. I would bring this into the classroom, because what I've figured out over seventeen years teaching university is that students don't know this stuff. Every time I teach the Indian Act it's, "How did I get through twelve or thirteen years of school and this never came up?" And I think that this will do the same thing. "How come nobody told me that this was happening?"

I think what these pieces show is that there's survival here. It doesn't matter what's been thrown at us, there's survival. It's constant. We haven't gone anywhere. Our communities aren't dead. We're victimized, but we're not victims. Our resiliency and survival is through all of these stories.

TARA: It was a lot of information to try and process. There are a few things I've been thinking about. Number one, how difficult it is to maintain a certain amount of hopefulness and positivity. I think that is so necessary, because the topic is so heavy and serious. There is a lot of pain around it. You can't avoid it. But at the same time I think that's how we need to be supporting each other—is to talk about the good things that are going on.

TRACY: As someone who educates, I kept thinking, how can I utilize this? How will my students react? My students always say on their evaluations, "I love the stories that you tell." That's what brings things home. This book has those stories that pull you in and make you remember, and make you full. The stories remind me of where I come from, and how blessed I am because of the strong women I have around me—and have had.

MAYA: What really struck me from this book was the need to create environments where we can be working like we are here today. You can't learn that from a book. So we have to create social environments. And the only way that we can be free, that we can change what we have—that violence, is to go back to fulfill those responsibilities that we have inherited from Creation. It's not like in English [where] freedom means to be free from obligation. That's not what it is in Anishinaabemowin. It's dibenindizowin: to have all the means necessary to fulfill one's responsibilities, as your Clan, as whatever you are in the world. So, I feel very free here in this gathering with my sisters.

I also thought about the word for "Love" in Anishinaabemowin. Zaagi'idiwin. To me, the root of that is zaaga'an. It's not a romantic thing—it's not a sexual thing. Zaaga'an means to go outside of yourself—to extend beyond yourself-ness. I think that's what we need today. I think we need that kind of love. The willingness to truly extend ourselves to one another. We can recreate those connections that we have, in order to have all the means necessary to fulfill our responsibilities and be free.

SYLVIA: So now we are at a point that we have the TRC [Truth and Reconciliation Commission] recommendations and we're launching a national inquiry into ending violence against Indigenous women and girls. It's this decade of issues that's going to swirl it all together like maybe none other ever have. I think that's the challenge—of not just education, but reconciliation; talking to mainstream to try to unpack some of this bundle for them. And so what I really need is for us to be as descriptive as we can be about our responsibilities. It won't be over in a decade but it's heating up. I think that it's a piece of a bigger puzzle that's going on.

Another issue is the perpetrators who are the authority themselves. Our big issue is young women in Northern communities. The police give them a ride to town for sexual favours. But there are laws. There are [traditional] laws. Do we need to promote them more? Yes. But in mainstream, there should also be a law. There should be a law telling police, *This is how you behave when it's an Indigenous woman.* You've got to go in to Ceremony and you've got to look people in the face and tell them "I did the best I could. I'm going to be accountable for this." There should be a law for judges. There should be for corrections centres. There should education provided for mainstream men. We know this problem is not only external to us. But there are institutions that perpetuate the environments where violence can occur, and they clearly need to be regulated, because they are not self-regulating.

I think there are concepts both traditionally and in terms of mainstream we could braid together to make our response stronger.

Critical Conversations, Vigilance, Life Giving

In addition to calling for more attention to systemic injustices, we also spoke about how to address lateral violence in communities— violence that comes from colonial oppression and patriarchy, and which works its way into Indigenous communities and so-called "traditional" ways. The group acknowledged the need to be vigilant, inclusive, and to focus on the future generations.

MARIA: All of the stories in the book are pretty powerful, but the one that really touches me is the one about Wenonah. So many times I've been in cultural teaching groups and somebody gets up and tells stories, that—when you really listen to them—are abusive to women. It's important that we have critical conversation about all kind of things, like "Women aren't supposed to have Pipes and that's a Teaching." What are we supposed to do—just sit there, listen, and not say anything, because we've been taught that we're not supposed to speak? I was raised with a Great Grandmother that was over a hundred and she raised us to ask questions, reminding us that if we didn't ask questions, we could die. You can't go out there and start walking on the ice and not pay attention. I think, for me that's what important. Wenonah opens the door for those kinds of conversations.

There is a word in our language—if you say something, some old lady might say kāya nānitaw itwē, "Don't say nothing!" Like it's okay for someone to smack the shit out of you—"just don't say anything." It seems to me that's what that piece is doing, more than anything else: it's telling us we have to question. Since reading it, I've become much braver—because there are some things I would just never talk about.

TRACY: These types of stories are great for teaching tools in the classroom as well. To say, yes, there are places where you can be critical. We teach them all of the time in university to critically analyze things. But, other [ceremonial] places—we're not as eager to tell people to be critical thinkers.

LYLA: I guess what we need to learn is to do it respectfully. How to be critical respectfully—while acknowledging the truth within it. But I was also raised to question.

MAYA: I think it's about aangwaamiziwin, vigilance—becoming skilled knowers of our environment. That is what the Elders ask us to do. You won't survive if you are not vigilant. They're asking us to do the same thing today, to deal with issues of violence in our community. We can't keep getting lulled into that [patriarchal, violent] way of thinking, without questioning.

So now moving forward, we're in this space where we have to deconstruct what is not ours, not our way. And we're starting to—especially with Idle No More and Missing Murdered work.

TARA: In the Wenonah article, Sy writes, "Must the burden of brutish, irresponsible, uncontrollably driven, and dehumanizing decisions veiled and distorted into natural, normal male inclinations be borne by the masculine spirit?" That was a line that stood out for me, because so much conversation seems to be focused on male violence perpetuated against women, when I see violence all around. I see violence between women. How do we have these conversations?

SYLVIA: There was a lack of gender continuum notions—that we're not strictly binary. So when you read these articles, woman is victim, man is the perpetrator. We know that's not true. It's not all women. It's children too.

LYLA: Questioning—we have to question. We can't move forward without questioning. It strengthens us. It finds different ways to press what we know and what we feel, and what we think we're ready for right now.

MARIA: What I want to do with our young women is talk about not only what we've experienced but what we then perpetrate. I mean, we're afraid to talk about that. It was easier to quit drugs and change my life than it is for me to deal with the violence that I lived with, because you never get rid of it. And then everybody says, "Women are sacred."

You know, why did we have moon lodges? So that women could reflect and use that power to do beadwork or to do whatever, to dream for the people. But they were thrown out; they are having to get beat up every day, having to deal with social workers and having all that stress in their lives. Then you'll hear some woman yelling at her little girl, or else her little boy, smacking her little boy on the head. She's not a bad person, but she just can't deal with anything anymore, and she's having to deal with all of the violence from the system, from her husband and whoever; who does she take it out on?

We can't have those kinds of conversations unless men do too, which they are starting to do in small ways. I know men who are meeting every couple of weeks and they ask me, "What do you think we should talk about?" So I've said, "Talk about violence; have you ever beaten women up? Why did you do it? How come you abandoned your children?" So they can have those kinds of conversations and I think it's like some floodgate is going to open.

We've already talked now about residential school; remember what happened to Phil [Fontaine] when he talked about being sexually abused? The Chiefs wouldn't talk to him. They were angry with him. And then all those old ladies stood up and supported him. It took a lot of courage. And out of that came all of this other stuff. So every so often something opens for us, and we have to be brave enough to jump through it.

LYLA: Our young women have to be educated. That was my Teachings, the knowledge I was given, was that the Grandmothers do that. This is part of this resurgence of us Grandmothers accepting and taking on that responsibility. And whatever little bit I know, I bring to the table and I put it there. We're going to weave new baskets. We're going to use different fabrics.

When we talk about this violence that women endure, there is so much going on in my head that I've seen happen in the past.

In my family one of my nieces was murdered by her partner. My sister asked me and my husband to help the family by coming to do the funeral. My husband and I thought, *We've never done anything like this, what they want us to do.* So I told my husband, "I think the only thing we can do is to provide a Sacred Fire where he dumped her body." It was between my brother house and my dad's house, our old home, right there in the middle. That's where he dumped her body. They left her body there for four or five days in the blazing heat, trying to investigate.

My niece had a son and daughter. I said, "I have to work on behalf of her son who was just a little baby. I'm going to bring in any man who wants to take care of the Sacred Fire." I said, "The Fire Keepers will be the guys of this land—of our home territory here. If you've been drinking or drugging, don't bring your drugs or alcohol here, but you are welcome to come take care of this Fire. I asked you to come this way because this is where we are as a community. Maybe some of you will change your ways. Maybe some of you, down the road, will see the young men trying to fill your boots the way you have. Maybe they will kick those boots aside and make their own. This is why I'm doing this—I'm giving us a choice. He left a son behind—a baby boy. We're doing this for him and all the other babies in our community who have suffered because of what's happened between the men and the women."

That's what we did. We had them sit at the Sacred Fire. Some of them had never done it before, but they came.

When somebody dies, what is it that we do? How do we honour that life and bring the families together?—For them to come together and look at this.

This was the first time that was ever done in my community. I know some of the things didn't follow traditional protocol, but it helped the family and it helped the people. And that young man—he's married. He's got two sons. Despite the struggles, he lives for his boys. That family still comes together no matter how things are going in the family. They still take care of each other.

So every one of us has life scars. We accept them. Those are some of the things I saw. But we have reason, women. We're on our feet. We're working. We're doing this—we're that wave. We don't have to be a big wave on top. You know that stream under the mountain? We're the water. We're helping the water. Anishinaabekwe. We use our tears. We honour our tears, because they are our healing. And every time we get together— I always tell people—behind you there are ten ancestors. Each one of us has that, and maybe more. So, we are never, ever alone. That's what I've been given to share.

CHRISTI: This morning I was thinking about this saying that
Maria texted me once—it was this beautiful thing—at the very
end she said, "Power to the babies." And last night I had a dream
that got me thinking of babies everywhere. Not just human
babies, but all of the babies everywhere. It got me thinking of
all of the children of the women who are still missing, and the
unspoken grief cloud that hovers over families. How do families recover from that kind of grief and that kind of trauma?
And then further, how do we as a People, as Peoples, as Nations—
how do we recover from that? I'm thinking of what you said
this morning, Maria, about how it's our job to be giving the
young people what they need.

TARA: That's what I think about a lot, because I really want to be
able to give back to the kids, but also to us, now today. We're
focusing our attention on the children who are coming somewhere in the future, but I also can't stop thinking of myself as
a child. I can't stop thinking about my mother as a child. And
think that part of this work is also for us as the children that we
still are. How immediate it is for us and how can we give back to
each other? There's also the people doing work quietly, going
about their business. You don't see them so much, you don't
hear from them, and you don't necessarily recognize they're
doing their thing.

BRENDA: The way our conversation ended up earlier was that we
hope young people will think, "I need to research this; I need
to do this; this doesn't exist; how come nobody talked about
this?"—and then go through it and have those that can help.

TRACY: If I go back to the editors' request to think about gaps
and what I see missing, I think about what I teach in gender
and sexuality. I've always seen a gap in healthy sexuality
stories. I went to New Zealand, and when I was on the Marae
with a bunch of Maori people we started trading stories about
Wesakechak. Their Trickster's name is Maoi. We went back and
forth, and the stories were very similar. As the night went on,
the stories get more bawdy [Laughter]. The night gets darker,

the stories get more exciting—right? I couldn't keep up with my stories of Wesakechak. I didn't know any. I knew he did things like that, but I didn't know the stories about them. So when I got back from New Zealand, I started looking, and they were just—not there. That started my research. So I see this gap constantly—that people don't talk about the healthy sexuality.

Then there's Moon Time—we know the process, and we know what we're not allowed to do. But I always wondered what are we allowed to do? If there's power there, I know we can use it somehow. But often you are sitting in a parking lot as Elders are having a Pipe Ceremony on the fourth floor of a government building, and you are the Indigenous woman, so you get sent out to the parking lot in January.

So I wanted to know the healthy part. I wanted to know the fun parts, the joy and the magic of sexuality and celebrate that. Maybe this book isn't the place—I don't know. That's one of the things I felt was missing, just because I *want* to see that.

MAYA: I really like rethinking about life giving. That would be a beautiful thing to write more about.

The last time I tried to kill myself (I was twenty-one), my friends broke me out of the Wellesley Hospital. I remember them calling my name on the intercom as we were running out of the hospital. I went to the Friendship Centre. And Vern Harper was there. I told him what had just happened—that I tried to take a bunch of pills, and that I was done. He said, "Okay, you're done. You're dead. Give your life to the community. That's all you need to do. You don't want to live your life for yourself—fine. Live it for your community." He was a life giver.

I said, "Okay." I started volunteering and I just gave my life over to that. It changed everything about how I could move forward and live. I think that's a beautiful way to start to rethink. What is this life giving? Our Friendship Centres are giving life. Miigwetch.

Stop in, Stock up, Stay over, Tell a Story

MADELEINE: In December [2015], Margo Greenwood hosted a conference,[2] and I was the closing keynote. Margo had phoned me and said, "What we'd like you to do is keep people engaged, and talk about how that can happen." It's almost the same thing as what we have been doing here—continuing the conversation.

I thought about it, and I thought of my sister. She just passed away in August. Miyos was her name. The Beautiful. That's her Cree name. Miyos. And Moise is her husband. When they knew we were coming back home to Alberta, they would always invite us. They would say three words to us.

Nakīstawinan. It means "Stop in." *Pimīcisok;* and that means "Stock up"—let's stock up together. We can share what we know, our experiences, and our stories. The third is *Kapēsik:* "Stay over." They would always say, "Stay over." That means spend the night with us—don't rush off. Stay with us.

So in talking about ways we can continue the dialogue, I was inspired by my sister, who was so kind, and who knew me and my family so well. She knew our needs implicitly. "Of course you're going to stop in. Of course we're going to feed you. And of course you can stay here as long as you want."

I thought, "Wow!" Those were the three ideas I tried to communicate at that meeting, and I was thinking about this gathering, and trying to unbundle three easy ways you might want to recommend to move forward. One thing that came to my mind—of course all these words have to rhyme in some way—it's just the way I think! I was thinking of *gratitude*, of course. Being grateful to the women who have let us into their lives. We've gone out of our comfort zones to be with them. That's what love is.

The other one I thought of is something like *latitude*. Give the reader—the critical reader—the latitude to think through this to come up with some transformative ways for the women to heal—for all of us to heal from this blot on the Canadian landscape. Especially for the women who are the hardest hit—the ones who experienced it so closely. Give people the latitude to think that through, to write about it, to make a film about it, to create digital stories about it. To make sure everybody will hear about it, because I think that's what a lot of people end up saying—"I didn't know about this." Even today—with the residential school issue—people say, " That's the first I heard of that." So I think we can give people the latitude to carry this conversation forward in the best ways they know how—through storytelling or whatever.

Then I was thinking when you were talking, Maya, about *platitudes*. You know we always talk about values and love, respect, and strength—well a lot of it becomes platitudes, because—I don't know—we overuse those words or we don't pay enough attention to them, and they become platitudes. We need to reclaim our platitudes, because they are so important.

You can go on to maybe write about attitudes or whatever—I have to think of things in association with one another, otherwise I can't make sense of it; I get so overwhelmed. But it's all so good—it's all so brilliant. We have to have good personal insights to really work through it.

That's all. Thank you very much.

Final Story

TANYA: I spend a lot of time listening to people talk. Some of it is through my work as a lawyer, going to residential school hearings and listening to testimonies. There's also an element of it that happens around Walking With Our Sisters. There is inevitably at least one person who comes around, seeking someone who will listen about their experience as a family member, or their experience as someone who was almost missing, or who was almost killed.

There was one old lady who came when I was in Whitehorse. She had sent a young man ahead the day before to say " There's a lady who wants to talk to someone here." I don't even think he understood what she wanted. So we tried as best we could to accommodate. We talked about helping her get some time with an Elder, but it ended up being me.

She was someone from the community, and had a level of discomfort in sharing with people that she knew—she wasn't ready. So we weren't sure what to expect. Did she want to talk to me as a lawyer? Did she want to talk to me as someone with Walking With Our Sisters?

So we go to a room, and we're sitting in there—her and I, privately. She seemed unsure of how to start. She's elderly—she must be in her late seventies, early eighties. I feel awkward—do I wait for her?—she's an elder. I feel like she wants me to start, so I just went right into it and said, "What is it that you would like to talk with me about today?"

She went on to share the story about how when she was a young woman she was kidnapped out of a bar by three or four young white men. They took her out to the bush, they tied her up, and they raped her. In telling me about all this, she described it very dispassionately, mechanically, without feeling.

She ended up getting freed and ran through the bushes, found her way to the highway, and came across a house. She was naked, and these people helped her and took her to the hospital. She told me everything—including that these young men were caught for what they did to her. They went to court. They were held accountable for what they had done.

And this was the point in the story when she broke down— when she told me about how when she went to court she saw the men all had their wives and their little kids there. That was what made her cry. She said, "I felt terrible. How could they do this to their wife and kids?"

I thought about what I hear in residential school stories, where a lot of the time the claimants break down in telling me what they saw and what they knew was going on that they couldn't prevent. And they carry this guilt within them. It leaves a person with an oppressive weight and then we in turn all carry the shame. It makes us unable to talk about it.

So, after this old lady tells me her story about this rape years ago, I said, "Why did you want to tell me this? What do you want me to do with your story?" She said, "I want you to tell it. I'm getting ready to go. I want you to tell my story." So I said, "Don't you have kids? Do they know about what happened to you?" She said, "No, they don't know. I was a terrible mom to them. Because of what happened to me, I was a terrible mom, and I did bad things to them. And they don't understand why I did that. They forgive me now, and they treat me kindly, and I'm always grateful for that, but they don't know." So I told her, "I think you need to tell them. They need to hear it from you— they shouldn't hear it from me, about what happened to you." So then she said, "Maybe. Maybe I'll tell them one day."

And then, that was it—it was over. I felt okay with how that was. She seemed happier—she hugged me and thanked me, and then she went.

I was thinking about that here, because I'm still thinking about the book in terms of what might be missing. I was really grateful to have Maya here today—to share her experience about where she came from, and what she went through to get here. We talk about holding each other up. Those are the kinds of stories I hear very often and I'm always in awe. [The resiliency] gives hope to young people, who are going through that right now. Then that hope translates into, how can we do something? And how do we move forward in reclaiming who we are?

NOTES

1. *Onkwehonwe* is a Mohawk word that translates as "original beings;" ista's are "mothers." Thanks to Bonnie Whitlow for assistance with Mohawk in this story.

2. Margo Greenwood is the academic lead for the National Collaborating Centre for Aboriginal Health.

Contributors

KIM ANDERSON is a Metis scholar working as an associate professor in the Department of Family Relations and Applied Nutrition at the University of Guelph. Much of her research is community partnered and involves gender and Indigeneity, urban Indigenous knowledge, Indigenous feminisms, and critical Indigenous masculinities. Her book publications include *A Recognition of Being: Reconstructing Native Womanhood* (CSPI, 2nd ed., 2016), *Life Stages and Native Women: Memory, Teachings and Story Medicine* (University of Manitoba Press, 2011), and *Indigenous Men and Masculinities: Legacies, Identities, Regeneration* (co-edited with Robert Alexander Innes, University of Manitoba Press, 2015).

STELLA AUGUST is from the Nuu-chah-nulth Nation in Ahousat, British Columbia. She was born in 1945 and is a long-time resident of the Downtown Eastside. When she joined the DTES Power of Women Group she learned that, as a woman in the neighbourhood, she had a voice and a collective group through which to support her people. Stella is also a member of the February 14th Women's Memorial March Committee.

TRACY BEAR is an assistant professor, cross-appointed in the Faculty of Native Studies and Department of Women's and Gender Studies at the University of Alberta. Her dissertation, "Power in My Blood: Corporeal Sovereignty through a Praxis of Indigenous Eroticanalysis," won the Governor General's Gold Medal in 2016. She is a Cree scholar from the Montreal Lake Cree Nation in Saskatchewan. Her research areas are rooted in decolonial methodologies often found within Indigenous studies. Specifically, she engages in the areas of Indigenous erotics and eroticanalysis, Indigenous feminism, gender and sexuality studies, sovereignty, land, body politics, and contemporary Indigenous art.

CHRISTI BELCOURT is a Michif visual artist with a deep respect for the environment, traditions, and knowledge of her people. The majority of her work explores and celebrates the beauty of the natural world. Her work can be found within the collections the Gabriel Dumont Institute (Saskatoon), the National Gallery of Canada, the Art Gallery of Ontario, the Wabano Centre for Aboriginal Health, the Indian and Inuit Art Collection (Gatineau, QC), the Thunder Bay Art Gallery, and Museum of Canadian History. She was one of the lead co-ordinators of Walking With Our Sisters.

ROBYN BOURGEOIS (Laughing Otter Caring Woman) is a mixed-race Cree woman currently residing in Haudenosaunee, Anishinaabe, and Huron-Wendat territory. She is an assistant professor in the Centre for Women's and Gender Studies at Brock University. Robyn's areas of scholarly focus are Indigenous feminisms, violence against Indigenous women and girls, Canadian colonial history, and colonial governance in Canada. She has published and presented nationally and internationally on these topics. Robyn is also an activist and has been involved in grassroots and community-based Indigenous and feminist organizing for almost twenty years. She is an artist, performer, and proud mother of three children: Raylena, Marvel, and Lydia Henry.

RITA BOUVIER is a (semi-retired) educator and researcher/writer and poet. In 2014, she received the Indspire Award for Education, recognizing her commitment to and extensive work in the field of education. Her third collection of poetry, *nakomowin'sa for the seasons* (Thistledown Press, 2015) was the 2016 Saskatchewan Book Awards winner of the Rasmussen, Rasmussen & Charowsky Aboriginal Peoples' Writing Award.

MARIA CAMPBELL is a writer, playwright, filmmaker, and activist who has worked as a volunteer with women and children in crisis for over forty years. She is the national grandmother for Walking With Our Sisters. Maria has published six books. Her first book, *Halfbreed*, was published in 1973. Her last book, *Stories of the Road Allowance People* was re-published in 2009 by Gabriel Dumont Publishing in Saskatoon. Maria is the Elder in Virtual Residence at the Centre for World Indigenous Knowledge and Research, Athabasca University, and the Cultural Advisor for the College of Law at the University of Saskatchewan. She is a mother, grand-mother, and great-grandmother.

MAYA ODE'AMIK CHACABY is Anishinaabe, Beaver Clan from Kaministiquia (Thunder Bay). Her family comes from the Lake Nipigon region in Northwestern Ontario. As a means to fulfill her Clan responsibilities, Maya works with First Nations communities as well as provincial and off-reserve Indigenous community advocacy bodies on issues of Indigenous human trafficking, trauma-informed culture-based models, community-driven research, language reclama-tion, Anishinaabe philosophy, restorative justice, and strategic planning. Maya also teaches Ojibwe language and culture at Glendon, York University.

DOWNTOWN EASTSIDE POWER OF WOMEN GROUP is based at the Downtown Eastside Women's Centre in Vancouver, British Columbia. The women are from all walks of life and are either on social assistance, are working poor, or homeless. DTES Power of Women Group members empower themselves through their experiences and raise awareness about the social issues affecting their neighbourhood. Many are single mothers who have had children apprehended; most have chronic physical or mental health issues; many have drug or alcohol addictions; and a majority have experienced and survived sexual violence. As Indigenous women, DTES Power of Women Group members are affected by residential schools and ongoing colonization and racism.

SUSAN GINGELL is mother to a Métis-African daughter and grandmother to two Indigenous grandchildren. She works to be a settler ally to Indigenous people in Canada and elsewhere. Susan has been a supporter of Iskwewuk E-wichiwitochik/Women Walking Together for many years, and became one of the Keepers of the Circle after retiring in 2014. She is professor emerita, University of Saskatchewan, where she was professor of English and women's and gender studies.

MICHELLE GOOD is a member of the Red Pheasant Cree Nation, a part of the Battle River Cree. Her work with Indigenous communities, focusing on grassroots capacity development began in the 1970s, in areas including education, administration, communications, and community development. At forty-three, she graduated law school with distinction in 1999 and completed an MFA in creative writing in 2014. Michelle has taught First Nations studies and history at the University of British Columbia Okanagan. She is published in *Best of the Best Canadian Poetry*; *Best Canadian Poetry 2016*, *The Puritan*, *Gatherings – volume 7*, *Standing Ground*, and *West 49th*.

LAURA HARJO is a Mvskoke scholar, founding member of the Green Corn Collective, and assistant professor in the Department of Community and Regional Planning at the University of New Mexico's School of Architecture and Planning. Harjo's research and teaching centers on Indigenous spatialities, community building, Indigenous feminist community planning praxis, and community-engaged knowledge production. Her recent research focuses on employing Mvskoke and Indigenous epistemologies, and theories of Indigenous space, place, and mapping in a community praxis of futurity. She has a forthcoming book with the University of Arizona Press titled *Spiral to the Stars: Mvskoke Tools of Futurity*.

SARAH HUNT is a Kwagiulth scholar whose anti-violence work is grounded in fifteen years of collaboration with Indigenous communities to address diverse issues related to justice, health, gender, and sexuality. She was awarded a Governor General's Gold Medal for her doctoral research, which investigated the relationship between law and violence in ongoing neocolonial relations in British Columbia, asking how violence gains visibility through Indigenous and Canadian socio-legal discourse and action. Sarah is assistant professor in First Nations and Indigenous Studies and the Department of Geography at the University of British Columbia. She is an activist, writer, educator, collaborator, and relation.

ROBERT ALEXANDER INNES is a member of Cowessess First Nation and an associate professor in the department of Indigenous Studies at the University of Saskatchewan. He is the author of *Elder Brother and the Law of the People: Contemporary Kinship and Cowessess First Nation* (University of Manitoba Press, 2013) and the co-editor of *Indigenous Men and Masculinities: Legacies, Identities, Regeneration* (co-edited with Kim Anderson, University of Manitoba Press, 2015). He has published in the *American Indian Quarterly*, *American Indian Culture and Research*, *Oral History Forum*, *Aboriginal Policy Studies*, and has co-edited with Winona Wheeler a special issue of the *Engaged Scholars Journal* on Indigenous community engagement.

BEVERLY JACOBS is a Mohawk lawyer from Six Nations Grand River Territory and an assistant professor in the Faculty of Law, University of Windsor. She is completing a PHD at the University of Calgary that includes Indigenous legal traditions, Aboriginal rights law, Indigenous wholistic health, and Indigenous research methodologies. The study includes a partnership with the Mohawk community of Akwesasne, and the title of her dissertation is "Impacts of Resource/Industrial Development on the Wholistic Health of the Mohawk Peoples of Akwesasne: A Human Responsibility and Rights Solution." Beverly is the former president of the Native Women's Association of Canada (2004–2009).

TANYA KAPPO is a nîhiyaw'skwew who defines herself according to the important relationships in her life. She is a daughter, a sister, a mother, a kohkom, and a wife. She holds a Juris Doctorate (JD) from the University of Manitoba, and was called to the Alberta bar in 2014. She is dedicated to the pursuit of bringing to life Indigenous ways of being, knowing, and existing with a focus on Indigenous women and girls. Tanya is from the Sturgeon Lake Cree Nation in Treaty 8 territory.

TARA KAPPO is a nîhiyaw'skwew of the sakâwiyiniwak from the Sturgeon Lake Cree Nation, Treaty 8. She is the daughter of Margaret Kappo and the late Harold Cardinal (Sucker Creek First Nation) and the traditionally adopted daughter of Harvey and Lorraine Raine (Smallboy Camp). Seeking to honour the lives and gifts of her grandmothers, Tara is currently completing an MA in Native studies at the University of Alberta with research exploring contemporary Indigenous governance, narratives, and beadwork. She is also deeply grateful for the honour of serving as contributing artist, local organizer, and national collective member for Walking With Our Sisters.

LYLA KINOSHAMEG is an Anishnaabe Ikwe from Manitoulin Island, raised with Anishnaabe Ahdzehwin teachings in a family of ten siblings. Lyla has been married since 1970 to Ray Kinoshameg from Wikwemikong, and together they raised a daughter and son in Sudbury. Today, Lyla is a very grateful Grandmother to a granddaughter and a grandson. She pursues Anishnaabe Ahdzehwin teachings and is active in the community in the promotion of collective well-being. Lyla provides mentoring and advocacy to individuals, families, and communities.

HELEN KNOTT is of Dane Zaa, Nehiyaw, and mixed Euro descent from Prophet River First Nation. She is currently completing her master's degree in First Nations studies at the University of Northern British Columbia. Helen has been involved with land defence in her traditional territory and has practiced social work in the Northeastern region of British Columbia. She is a poet, writer, facilitator, and, most importantly, a mother.

SANDRA LAMOUCHE is Nehiyaw Iskwew from Northern Alberta. She is a wife, mother, hoop dancer, and blogger. She currently works as the First Nations, Métis, and Inuit Success Coordinator for the Livingstone Range School Division. Her passion for dance and thirst for knowledge are the driving factors in her writing, choreography, research, work, family, and ceremonial life! She is the only First Nations person on the International Dance Council and the first adult champion of the Intermountain All-Women hoop dance contest. She is also working on a thesis on Indigenous dance and well-being.

JO-ANNE LAWLESS is an Acadian Métis PHD candidate in the Department of Law and Legal Studies at Carleton University in Ottawa, Ontario. Her work as a research assistant includes topics such as the incorporation of Indigenous cosmology in water infrastructure, the role of knowledge transfer in an urban Indigenous organization, and the state of Métis self-governance in Canada. Currently, she is completing her dissertation on the constitutive influence of the law on Métis identity in Atlantic Canada. The first of her publications, co-authored with Brenda Murphy in 2013, was "Climate Change and the Stories We Tell." She has four children.

DEBRA LEO is a resident of Vancouver's Downtown Eastside and is happy to have a life where she can start over. She wishes others could do so. She likes the DTES Power of Women Group. She is also an active member of Sex Workers United Against Violence.

KELSEY T. LEONARD is a citizen of the Shinnecock Indian Nation from Long Island, New York. She is pursuing a PHD in comparative public policy in the Department of Political Science at McMaster University in Hamilton, Ontario, where she focuses on Indigenous governance. Kelsey has worked for the National Congress of American Indians as a legislative associate on the Tribal Law and Order Act and Violence Against Women Act. She holds an AB in sociology and anthropology from Harvard University, an MSC in water science, policy, and management from the University of Oxford, and a JD from Duquesne University.

ANN-MARIE LIVINGSTON is a member of Pacheedaht First Nation on the west coast of Vancouver Island and has lived in Victoria her whole life. Following a ten-year career in Treaty negotiations, Ann-Marie graduated with a bachelor of business administration, which led to work in the area of First Nations land management. She is committed to empowering women and has participated in lectures, marches, and films, speaking about the issue. Along with her sister Donalee Sebastian, Ann-Marie participated in the Missing Women Commission of Inquiry in Vancouver. She is the proud mom of one son and stays busy with her family and community.

BRENDA MACDOUGALL is the chair of Métis Research at the University of Ottawa and holds a PHD in Native studies from the University of Saskatchewan. She specializes in Métis and First Nations histories blending Indigenous intellectual traditions with conventional historical methodologies. Her first book, *One of the Family: Metis Culture in Nineteenth-Century Northwestern Saskatchewan* (UBC Press, 2010), was the winner of the 2010 Clio

Prize for best book in western Canadian history. She has published numerous articles and was co-editor (with N. St-Onge and C. Podruchny) of *Contours of a People: Metis Family, Mobility, and History* (University of Oklahoma Press, 2012).

SYLVIA MARACLE (Skonaganleh:ra) is a Mohawk from the Tyendinaga Mohawk Territory and a member of the Wolf Clan. She has served as the executive director of the Ontario Federation of Indigenous Friendship Centres (OFIFC) for almost forty years. Sylvia holds an honorary doctorate of laws in management and economics from the University of Guelph and an honorary doctorate of laws in education from York University. Other awards include a Queen Elizabeth II Diamond Jubilee Medal and a National Aboriginal Achievement Award in Public Service. Ms. Maracle is a storyteller and lectures regularly on urban development, women's issues, and the cultural revitalization.

JENELL NAVARRO (Cherokee descent) is an assistant professor of Ethnic Studies at California Polytechnic State University, San Luis Obispo. Her scholarship focuses primarily on Indigenous hip-hop, Indigenous feminism, and Indigenous art in the Americas. Currently, her work has also aimed to build greater alliances between Indigenous and black communities, and her co-edited anthology *Otherwise Worlds: Against Settler Colonialism and Anti-Blackness* is under review with Duke University Press. She is also a bead artist and zinester, and her current zine series is titled *Beadwerk*. She is a founding member of the Green Corn Collective, a constellation of Indigenous feminist bosses.

DARLENE R. OKEMAYSIM-SICOTTE is a nehiyaw iskwew from Beardy's & Okemasis First Nation near the town of Duck Lake, Saskatchewan, and was educated at Rivier Academy in Prince Albert and the University of Saskatchewan. Darlene has been working with the Gordon Tootoosis Nikaniwin Theatre since 2013. Her previous workplaces include the Saskatchewan Indian

Institute of Technologies and the University of Saskatchewan Native Studies, where she worked as departmental secretary. Darlene is a twelve-year member of the local ad hoc concerned citizens group Iskwewuk E-wichiwitochik (Women Walking Together), whose focus is on missing and murdered Indigenous women and girls. She received the Queen Elizabeth II Diamond Jubilee Medal in January 2013 for this volunteerism.

PAHAN PTE SAN WIN is a spiritual caregiver to incarcerated youth at the Manitoba Youth Centre. With a degree in social work from the University of Calgary, Pahan has provided counselling support to residential school survivors, traumatized women, and incarcerated men. Her storytelling pursuits include awards for best writing by an Aboriginal Student, Grant MacEwan College; host and producer of the *Good Medicine Radio Show* for CKLB Radio in Yellowknife, NT; and a blog titled, *I Married a Holy Man*. Pahan's vision to have a Sundance of Women that honours our stolen sisters began in 2017.

RAMONA REECE is a human rights advisor for the Human Rights Legal Support Centre in Toronto, Ontario, and serves as Keeper and Planning Committee member for Walking With Our Sisters–Toronto. She draws on experiences as a 2015 Early Researcher Award recipient for an Indigenous knowledge transfer project, graduate studies in political theory and environmental politics at the University of Toronto, and over two decades as a paralegal to explore urban Indigenous governance and legal theories in climate change politics. Ramona and her ancestors are from the Karankawan and Caddoan borderlands of the Texas Gulf Coast.

KIMBERLY ROBERTSON (Mvskoke) is an artivist, scholar, teacher, and mother who works diligently to employ Native feminist theories, practices, and methodologies in her hustle to fulfill the dreams of her ancestors and to build a world in which her daughters can thrive. She earned an MA in American Indian studies and a PHD in women's studies from the University of California, Los Angeles, in 2012. She is an assistant professor of women's, gender, and sexuality studies at California State University, Los Angeles, and is also a founding member of the Green Corn Collective, a constellation of Indigenous feminist bosses.

LEANNE BETASAMOSAKE SIMPSON is a renowned Michi Saagiig Nishnaabeg scholar, writer, and artist, who has been widely recognized as one of the most compelling Indigenous voices of her generation. She is currently faculty at the Dechinta Centre for Research & Learning in Denendeh and a Distinguished Visiting Scholar in the Faculty of Arts at Ryerson University. Leanne is the author of five books, the editor of three, and she has released two records. She was most recently named a finalist in the Rogers Writers' Trust Fiction Prize. Leanne is a member of Alderville First Nation.

BEATRICE STARR is in the spirit world. Originally from Bella Bella, she lived in Vancouver for thirty-five years. She spent thirty years sober and volunteered at the Downtown Eastside Women's Centre. She loved being part of the DTES Power of Women Group because the group fights for everything she had been through—from violence and abuse to child apprehension—and it gave her a voice! She also regularly marched in the February 14th Women's Memorial March Committee for her murdered sister and niece.

MADELEINE KÉTÉSKWEW DION STOUT is a fluent Cree speaker, an independent scholar, and honorary professor at the University of British Columbia. She was a professor in Canadian Studies and founding director of the Centre for Aboriginal Education, Research and Culture at Carleton University. Now self-employed as the president of Dion Stout Reflections Inc., Madeleine adopts a Cree lens in her research, writing, and lectures. Her work has shaped the way health and health care equity is best encouraged, cultivated, and disciplined for Indigenous peoples; other research interests include Indigenous knowledge and example setting, violence against women, lateral violence, resilience, colonization, racism, mental health and trauma.

WAASEYAA'SIN CHRISTINE SY is a lecturer in Gender Studies at University of Victoria. Her PHD dissertation, "Following the Trees Home: Anishinaabeg Womxn's Relationship with the Sugar Bush," is an anishinaabe material feminist analysis of archival, cultural, and oral sources that make present and absent this relationship in Anishinaabewaki. Cultural productions of her own relationship with the sugar bush operate in tandem to further historicize and elucidate gendered land-based relationships. More broadly, she is interested in Indigenous economic sovereignties and the (a)gendered subject within Indigenous-settler-global-celestial spaces and in understanding the differential ways in which Indigenous womxn's interests are dismissed or mobilized.

ALEX WILSON is from the Opaskwayak Cree Nation, and is a full professor and the academic director of the Aboriginal Education Research Centre at the University of Saskatchewan. Her scholarship has greatly contributed to building and sharing knowledge about two-spirit identity ("coming in"), history and teachings, Indigenous research methodologies, and the prevention of violence in the lives of Indigenous people. She is one of many organizers with the Idle No More movement, integrating radical education movement work with grassroots interventions that prevent the destruction of land and water. Having co-developed a master's focus in land-based education, she is now in the process of creating an international Indigenous land-based PHD program.

343

Index

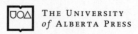